Wendell Fertig and His Guerrilla Forces in the Philippines

Fighting the Japanese Occupation, 1942–1945

KENT HOLMES

McFarland & Company, Inc., Publishers

Jefferson, North Carolina

LIBRARY OF CONGRESS CATALOGUING-IN-PUBLICATION DATA

Holmes, Kent, 1933–
    Wendell Fertig and his guerrilla forces in the Philippines :
fighting the Japanese occupation, 1942–1945 / Kent Holmes.
      p.   cm.
    Includes bibliographical references and index.

    ISBN 978-0-7864-9825-3 (softcover : acid free paper) ∞
    ISBN 978-1-4766-2118-0 (ebook)

    1. Fertig, Wendell W.   2. World War, 1939–1945—
Underground movements—Philippines—Mindanao Island.
3. Guerrilla warfare—Philippines—Mindanao Island—History—20th century.   4. Mindanao Island (Philippines)—
History, Military—20th century.   I. Title.

D802.P52M564 2015
940.54'25997—dc23   2015008126

BRITISH LIBRARY CATALOGUING DATA ARE AVAILABLE

On the cover: *left to right* Moro troops of the 108th Division
under the command of Lieutenant Colonel Charles Hedges
(center with wide-brim hat); Colonel Wendell W. Fertig
wearing a Moro hat; *The Athena,* a two-masted sailing vessel of
the Mindanao guerrilla navy, captained by Vicente Zapanta (all
images courtesy MacArthur Memorial Museum and Archives)

Printed in the United States of America

*McFarland & Company, Inc., Publishers
  Box 611, Jefferson, North Carolina 28640
  www.mcfarlandpub.com*

To the brave Filipinos, Americans and other nationalities in
Mindanao that made up the World War II guerrilla force of the
Tenth Military District, United States Army Forces
in the Philippines

Table of Contents

Maps   viii

Preface   1

Introduction   3

1. Fertig's Background and Engineering Experience   9
2. Assessment of the Situation   23
3. Development of a Guerrilla Movement   37
4. Connectivity with Australia   48
5. Japanese Presence, Disposition and Tactics on Mindanao   69
6. Guerrilla Organization, Strength, Disposition and Tactics   79
7. Logistical Support for the Mindanao Guerrillas   122
8. Intelligence Collection   134
9. Critique of Fertig's Leadership   145
10. Magnitude of Responsibilities   159
11. Leadership Assessment   171
12. Legacy and Reflections on Guerrilla Warfare in the Philippines   184

Appendix: History of the Mindanao Guerrillas   191

Chapter Notes   219

Bibliography   225

Index   227

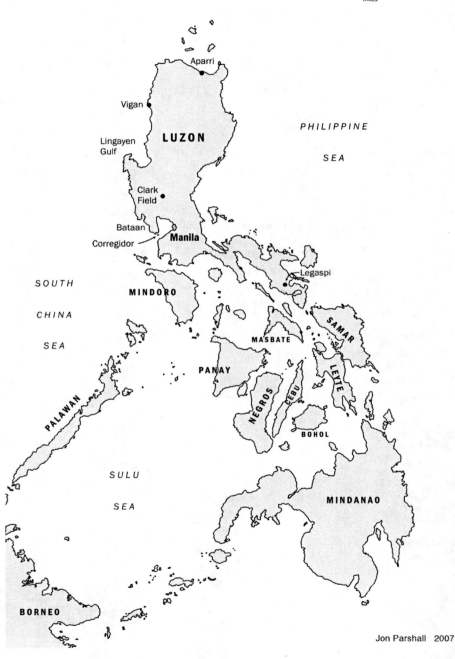

The Philippines (map by Jon Parshall).

Preface

My interest in writing this book about Colonel Wendell W. Fertig was kindled when I was assisting my wife, Virginia Hansen Holmes, with her memoir, *Guerrilla Daughter*. Her book describes her family's struggle to survive the Japanese occupation of Mindanao during World War II. Part of that struggle was the service of her father and two brothers in the guerrilla organization assembled by Fertig following the surrender of the American and Filipino forces in May 1942. My father-in-law, Charles Hansen, like Fertig, had been in the mining business during the 1930s. Because of his World War I service, he retained a U.S. Army commission of captain in the reserves. Like many American businessmen on Mindanao, he refused to surrender to the Japanese and suffer internment for himself and his family. As Fertig organized the guerrilla movement, Hansen and his teenage sons, Rudyard and Henry, became eager volunteers for this growing armed force to oppose the Japanese occupation.

Prior to my wife's published memoir, John Keats' book, *They Fought Alone*, had become one of the few historical sources on the activities of the guerrilla movement in which her father and brothers served. In fact, we still retain a much-used copy of the book that was autographed by Fertig.

As my wife began research for her memoir, she increasingly turned to other sources for additional information on the guerrilla movement on Mindanao. Important contributors were members of the "American Guerrillas of Mindanao (AGOM)," a veterans group whose members had served in the movement under Fertig during World War II. Several of these veterans had served with my father-in-law. Attending their annual reunions during the 1990s, we gleaned much background material about the guerrilla organization and the role of Fertig at various periods of the war.

A key element for us in researching the Mindanao guerrilla movement was finding my father-in-law's military records that included orders and memos written and received by him from early 1943 to mid–1945. Subject matter in this material included special orders written by Fertig and other guerrilla commanders.

This collection of original documents was most useful for my wife because it provided background information and timelines on the ebb and flow of the war. However, many aspects of this material could not be used because her story was about the everyday experiences of her family in evading the Japanese. Thus, much of the information was not used or was relegated to a footnote in my wife's memoir.

This information about the guerrilla movement, such as Fertig's command problems in the early days of the movement in Misamis Occidental, prompted me at a later date to consider writing a comprehensive focus on Fertig as a major guerrilla commander in the Philippines during World War II. This book is my effort to put Fertig in perspective, particularly in the leadership role he played in orchestrating the movement as an effective force against the Japanese occupation of Mindanao. This force, with its intelligence collection from the coast watcher stations and the military capability of the guerrilla divisions to augment U.S. military forces in the liberation of Mindanao in 1945, demonstrated a capacity that was unique in the history of unconventional warfare.

While a large proportion of Fertig's guerrilla forces were Filipino officers and enlisted personnel, the focus of this book is on the multitude of command problems with which he was confronted, especially in the initial phases of organizing the movement. The leadership contributions of Filipino officers are discussed only in specific situations, but this in no way downplays the vital role the Filipino guerrillas played in the overall resistance to an aggressive Japanese military campaign to control Mindanao; rather, the emphasis of the book is providing the reader with an account and evaluation of Fertig's leadership efforts in forming and maintaining a viable military counterweight to the Japanese presence on the island.

Many of the photographs included in the book were taken during the war but the film could not be developed until war's end, causing major degradation in quality.

During and after World War II the preferred spelling of the term was "Moslem." Since that time this has changed. For reasons of currency and standardization, the present author has opted for the spelling "Muslim" except of course in direct quotation.

I am most grateful to my wife, Virginia (Ginger) Hansen Holmes, for her tireless efforts in assisting me in the preparation of this book.

Introduction

Wendell Fertig and His Guerrilla Forces in the Philippines is an account and evaluation of Colonel Fertig's effort to organize a guerrilla movement on the island of Mindanao following the attack and occupation of the Philippines by the Japanese army after the outbreak of World War II. In addition to Fertig, there were indeed some remarkable Filipino and American guerrilla leaders that emerged to oppose the Japanese during the occupation. Because of the many islands making up the country, leadership that emerged varied from island to island. Moreover, it was diverse in its development and organization. The island of Luzon had several leaders but most notable was Lieutenant Colonel Russell Volckmann. Panay was fortunate to have a leader like Lieutenant Colonel Macario Peralta, who refused to surrender and was able to transition much of the Filipino military force into a guerrilla mode that would oppose the Japanese from the countryside. Furthermore, he was able to develop a military radio capability to communicate with General Douglas MacArthur's headquarters in Australia. Much later, in October 1943, Colonel Ruperto Kangleon, after a bitter struggle with other contenders, was recognized by MacArthur as the guerrilla leader of the Ninth Military District, comprising the islands of Leyte and Samar.

The emerging guerrilla movement on the southern island of Mindanao was somewhat different from what was taking place on the other islands in the archipelago. Because of its size and the lack of meaningful Japanese control in the early months following the outbreak of hostilities, a fragmented but growing opposition emerged around an array of undefined leaders and very general goals. This included two American officers who had not surrendered: Major Ernest McClish in Agusan province and Major Robert Bowler in the nearby provinces of Bukidnon and Misamis Oriental. Both would later join Fertig's guerrilla organization and command divisions in the Tenth Military District that was designated by MacArthur for the Mindanao and Sulu areas. At the same time the Filipino people were coming to the conclusion that the Japanese occupation was not as friendly as suggested by propaganda coming from Manila. Increasing acts of Japanese brutality against Filipino civilians were generating public hostility toward the occupation. At some point this growing resentment would result in a call for leadership to actively oppose the Japanese. If a Filipino leader did not emerge, then an American, probably a military officer who had not surrendered, might be asked to lead. Such a leader would demonstrate a multi-tasked skill set that focused on justice, tactics, diplomacy, logistics and supply. In addition, he would have the poise and stature of command. Most important, the leader had to have the same aspirations that were shared by a diverse population—defeat of the Japanese and liberation of the Philippines. Wendell Fertig, the eventual leader of the guerrillas on Mindanao, did in fact emerge with the qualities I have just described. With his years in the Philippines as a mining engineer, he brought a wealth of practical experience that would lay a foundation for a resistance movement that could make a contribution to the eventual liberation of the island by U.S. forces.

Creating a viable guerrilla movement presented Fertig with some formidable challenges. Unlike other islands in the Philippines, Mindanao had a large Filipino Muslim (Moro) population which was concentrated in the western provinces of the island. For a century or more cultural and religion strife was common between the Moros and the Christian Filipinos. Pacification of the Moros was a priority during the early years of the American administration of the Philippines and was finally achieved by General John J. Pershing, using a combination of force and fairness with the Moros. With the surrender of the United States Army Forces in the Far East (USAFFE) in May 1942, the Moros, sensing a power vacuum, attempted to gain an upper hand by taking back property they had sold the Filipinos. Filipino armed bands, calling themselves guerrillas, went after the offending Moros. As a result a minor civil war developed between the aspiring guerrillas and the Moros. Unlike the Filipino Christians, the Moros had not yet been convinced that the Japanese occupation was bad for them. If a guerrilla movement was to be successful it could not fight both the Moros and the Japanese. This reality faced Fertig and he would have to find a solution if an effective guerrilla movement was to be formed.

Another problem facing Fertig was his lack of communications capability—unlike Peralta on Panay, who had communications with Australia and MacArthur by November 1942. It would take a good deal of time and ingenuity to acquire resources and personnel that could solve this problem.

Though Fertig had willing personnel to join the movement, they lacked adequate arms and ammunition to combat the Japanese. Some Filipino military personnel had kept their Enfield or Springfield rifles when they melted into the jungle. Hidden ammunition caches were available but not in any great abundance. If they were to survive logistical support from MacArthur's head-quarters in Australia would be required.

While Filipino foot soldiers for the movement were available, what about leadership for the force? Fortunately, unlike the other islands, there were about 190 American military and civilians that had either refused to surrender or had escaped from Japanese POW camps, and were now available to serve the movement. This was a resource that would make the guerrilla movement a success and was unique to Mindanao. Many of the civilians had been businessmen and had military experience in World War I. The military, both officer and enlisted, brought a variety of skills and leadership capabilities that would be useful to Fertig as the movement expanded.

An important element that Fertig sorely needed was external support from Australia to bolster his island-wide organizing effort. Just as the movement was developing, MacArthur's staff in Brisbane was formulating methods of supplying logistical support to guerrilla organizations in the Philippines. The information available to them in late December 1942 was somewhat sparse but they did have contact with Peralta on Panay. In January 1943 three of Fertig's fellow mining engineers successfully reached Australia from Mindanao on a small boat and they were able to brief MacArthur's staff on Fertig's growing movement on Mindanao. Planning now moved ahead on getting much-needed supplies to these potential guerrilla groups. Since submarines had been successful in supporting Corregidor before the surrender, this would be the preferred method in supplying the guerrillas.

Once Fertig had firmly established his guerrilla movement in the province of Misamis Occidental, he now took bold steps to broaden the movement. Utilizing the persuasive skills of his chief of staff, Luis Morgan, a former Philippine constabulary officer, he began an outreach program to other guerrilla groups on Mindanao. Realizing the importance of the Catholic Church and prominent families in the province, he cultivated both entities to gain their support. He also encouraged Filipino civil servants to return to the positions they had vacated after the Japanese occupation and urged them to again serve the people. Fertig felt this was important not only for the province but also for the movement. In his discussions with the civil authorities he learned that President Quezon, prior to his departure for Australia, had authorized a Provisional Emergency Currency Board to print money, up to ₱3 million. This funding had never been used because of the lack of plates and paper. This was a positive discovery for Fertig, who could now print money for both the provincial governments and the guerrillas. In a symbolic move Fertig established his command headquarters in the old Spanish fort within Misamis City. Flying both the American and Filipino flags from its ramparts, it became an outward sign to the public that the guerrilla movement was behind the local government and the people in opposing the Japanese occupation.

Though Fertig's guerrilla movement of 25,000 to 40,000 men was largely successful, both as an armed force and as collectors of intelligence for MacArthur's staff in Australia, achieving these goals was not without problems. Perhaps the most dangerous phase in the developing movement was the June–July 1943 period when the Japanese moved additional troops into Mindanao to put down the threat posed by the fledgling guerrilla group. Fortunately the movement survived this threat. However, the Japanese pressure would continue in all areas of Mindanao until preparations for the invasion of Leyte would begin to destroy Japanese capabilities.

Keeping the Moros in the movement was a continuing administrative and command problem. However, the logistical support arriving from Australia would mitigate the challenge of dealing with them. By far, the most serious problem that Fertig faced was the separatist tendencies of his chief of staff, Lieutenant Colonel Morgan. This came to a head in late August 1943. As a result, Morgan was ordered by Fertig to take a staff position in Australia and he departed by submarine in September 1943. Along with these problems faced by Fertig was the mounting load of administrative and command problems he encountered during the course of the movement. Fortunately he was able develop a strong command organization that was built around six geographic divisions. Each division commander was an American officer who had either World War I experience or command responsibilities during the early days of the war. Perhaps the epitome of his commanders was Colonel Frank Mc Gee (West Point 1915). After distinguished service in World War I, he retired with a disability in the Philippines and became a successful businessman. Having worked with Moros since his arrival in the Philippines, he was most effective in developing their allegiance to the movement when he was commander of the 106th Division. Unfortunately, he was killed in action in the last days of the war.

While a number of sources have been used to write this book about Fertig, extensive attention was focused on Fertig's personal diary 1941–1945 (approximately 250 pages) and his narrative of the diary written after the war (approximately 600 pages) which was, in effect, his draft manuscript on his wartime experiences as a guerrilla leader. This latter document became the basis of the book, *They Fought Alone,* which was written by John Keats when he was a recipient of a Guggenheim fellowship. Keats describes the writing process as follows:

> Selection was my most difficult problem. For while the story is told in the form of a novel, it depicts real events and real people. The problem was to choose from diaries, memoranda, documents and tape-recorded conversations of those events that gave form and meaning to the whole adventure.

In 1959 Keats accompanied Fertig on a trip to the Philippines. They visited some of Fertig's World War II haunts and talked with Filipinos who had served under Fertig. *They Fought Alone* was published in 1963.

It was not until the 1980s that some veterans who had served with Fertig began to complain about the book and the way certain events and members of the guerrilla movement were depicted. The major critic of the book and of Fertig's command performance was retired Lieutenant Colonel Clyde Childress. He served in Fertig's Tenth Military District throughout the war. Initially chief of staff of the 110th Division, he was later designated by Fertig as the commander of the 107th Division.

Why was criticism so long in coming? The personal papers and diaries used to write the narrative remained with the family after Fertig's death in 1975. Several years later the MacArthur Memorial Archives and Library in Norfolk, Virginia, acquired these papers and diaries. It was at this point that Childress visited the library and reviewed Fertig's documents. As a result of this research Childress wrote a scathing critique that was published in the *Bulletin of the American Historical Collection* published by the American Association of the Philippines, Metro Manila, Philippines. This critique is discussed in Chapter 9.

1

Fertig's Background and Engineering Experience

Wendell Welby Fertig was born in Colorado on December 16, 1900, in the high plains of the southeast part of the state. With his parents, Welby Fertig and Olive Baxter Fertig, he was reared in the small town of La Junta, an area that was in no small measure a product of the frontier west. As he was growing up he experienced first-hand the rigors and responsibilities of the unlimited nature of the outdoor world around him. Graduating from La Junta High School, he attended the University of Colorado, majoring in chemistry. Later he decided he wanted to be a mining engineer and transferred to the Colorado School of Mines in Golden. There he prepared himself for a profession in mining and engineering. While at Golden he also enrolled in the Army Reserve Officer Corps. During the summer breaks he attended additional military courses at Fort Sam Houston in preparation for becoming an Army engineer. Upon graduation he was commissioned a reserve second lieutenant in the U.S. Army Engineering Corps. In 1924 Fertig married Mary Ann Esmond of Golden.

Fertig's first civilian position was with Kennecott Copper Company in Ray, Arizona. Later he moved to Alma, Colorado, where he was manager of American Mine. He next took the position of mine manager at Shenandoah Mines in Silverton, Colorado.

Since the Great Depression had brought hard times on the mining industry in the U.S., Wendell and Mary decided to strike out for an area where mining was booming; their choice was the Philippines. They arrived in Manila with their two young daughters, Patricia ("Pat") and Jeanne, in 1936. Fertig's initial job after arrival was in the province of Batangas, south of Manila. As a mining engineer, he was an on-site supervisor for a new start-up mine. Later he would move to northern Luzon where he was a mining engineer for Baguio Gold Mines. Fertig's brother Claude and his wife Laverne would join Wendell and Mary in the Philippines in 1937. Claude was four years younger and had the same professional track as Wendell—Colorado School of Mines and ROTC.

One might ask what a mining engineer does and how this might have prepared Fertig to become a guerrilla leader. Mining engineers are hired to determine if a deposit of a mineral can be made profitable for a mining firm. If the determination is favorable the engineer proceeds to ascertain the best process for bringing the mine into operation. He will consult all available geological information on the area to be mined as well as obtain additional rock and sediment samples. This approach will then begin to suggest the extraction process to be used. If underground, the engineer will propose designs for the shafts and tunnels to be used in the extraction. Should surface mining appear to be the best option, a whole new set of engineering considerations will emerge. These would include decisions on the pit site; disposition of the soil and rocks that are displaced in the extraction process; erosion and run-off considerations; and, conformance of the site operation with local and national laws. Once the final decision is approved for the project, the mining engineer will then proceed to formulate the day to day operations of the mine. This may entail the possible design of the equipment to be used and the training of mine workers. Safety concerns will be closely monitored by the engineer— these will cover the possible presence of toxic materials and proper ventilation if the extraction process is underground.[1]

The foregoing briefly describes the type of work Fertig was doing in the Philippine mining sector during the 1930s. The broad range of his engineering work in the mining industry, both as an engineer and consultant, would auger well in bringing life and vitality to the guerrilla movement on Mindanao.

Moving to Manila after his work with Baguio Gold Mines, Fertig took on consulting positions with various firms such as Anakan Lumber Company, a subsidiary of the Elizalde Corporation. Life in Manila for Fertig and his family was most pleasant and gracious. He had memberships in the polo club and the yacht club. In his consulting positions he made several business trips to Japan from the Philippines. The Japanese were major importers of minerals and lumber and these visits most certainly did not go unnoticed by Japanese intelligence. Moreover, this travel to Japan made him most sensitive to the ongoing military adventures that this nation was undertaking in China and Indochina. Certainly the question of Japan's next step in Asia was in the back of his mind.

During 1941, while on leave in Manila from a mining management position for Samar Iron Mines, Fertig paid a visit to the Department of Engineers, Philippine Department, U.S. Army. General Hugh J. Casey, under General MacArthur, was chief engineer. During this visit it is assumed that Casey filled

Fertig in on the major project with which the engineers were involved—the upgrade of Philippine airfields to support the forthcoming deployment of B-17 bombers.

With war fever in the air relative to Japan's ambitions in the Far East, the mining business had begun to decline. In the summer of 1941 President Roosevelt issued a directive freezing all of Japan's bank deposits. Without this funding Japan could not purchase U.S. goods, including iron ore from the Philippines. This action did not bode well for mining operations in the Philippines. Since the U.S. Army in the Philippines needed experienced engineers, and with the encouragement of General Casey, Fertig made the decision to go on active duty in June of 1941, with the rank of major. One month later, on July 26, President Roosevelt issued a military order establishing a new command in the Philippines: U.S. Army Forces in the Far East (USAFFE). All military units in the Philippines would come under the new command. At the same time, General MacArthur was recalled to active duty from his position as Field Marshal in the Philippine army and assumed command of USAFFE. As military dependents were being sent back to the U.S. in the summer of 1941, Fertig decided that his family should also return to Colorado. At this time his brother Claude was working as assistant general manager for Capsay Mine on the island of Masbate, south of Luzon. Still on reserve status, he and Laverne remained there.

Going on active duty, Wendell Fertig's initial assignment was that of assistant engineer, Bataan Field Area. By November 1941, he had been elevated by General Casey to the position of head, Construction Section, General Headquarters. In this period prior to the Japanese invasion, he was involved in implementing the upgrade of airfields throughout the islands. Also, during time frame he was promoted to lieutenant colonel. This construction effort was a major project for the U.S. Army engineers in support of the ongoing B-17 bomber deployment to the Philippines. The deployment of these aircraft was the War Department's solution to quickly building a defensive capability in the Philippines. The Del Monte airfield on the island of Mindanao, 500 miles south of Clark Field, was the centerpiece of this effort and involved some 1,500 construction workers. Previously, this airfield was a small facility used mainly to support the small corporate aircraft of the California Packing Corporation's Del Monte pineapple plantation and canning operations located near the Bukidnon-Misamis Oriental provincial border. With more B-17s being sent to the Philippines, it was urgent that a number of strategically placed airfields be upgraded to handle these heavy bombers. While Clark Field was the primary military U.S. Army Air Corps base for supporting B-17s, alternate facilities like the Del Monte airfield were needed to support this influx of heavy bombers. A military concern was having too many aircraft in just one location such as Clark. On December 5, after a hasty upgrade of the airfield's length to one mile, 16 B-17s were moved to Del Monte and managed to avoid the destruction wreaked by the first Japanese attacks on Clark on December 8.

The plan for the Japanese invasion of the Philippines was skillfully developed. The force would contain two elements. The first invasion force would be marshaled in the Formosa Island area and target the Batan Islands north of Luzon, as well as Aparri on the east and Vigan on the west of northern Luzon, and Lingayen further south. The Batan Island landing force was launched on December 8 in order to capture potential airfields. Aparri and Vigan would be the sites of the next landings on December 10. The largest landings would be on December 22 at Lingayen Gulf.

The second invasion force was assembled on Palau Island. Part of this force would land in southern Luzon on December 12 at Legaspi, southeastern Luzon. Two battalions would land at Davao, Mindanao on December 20. The immediate purpose of the Davao landings was to secure a base for thrusts into Borneo. Also, there was a large Japanese population in the Davao area. The last group in the force would land at Lamon Bay, southern Luzon, on December 21.

After the December 8 Japanese air assault on northern Luzon, the first ground invasions against Luzon would commence two days later at Aparri and Vigan. The follow-on Japanese air raids on December 10 against Clark, Nichols Field and the Cavite Navy Yard were so destructive that U.S. air and naval capabilities ceased to be a threat to the Japanese. MacArthur's land forces would now be without air and naval support. Within a few days the Asiatic Fleet would be underway for Borneo with two cruisers and several destroyers. Only damaged ships, torpedo boats and submarines would remain. Those remaining B-17s at Del Monte on Mindanao would now deploy to Australia. As of mid–December U.S. air capability had been reduced to a handful of fighter aircraft.

As the Japanese advance southward accelerated after their landings at Lingayen Gulf, the U.S. and Philippine defensive lines were rapidly breached. First, on December 25 the Japanese units broke through defensive positions along the Agno River and the town of Carmen. Next, on December 27 the Japanese forward forces began reaching the defensive line that extended across the central Luzon plain from Santa Ignacia to San Jose. This was the midpoint between Lingayen Gulf and the major town of San Fernando. A few days earlier, on December 23, General MacArthur made the decision to withdraw all U.S. forces to Bataan. Moreover, Manila was to be declared an "open city" which meant that all U.S. combatants would need to move out of the city. Unfortunately, many of the military supplies in Manila were needed for the Bataan operations and would have to be moved there with dispatch. On December 26 Manila was officially declared an "open city." In his diary Fertig records the chaos of withdrawal from the Manila area. Both land and sea transport was in short supply and only a modest quantity of military materiel would reach Bataan. In many situations the Army engineers were pressed into support duties that were more akin to those performed by quartermaster corps. The goal here was to get as many U.S. Army supplies out of Manila as possible. Fertig estimates the quartermaster corps did not get more than 40 percent of the needed stores out of Manila to Bataan.[2]

The air raids of December 29, 30 and 31 did extensive damage to Corregidor. Fertig notes in his diary that now U.S. lines have fallen back to a point south of San Fernando. Bridges south of this point were being blasted by U.S. Army engineers. Fertig, having been promoted to Lieutenant Colonel in December,[3] now had responsibility for both supply and construction. Moreover, his engineering personnel were building airfields at Hermosa and Orani. Once in Bataan, Fertig's engineers were met with a multitude of responsibilities, including the construction of a new camp that was to house a command center. He proudly notes that it was a tent-covered facility on a platform with bamboo floors. It also had a good supply of foodstuffs. He remarks in his diary that General Casey had stayed there before departing for Australia.[4]

The U.S. Army history *The Fall of the Philippines* has an excellent review of the efforts and problems with which the U.S. Army Corps of Engineers was confronted in the retreat to Bataan. (Many of these problems were some of the same experienced by Fertig and noted in his diary.)

> Engineer supply, like that of other services, was limited and carefully controlled. The engineers had managed to ship to Bataan and Corregidor more than 10,000 tons of their supplies, in addition to organizational equipment, by the end of December. These included 350 tons of explosives, 800 tons of valuable barbed wire, 200 tons of burlap bags for use as sandbags, and large quantities of lumber, construction material, and depot stocks. During the withdrawal, engineer supplies had been evacuated from advance depots along the route of retreat and moved to Lubao, a short distance from Bataan. From there they were transferred to two locations on Bataan. Despite congestion along the roads, the shortage of transportation, and the confusion of retreat, the final evacuation of engineer supplies from the Lubao depot was completed by 6 January.
>
> The first engineer troops to reach Bataan were put to work immediately on airfield construction to accommodate the few fighter craft still left and those which, it was hoped, might yet arrive from the United States. Work was also begun on access roads to the main highway along the east coast of Bataan and on the lateral road from east to west across the slopes of the Mariveles Mountains.

The main work on fortifications along the front was performed by the infantry and artillery, but the engineers improved these positions, strung wire and laid mines. They maintained roads and bridges and prepared demolition charges where necessary. In addition to serving the troops along the front, they built camps for the 26,000 civilians who had taken refuge on Bataan, sawmills to provide lumber for buildings and bridges, and rice mills to feed the men. The greatest handicap to engineering activity was the lack of trained engineer troops. Civilian labor was used whenever possible, but there was no substitute for trained engineer officers. So small was their numbers that in one instance a civilian served for a time as the commander of an engineer battalion.[5]

In his draft manuscript Fertig expressed his feeling about the state of the war. As the Japanese invasion pushed the American and Filipino forces further into a retreat mode, he noted that he began to have thoughts about where this war was going and how he would survive without becoming a prisoner of war. As the Japanese army came ever closer to controlling Luzon, it was Fertig's intention to take to the hills to avoid capture. Early in February 1942 he had been directed by General Casey to support a group that would be operating behind Japanese lines north of Mount Mariveles. This operation stimulated Fertig's imagination for guerrilla warfare should the opportunity arise. Again, both of these statements about not surrendering and guerrilla warfare were in his draft manuscript, but not in his diary.[6] The question might be asked as to whether he actually had such thoughts in the hectic period of his Bataan assignment or whether such thoughts came to him after the war when he was attempting to tie the experiences of Bataan to his eventual role as a guerrilla leader.

Fertig at one point was asked to report to Major General Edward P. King, Commander, Luzon Force, to receive instructions on demolition work to be done in advance of Japanese movement toward U.S. lines. King said the situation looks bad but not hopeless. In the meantime, the engineers were given the order to destroy the equipment of contractors. Last to be destroyed would be the equipment used by the engineers. Once equipment and buildings were destroyed it was decided that all engineering officers would be evacuated to Corregidor. The move to the island from Mariveles was accomplished on April 8.

Just after daylight Fertig and his fellow engineers arrived by launch at the Mine Dock on Corregidor. They had been waiting on a Mariveles beach for their transport since 0300 on the morning of the evacuation. Once they arrived, they were hurried to the middleside tunnels to await Japanese planes that were about to make their bombing run on the island fortress. Here Fertig ran into many of his colleagues from the mining sector that had been recruited to drive new tunnels for additional protection to personnel and supplies. Barely arriving in their assigned tunnel, the Japanese bombs commenced hitting the island. Despite the dust and noise generated by the Japanese aerial assault Fertig and his fellow engineers managed to get some much-needed rest. Fertig comments about this first rest on Corregidor as follows:

> Actually my ability to sleep under these conditions were all part of the "don't give a damn" attitude that had developed during the past weeks, and was compounded more of fatigue than of courage.[7]

Now on Corregidor, the Department engineers were expected to assist in the defense of the island. Fertig's section was assigned maintenance work on the fortress. Fertig describes the work as endless in what had to be repaired or replaced. A backdrop to these duties was the almost constant bombing and the difficulty of sleeping in a tunnel.

With the passage of time on Corregidor, Fertig was devoting more time on physical exercise; he was attempting to restore his physical condition to the level prior to the siege of Bataan. Although on reduced rations, he had managed to regain some weight. Also, he had a growing feeling of being able to evade capture by leaving Corregidor. This was due to his experience with five failed evacuations by air.

On the evening of April 29, two Catalina patrol aircraft arrived to transport American nurses from Corregidor to Australia. Four officers were also chosen to be evacuated on the basis of operational need. Fertig had a Priority 1 (which he also had on previous flights but had not been selected), but this flight would be different and he was among the four officers slated for the trip. When informed that he was on the manifest, he had only minutes to meet a launch at the island's south dock. The officers and nurses were taken by two launches to the waiting aircraft and upon arrival climbed from the launches through the open Plexiglas blister on the port side of their assigned aircraft. The aircraft was sparse and without seats so the only recourse for the passengers was to crouch on the cold aluminum floor of the hull during take-off; in Fertig's mind, this was a minor sacrifice made for the opportunity to leave the dwindling defensive bastion of American military presence in the Philippines. Fertig found a spot near the aft gun turret. Once the passengers on his seaplane were situated the pilots revved up for takeoff. Moving through the water the Catalina's hull made slapping sounds as it met the wavelets. This quickly changed to a hiss and the aircraft pulled free and was airborne. A few minutes later Fertig and his fellow passengers were flying over Cavite province, passing near Pico de Oro, the highest point on the Cavite coastline. The aircraft then headed southward past Taal Volcano and toward the island of Panay. From this island the aircraft continued its low altitude flight path, using a southward compass heading toward Lake Lanao on the island of Mindanao.

Despite their cramped and uncomfortable seating arrangements, the passengers did experience one luxury on this stripped-down patrol aircraft—one of the crew brought out fresh hot coffee. All were shocked at this luxurious treat since coffee had been severely rationed on Corregidor and Bataan. Fertig mulled over his good fortune in catching the flight. He was now one step closer to obeying General Casey's final directive: that he should attempt to obtain an Army Air Corps flight from Del Monte to Australia where he was slated to take command of the Construction Division under Casey.

Finally arriving in the vicinity of Lake Lanao they were greatly disappointed to discern that the lake was fogbound and this forced the aircraft to abort a landing. The aircraft then flew to Panguil Bay, a few minutes to the southwest of Lake Lanao. (Ironically, Fertig would cross Panguil Bay within six months as a guerrilla leader taking control of Misamis Occidental province with a 200-man guerrilla force.) On this occasion, however, the water in Panguil Bay was smooth and the aircraft experienced an uneventful landing.

As morning approached the pilot readied his aircraft for the flight back to Lake Lanao. However, he observed that after landing they had taxied into the mouth of a fish trap. These traps were built by local fishermen in shallow water to guide the schools of fish into narrow channels so they would be easily caught. Heading for the weakest point in the trap, the pilot went to full power for a successful takeoff. As the Catalina gradually gained altitude, loud thumps were heard as the body of the aircraft struck the poles of the fish trap. By the time they arrived at Lake Lanao the fog had lifted and the pilot landed without incident.

Immediately after landing the plane taxied into an area sheltered by tall bamboo along the shore. The passengers disembarked and were invited to breakfast in an area surrounded by large trees ringing the lake. Fertig described this first meal in Mindanao:

> It is difficult to imagine such a breakfast and its appeal to us unless you have lived for weeks on monotonous and insufficient rations. Peanut butter made from freshly roasted peanuts, hot coffee from local berries, hot pancakes covered with coconut honey, all the eggs you wanted to eat and fresh meat. We all gorged ourselves to complete capacity with the feeling that heaven was with us again and things were not nearly as black as they appeared a few hours earlier.[8]

Fertig then boarded a truck for the trip along the lake to Camp Keithley at Dansalan which was also located on the lake. Lake Lanao is interesting because it occupies what was once an ancient volcano. The surrounding hills were eroded and rounded, forming gradual contours farmed by the Moros.

On arriving at Dansalan and Camp Keithley, Fertig focused on the following memories of the past:

Although the war had been in progress for four months, Dansalan still presented almost a peacetime appearance. In my many trips to this area, I had learned to know and admire the country and the people. It was a pleasant homecoming, after four months of shelling and bombardment, although I was aware of the fact that it was only an interlude. Our truck stopped three or four times in the fifteen mile ride in order to avoid strafing from planes that passed overhead on their constant patrols. [A Japanese force with tanks had landed on April 29 at Parang and Malabang and was pushing toward Lake Lanao.] We finally arrived at Camp Keithley, an old Army post which General Pershing and General Douglas MacArthur had served in their youth. The post had passed to the Control of the Philippine Constabulary and was well preserved; a pleasant place with huge acacia trees shading the perimeter of the parade ground. Truly Mindanao was a land of milk and honey, but here was planted the first thought that should I not be able to go to Australia as planned, these hills were free, food was plentiful and I had no intention of spending my years as a prisoner of the Japanese.[9]

Later in the day Fertig met an old friend of his, Charles Hedges, formerly the logging superintendent of the Kolambugan Lumber Company. Their mills were on Panguil Bay. Hedges, now a captain in the Quartermaster Corps, was assigned as transportation officer of General Guy O. Fort's Division, the 81st Philippine Army Division. Their division had been charged with the defense of the Malabang area which controlled the approach to the southern end of Lake Lanao.

Fertig's reunion with Hedges was interrupted by the arrival of General William F. Sharp, now a major general and commander of the Visayan-Mindanao Force. General Sharp welcomed Fertig and the three officers that had accompanied him from Corregidor and asked them to join his staff. He specifically asked Fertig about his plans—they had worked together prior to the war and Sharp was aware that Fertig was still a member of General Casey's engineering staff. Fertig indicated that he expected to go to Del Monte for transportation to Australia to head the Construction Division under Casey. Sharp informed him that the last flight to Australia had already departed from Del Monte and indicated to Fertig that he wanted him to join his staff as his engineering officer. Fertig responded that he would only accept Sharp's offer when it was clear that he would be unable to leave Mindanao for Australia.

In view of General Sharp's comments about cessation of flights to Australia, Fertig wrote a letter to his wife Mary, who was now in the United States with their two daughters. This letter was to be taken to Australia by a navy commander who was joining the Seventh Fleet. Fertig wrote the letter in a cryptic fashion to avoid any U.S. censorship or benefit to the Japanese should it fall into their hands. The heading in the letter was simple: "Pineapple for Lunch." Mary knew his enthusiasm for the island of Mindanao and the pineapple plantation operated by the California Packing Corporation at Del Monte, where a bit of the United States had been transplanted. The American quarters and club, together with a golf course, offered a restful environment for Americans and Fertig had spent enjoyable visits there on many occasions. Mary would understand the reference to "Pineapple for Lunch" and realize that he was on Mindanao and free from Bataan and Corregidor.

The letter given to the navy commander was mailed in Australia and eventually arrived at Mary's address in Colorado. Later in the war it was used by Army intelligence to authenticate Fertig's position as an American guerrilla on Mindanao.[10]

With the Japanese advances on Mindanao canceling all air operations out of Del Monte, Fertig was resigned to remaining on Mindanao. His mission now changed—he was ordered to oversee the demolition of bridges and roads. As he commenced these duties the Japanese were within days of arriving in the Dansalan-Iligan area.

During this period Claude Fertig, still living with his wife on Masbate, was called to active duty by USAFFE, with the rank of Major, and ordered to report to the 61st Division (PA) on the nearby island of Panay. However, prior to departing for Panay he was directed to survey available mining equipment on Masbate that should be transported to Panay for use by USAFFE forces. In February 1942 Claude and Laverne would travel by fishing boat to the north coast of Panay, closer to the U.S. military presence.[11]

MacArthur's Departure for Mindanao

With Fertig's arrival on Mindanao from Corregidor, it might be interesting to contrast his trip with that of General MacArthur's exit from the island fortress to Australia via motor torpedo boat to Mindanao and thence by B-17 to Australia. While Fertig's trip on a Navy patrol aircraft was a matter of hours, MacArthur's 500 mile trip by PT boat lasted two and a half days and occurred some eight weeks earlier, when the struggle to resist the Japanese onslaught against USAFFE forces on Bataan and Corregidor was approaching its inevitable conclusion. On April 29, the day Fertig arrived in the Lake Lanao area of Mindanao, the Japanese were already in the process of invading Davao province in southern Mindanao, their first landing point on that large island. The surrender of USAFFE forces was close at hand, finally happening on May 8 for the forces on Luzon and May 10 for those on the other islands, including Mindanao.

The decision on MacArthur's leaving the Philippines for Australia was broached as early as February 4. General George C. Marshall, Army chief of staff, suggested to MacArthur that he consider leaving Corregidor and establish a new command in Australia, but MacArthur refused to consider Marshall's proposal.[12] Even as Marshall was attempting to convince President Roosevelt that MacArthur should be ordered to leave the Philippines, his colleagues in the president's cabinet believed otherwise. However, developments from another quarter changed Roosevelt's mind. Apparently there were British-Australian differences on their respective views on defense policy in Asia. The Australian prime minister had indicated that Australia was looking for American assistance in the war against Japan. Shortly thereafter Marshall sent a message to MacArthur, as follows: "The President directs you to proceed to Australia via Mindanao. There you will assume command of all U.S. Forces." After agonizing over the presidential order, MacArthur sent a message to Marshall requesting permission to make his own decision on when and how he should depart Corregidor.[13]

There was good reason for MacArthur's request. He disliked traveling in closed spaces, as would be the case on a submarine or small aircraft such as a PBY. Instead, he preferred the open sea and consulted with one of his subordinates, Navy lieutenant John Bulkeley, commander of Motor Torpedo Boat Squadron 3 (MTBRON3), whose boats had effectively participated in missions against Japanese shipping. For several months Bulkeley had reported to MacArthur on a daily basis, earning his respect and trust.[14]

MacArthur's concern at that point was whether his wife Jean and young son could make the trip on one of Bulkeley's boats. To this end he asked Bulkeley to take Jean on a short run around the island and when she returned she indicated that she had no objections to traveling on a PT boat. Later that same night MacArthur conferred with Bulkeley, telling him the president had order his departure from Corregidor and his plan was to leave for Mindanao after dusk on March 11. His family and staff would make the trip on Bulkeley's PT boats, consisting of Boats 32, 34, 35 and 41. It was decided that MacArthur and family would travel on Boat 41.

Bulkeley possessed many character traits that appealed to MacArthur and may have affected his decision toward a PT Boat option. Bulkeley was described as "a swash-buckling pirate in modern dress, sporting a long, unruly beard and carrying two ominous-looking pistols at his side. His eyes were bloodshot and red-rimmed from staring out on his nightly missions and from lack of sleep. His nervous energy was tremendous and the supply of it never seemed to give out. He walked with a cocksure gait and one could always count on him to raise particular hell with any Jap who crossed his path. High-strung, temperamental and gallant. Bulkeley was one of the more colorful figures in the Philippine Campaign."[15]

After being advised of MacArthur's decision to leave Corregidor bound for Mindanao via PT Boat, Marshall sent a message to Major General George Brett, U.S. Army commander in Australia, ordering him to supply aircraft for transporting MacArthur and his family and staff members from Mindanao to Australia.

As preparations were being made for MacArthur's departure from Corregidor, the question arose as to how many of MacArthur's staff would accompany him. Marshall had authorized only his family and Sutherland to accompany him. According to Master Sergeant Paul P. Rogers, Sutherland's stenographer and typist, it was Sutherland who selected staff members to be placed on the list of passengers that would accompany MacArthur. These included thirteen Army officers, one enlisted man, two Navy officers, Jean, her son Arthur and his amah.[16] Among the Army officers was Brigadier General Hugh J. Casey, Fertig's superior officer who arranged his departure from Corregidor eight weeks later. It was Casey's plan that Fertig would join him in Australia as his chief of construction.

On the evening of March 11 Bulkeley's four PT boats drew up at Corregidor's North Dock. MacArthur, his family and his selected staff members departed on the four boats.

As PT-41 moved away from the dock its powerful engines, driving its three propellers, opened up to full power. The four boats, in a diamond formation, headed south toward Mindanao. Once they had cleared the minefields around Corregidor, their speed at this juncture was about 30 knots.

At some point in the evening the four boats became separated. The skipper on PT-32, carrying Casey and other staff members, thought he saw a Japanese destroyer coming toward them. The skipper ordered the dozen 50-gallon fuel tanks cut loose as he prepared to torpedo the destroyer. At the last minute he realized that the vessel he thought was a Japanese ship was really PT-41. With PT-32 now without sufficient fuel to make it to Mindanao, Casey and the other staff members transferred to PT-41. Pt-32 and crew would remain in area near the island of Cebu. PT-34 at this point was missing and presumed lost. The trip southward would continue with two overcrowded boats—PT-35 and PT-41.[17]

On the morning of March 13 the northern shore of Mindanao came into view. The two boats entered the small port of Cagayan de Oro in Misamis Oriental province, approximately five miles from the Del Monte airfield, at approximately 7:00 a.m. The missing boat, PT-34, arrived one hour later. All who had departed Corregidor had successfully made the 500-mile trip to Mindanao. Thirty-six hours had elapsed since leaving the North Dock on Corregidor. This would mean a speed of advance of approximately 14.5 knots per hour for the trip to Mindanao.

The Army commander on Mindanao, Brigadier General William F. Sharp, with an honor guard, was on the dock to greet MacArthur. Before leaving PT-41 MacArthur thanked Bulkeley. He told him, "You've taken me out of the jaws of death and I won't forget it."[18]

Prior to leaving for the Del Monte airfield, MacArthur bade farewell to Bulkeley and members of MTBRON3. He congratulated them on successfully carrying out their mission and awarded the Silver Star to every member of the squadron.[19]

Arriving at Sharp's headquarters, MacArthur was informed that the president of the Commonwealth of the Philippines, Manuel Quezon, his vice president, Sergio Osmeña, and members of his cabinet were evading the Japanese on the island of Negros Oriental. MacArthur decided to send a message to Quezon, urging that he and his family join MacArthur in Australia. Once again, MacArthur called on Bulkeley, entrusting him to deliver the message to Quezon and bring him and his family to Mindanao.[20] Late in March PT Boats 34, 35 and 41 went to Negros Oriental to pick up Quezon and his family, along with his vice president and other government officials and brought them to the same port of Cagayan de Oro where MacArthur had landed earlier that month. They proceeded to Sharp's headquarters at Del Monte to await aircraft to transport them to Australia and then on to the U.S. to establish a Philippine commonwealth government-in-exile.

When MacArthur arrived at Del Monte he expected four B-17s to be waiting for him, but the only bomber he could see was battered and covered with oil. While four aircraft had been dispatched from Australia, two had to abort after taking off and a third had crashed into waters off of Mindanao. MacArthur sent a nasty message to Brett in Australia demanding that four additional B-17s be dispatched to Mindanao, but Brett could only send three aircraft. To make matters worse, one had to abort after take-off and only the remaining two would land at Del Monte.

At approximately midnight on March 16 MacArthur, his family and staff boarded the two B-17s, crowding into the limited space available for passengers. After a 10-hour flight the two aircraft landed at Batcheler Field, 40 miles from Darwin in northern Australia. After landing MacArthur had the crews of both aircraft line up. He shook their hands as he awarded each one the Silver Star.[21]

When MacArthur arrived he had visions of a large American army being in Australia. Instead, a ragtag honor guard from an anti-aircraft unit greeted him in Darwin. He asked the officer in charge where the American army in Australia was based. "There are very few troops here," was the reply. MacArthur could not believe it![22]

At this point it might be appropriate to insert a footnote regarding the fate of the boats of MTBRON3 that had played such an important role in making it possible for MacArthur to be successfully evacuated from Corregidor for his eventual trip to Australia in accordance with President Roosevelt's orders.

During the trip to pick up Quezon and his party PT-35 had to be scuttled off Negros Oriental because of engine failure and the crew members were loaded onto the two remaining boats. On April 8 PT-41 and PT-34 were attacked by a Japanese cruiser off the island of Cebu but escaped with minor damage. The following day the two boats were attacked again, this time from the air, and PT-34 was sunk. Two crewmen were killed and the remainder of the crew boarded PT-41.

PT-41 returned to Mindanao on April 20, landing in Iligan in Lanao province, where it was put on a trailer for transport to Lake Lanao for possible use by the guerrillas there. The road to the lake had many sharp turns and when the trailer and boat were no longer able to proceed further they were abandoned. Eventually the Japanese pushed them off a cliff to make the road passable for their vehicles and equipment. This was an inglorious end to a very famous boat that had transported both MacArthur and Quezon and their families and staff to Mindanao, saving them from possible capture by the Japanese.[23]

It is also worth noting that 10 members of MTBRON3 joined Fertig's guerrilla organization. Following are the names of these naval personnel:

William H. Johnson	Dewitt Glover
William F. Konko	Paul L. Owen
John L. Lewis	Henry Rook
Francis J. Napolillo	John L. Tuggle (engineer on PT-41)
Marvin H. DeVries	Elwood L. Offret

2

Assessment of the Situation

After the initial Japanese invasion of Mindanao in the Cotabato area on April 29, 1942, Fertig commenced an inspection of previously laid charges along Route 1 leading to the Lake Lanao area. Because of recent heavy rains, he found these charges to be defective and inadequate. Returning to Dansalan he discussed the matter with Brigadier General Guy O. Fort, commander of the 81st Division (PA). General Fort asked Fertig to do what he could to close the road leading to Lake Lanao. Returning to the task at hand, Fertig, assisted by Charles M. (Charlie) Smith, an old mining engineer acquaintance completed the demolitions as requested by General Fort. They were accompanied on this mission by Father Andrew Cervini, an American Jesuit parish priest from Iligan, who had expressed his desire to join the troops and administer the sacraments to those preparing for battle.[1]

On the night of May 2, Fertig received an order from General Sharp to return to Del Monte. Fertig's old friend and colleague, Captain Charles Hedges, a logistics officer in the USAFFE forces, had received a similar order for the division motor pool which he commanded. He and his unit had left Dansalan a day earlier but were delayed by a minor accident. While moving toward Cagayan City, Fertig by chance met up with Hedges and his unit on the road. The two old friends decided to team up and travel together to Del Monte. As they approached Cagayan City they found that bridges were in flames and the Japanese were shelling the area. The landings by the Japanese would commence the following morning, May 3. At this point Fertig and Hedges decided against proceeding to Del Monte and opted for a back road/trail trip back to Lanao province. Before arriving in the Lanao area, they learned that General Sharp had surrendered on May 10 but that General Fort's troops were still fighting. As they neared Iligan the news was spreading that General Fort had also surrendered. This attempt to join General Sharp had been a failure. It had taken Fertig and Hedges and his men twenty days to travel 240 kilometers. Much of this trip had been made with detours over mine roads and trails and in some cases motor transport was not available.[2]

Fertig and Hedges, not wanting to be captured by the Japanese, headed away from the coast and moved toward the Lake Lanao area. They were accompanied by Hedges' deputy, Chief Petty Officer Elwood Offret. Fertig personally felt that the order to surrender from General Wainwright and General Sharp did not apply to his status because he was still under orders of General Casey. Though Hedges' case was different, he felt that his detached status exempted him from the surrender order.

From the surrender in May until mid–August the Americans would be constantly on the move. This evasion travel took them into the jungle, along difficult trails but away from Japanese troop concentration. During this travel they heard stories about the American and Filipino forces surrendering to the Japanese but learned few details. Now they wondered what their future official status would be. Since both Fertig and Hedges were on detached duty, neither had received an official order to surrender. More and more the officers became reflective of what the American surrender would mean and how they would deal with it relative to their individual lives.

In their flight from the Japanese presence, the three Americans heard about and visited an evacuation area used by other American servicemen that refused to surrender to the Japanese. It was called Deisher's Camp. The camp had been conceived by a former Spanish-American War veteran, Jacob Deisher. He had settled in the region in 1902 and had several enterprises that included a coconut plantation, sawmills and mines. In February 1941, concerned with the Japanese expansion in Asia, he applied for U.S. passports for himself and his family. When the Japanese launched their invasion of the Philippines the passports had not arrived and the family was stranded. Not wanting to be taken prisoner, he made plans to build an evacuation camp in Bukidnon province but near the border with Lanao province, some nine hours from his plantation. The camp became a reality on May 4, 1942, when Deisher and his family, plus eight U.S. servicemen, arrived at the camp. Later, additional U.S. military personnel would come to the camp.

The first task for the inhabitants of the camp was to construct huts for housing. The camp was near a stream so water was not a problem. Deisher had made arrangements for rice to be delivered every few weeks by Filipino *cargadores* (bearers).

Fertig, Hedges and Offret did not remain long at Deisher's Camp. Keats in his book *They Fought Alone* had the following negative comments about the camp:

Deisher's camp was nothing but a wet hole in the jungle. The thirty-some American soldiers at Deisher's were as impossible as the camp's location. They wanted only to be left alone. They resented officers, would not take orders, and would do nothing but sit there, rotting in the jungle, living off the store of army rations which Deisher, an old prospector and boar hunter, had somehow acquired. Fertig wondered what they would do when the food was gone. The young Americans did not seem to know or care.[3]

Fertig's diary does not mention the visit to the Deisher camp. However, his draft manuscript devotes several pages to the visit. Some negative elements emerge on the atmosphere of the camp but are not nearly as caustic and negative as the paragraph contained in Keats' book. Both Keats and Fertig should have perhaps given more consideration to the psychological state of the American military personnel on the heels of the Japanese victory and the confused outlook that many had on their future just a few months away from the surrender. Fertig himself had the same confusion in the aftermath of the surrender and expressed this in his draft manuscript (see the next paragraph). It should be noted that all the servicemen at this camp would later join the guerrilla movement to be created by Fertig and Luis Morgan.

A turning point in Fertig's reflective mode came on July 4, 1942, when both he and Hedges, from a hidden vantage point, observed the forced march of American prisoners of war (POWs) along the Philippine National Highway from Dansalan to Iligan. This scene became a turning point in Fertig's decision to confront the Japanese occupation on Mindanao. Listening to the rumors from Iligan and shaken by what he had seen on the road, Fertig found himself hounded by a thought that he had with increasing frequency—a decision must be made one day soon on his future role in a movement to oppose the Japanese occupation.[4] In the meantime, Fertig had located himself in a house, with a garden, in the Abaga/Momungan area of Lanao province. This area was somewhat away from the active Japanese presence. As he worked in his garden, dressed in his uniform and sun helmet, he subconsciously began thinking about the future by sorting out the stories he had heard of what had happened to the American prisoners he had observed on the road. He then projected this reality into a possible role he was capable of playing in confronting the Japanese. More important, he rationalized his future involvement in confronting the Japanese as a way of diminishing the tyranny that they inflicted on the Americans and Filipinos on Mindanao. In Keats' book Fertig's thoughts on the way ahead are as follows:

No man can forever sit idle with a gun in his hands and watch his friends being bayoneted. Moreover, no man can ever hide from an evil or pretend that it will go away of its own accord.[5]

Being a mining engineer suggested that Fertig had skill sets that could be essential in building an effective guerrilla movement. Foremost was his management experience in running mining operations. There are similarities between bringing a mine along as a productive enterprise and developing a military organization to the point where it can perform against an occupying power while at the same time inspiring the populace to maintain the fight against the enemy.

Reading Fertig's diary as it records early events after the surrender, one is struck with the impression that his mind was working like that of an engineer—analyzing the problems and coming up with options that will eventually bring a positive outcome. His analysis reflected that there was a tipping point when the Filipinos would be inspired to fight the Japanese. When this occurred, he and other Americans would have to be ready to take on the mantle of leadership if it was offered by the Filipinos. This is precisely what happened. A guerrilla group in Lanao province, led by a former Philippine constabulary officer named Luis Morgan, had loosely organized themselves after the surrender to oppose the Japanese. However, Morgan and his Filipino colleagues soon realized that American leadership would be required if they were to move beyond their poorly focused guerrilla group and be successful in capturing the growing opposition of the Filipino people against the Japanese occupation. Most interestingly, they were aware of the nearby presence of Fertig, an Army lieutenant colonel, who had refused to surrender and was observed each day in uniform tending his garden in a thoughtful and imposing manner. This American officer fit the role and stature of a leader they envisioned could galvanize a guerrilla movement against the Japanese occupation.

Though Fertig in his mind had resolved to confront the Japanese, he would continue his gardening pastime until conditions were right for him to assume a command role in a guerrilla organization that could effectively confront the ever-present Japanese occupation. Though there were indications of a growing Filipino opposition to the Japanese occupiers, he felt that it was necessary that the Filipinos come to him and ask for his leadership. He was sensitive to the Filipino outlook as to what had happened—the Americans had been defeated and there was no sign of the promised "aid" arriving. Even so, there was smoldering opposition to the Japanese as they treated the ordinary Filipinos with contempt and cruelty. This attitude would harden as the months passed and the Japanese became more oppressive. By August 1942 a tipping point was now at a critical juncture when Fertig would be asked to play a role in a guerrilla movement.

Aside from the Filipinos who were developing a growing resentment against the Japanese, there were a number of Moros (Filipino Muslims who

occupied much of the central and western parts of Mindanao) that were unde-
cided and hesitant about confronting the Japanese. Historically hostile to the
Filipinos (who were mostly Christian), the Moros would not fully support a
movement against the Japanese if the leadership were to come from the Filipinos. On the other hand, should the leadership come from the Americans
this would be a more favorable condition upon which the Moros could pledge
their support. Fertig was sensitive to this and gleaned much from his colleague
Charles Hedges, who had dealt with both groups during his many years as a
businessman in Mindanao.

During the months following the surrender of the Americans, the population in Mindanao, like other parts of the Philippines, was slowly becoming
disenchanted with the Japanese presence. This fostered a growing military
opposition to them. Unfortunately this military response was unfocused and
was not inspiring an effective opposition. Morgan's group was symbolic of
this unfocused approach. Promoting himself to the rank of captain, he, along
with William Tait, his deputy, had organized their bandit group into an effective operational force that had attacked both Japanese troops and Moro population centers. In Morgan's view these latter operations were launched to root
out Moro bandits.

Tait had an interesting background. His father had been a black veteri-
narian with the U.S. Army Cavalry in the Philippines. His mother was a Moro
woman from the southern Philippines. Morgan himself was an American *mes-
tizo*—his father was an American and his mother a Filipina. Henry Hansen
was with his father, Charles Hansen, when Morgan paid a visit to the Surigao
area to recruit guerrillas for Fertig's movement. He recalls that Morgan arrived
in a big sailing banca. While outgoing, he was demanding and almost arrogant.
Morgan, he also remembers, had a swashbuckling air about him, with a Tommy
gun strapped across his chest. Later on in the war, after young Hansen had
joined the guerrillas, he recalls Morgan bragging about his American name—
after he had consumed several glasses of tuba, he would talk about his American heritage and the fact that there had been Morgan warriors fighting in the
Civil War.

Through Tait, Morgan initiated an approach to Fertig in August of 1942
for assuming command of approximately 500 insurgents that were loyal to
Morgan. One might ask why Tait was used to make the approach to Fertig.
Comments by American guerrillas suggest why this happened. Following the
surrender, Tait had assisted Americans in traveling to Misamis Occidental to
join guerrilla opposition to the Japanese occupation. During his efforts to help
the Americans his personality became patently clear. He was big, he was
impressive, and he was convincing. In his youth he was often in trouble but

was developing a personality and manner to please and convince those with whom he was in contact. During the early days of the occupation he had led the Japanese to believe that he could act as an informer and provide them with information on any Filipino opposition. They accepted his offers without question. This caused them dearly in terms of lost personnel and weapons. They did not know that he was on the American/Filipino side and was using his so-called cooperation to fleece the Japanese of their weapons and personnel. Tait was a natural and convincing salesman for Morgan in making his offer to Fertig.[6]

It should be noted that in a letter Fertig wrote to General Casey in July 1943 Fertig said that he and Tait had discussed guerrilla activity. He advised Tait to contact Morgan regarding this possibility.[7] Again, it is unclear why Fertig would change the version of meeting Tait in his draft manuscript.

Putting aside the time line of Morgan and Fertig meeting, there is the question of why Morgan would be motivated to come to Fertig. The reasons were probably complex and varied. Perhaps Morgan had realized that if "the Aid" were ever to come to Mindanao it would have to be through an American commander, not Filipino, who had the backing of General MacArthur's headquarters. A second reason could have been the recognition by Morgan that he had limitations in the administration and command of the troops he had. An American commander, with Morgan as deputy, would be more attractive to MacArthur and future military assistance. In addition, this arrangement would free Morgan from the administrative burden of command while allowing him to focus on the operational aspects of the movement. This way he could still retain the levers of power within the organization. Also, with American leadership, the movement would have more attraction for the Moro population than had been the case with Morgan. For Fertig, the offer made by Morgan had appeal since he had already made an emotional and mental decision to oppose the Japanese as a guerrilla. However, throwing his lot in with Morgan would be difficult. Moreover, his old friend Hedges was not enthusiastic over the prospect.

As Tait continued in his initial meeting with Fertig, he proposed the following:

> We will start a rumor that an American general has come from General MacArthur in Australia to assume command of all guerrillas on Mindanao. No one will question an American general from Australia, sir. Everybody is feeling good that General MacArthur has remembered and sent us a general.[8]

Fertig at this point prompted Tait to acknowledge that under his proposal Fertig would be the general. Tait affirmed that this indeed would be the plan as he had proposed. Fertig gave Tait's bold proposal much thought. At first blush it appeared unrealistic, but as he gave it more consideration it became more plausible. It was clever and had propaganda potential. Despite the surrender, MacArthur would continue to be a hero for the Filipinos. Assuming the role of a newly-arrived general officer from Australia could easily gain him respect and quickly move him into a command and leadership role that could sublimate the differing guerrilla groups on Mindanao.[9]

As Tait rose to leave, Fertig stated that he would advise Morgan of his decision on the proposal that had just been made. Hedges, who was present, could not believe what he had just heard and cautioned Fertig not to go along with Tait and Morgan's proposal of making him a general who had been sent by Australia. Even so, Fertig thought it had merit and believed that it was the opportunity he had been waiting for relative to commanding a guerrilla movement against the Japanese.[10]

By far the most pressing problem facing the guerrilla movement was gaining the allegiance of the Moro people in opposing the Japanese occupation. The movement on Mindanao could not be successful if it was forced to fight both the Japanese and the different Moro groupings, which in Mindanao amounted to about a third of the population. This was a problem not faced by guerrilla leaders on the other islands. One of the reasons that Morgan may have asked Fertig to join the movement was that he realized that he did not have the standing to form an alliance with the Moros. Historically the separatist nature of the Moro people had plagued both the Spanish and American administrations of the Philippines. Even today it continues to be a vexing problem for the Philippine government.

The Muslim influence came to Mindanao from Indonesia. Migration and traders moving through the many islands that form a loose boundary between the two countries created the various Muslim population centers in the southern Philippines in the 15th century. The Spanish colonial administration attempted to dislodge the Islamic faith with Christianity but was unsuccessful.

With the arrival of the Americans in 1898 a completely different policy was established. The Americans wanted to end the violence on Mindanao. Firepower was introduced by the U.S. Army. The Moros had not experienced this under the Spaniards. The effect of this action by the U.S. military was a heated rebellious conflict lasting until 1913 when the American campaign ended and the Moros recognized the sovereignty of the U.S. over the Moro population centers of Mindanao. Created in 1901, the Philippine constabulary (with American officers) would play a major role in law enforcement in the Moro population centers. The U.S. allowed the Moros to practice their religion. Also, with this came an administrative system that provided for fair treatment and security. General John J. Pershing served in the campaign and was a legendary figure with the Moros. He earned their respect and allegiance. The precedent set by Pershing and other American military leaders would provide a good basis for obtaining Moro support for an American-led guerrilla movement in the 1940s. Had the movement been Filipino-led it is doubted that the Moro people would have backed and supported the movement. On the other hand, an American-led organization would in the minds of the Moros ensure that they would be fairly treated.

With the invasion of Mindanao by the Japanese and the resultant surrender of the USAFFE forces, both Americans and Filipinos "lost face" in the eyes of the Moros. The Moros now saw an opportunity to take revenge for past grievances. With the dissolution of the Philippine constabulary (this primary law and order organization had been absorbed into USAFFE after the war commenced), the way was now clear for the Moros to take action. They went on a rampage killing and wounding many. Some Moros tried to take back land from the Filipinos that had bought the land in good faith. At this point people like Luis Morgan stepped in with guerrilla forces to retaliate against the Moros on behalf of the Filipinos. With this civil war type environment going on between the Filipinos and he Moros the net advantage was going to the Japanese at the expense of the guerrilla movement.

As Fertig considered Morgan's offer of taking over his guerrilla organization, he was painfully aware of the intensity of animosity that Morgan's forces were generating among the Moros for protecting the Filipinos. Toward understanding better the problem that now faced the guerrilla movement, Fertig would have a number of in-depth conversations with Charlie Hedges and Charles Bolt about the Moro problem. Hedges was a long-term businessman on Mindanao who had worked with and employed Moros in his business dealings. Bolt, another American long timer in the Philippines, lived in the Kapatagan valley. He had several Moro tenants on his property and had many dealing with the Moros over the years. Fertig would also have conversations with Edward Kuder, a former American educator and retired superintendent of schools in the Moro area. In fact, Salipada Pendatun, son of a Datu and a Moro leader, had been reared in the Kuder household. In this environment he had received the personal attention of Kuder. Kuder, who had schooled many of the Moro leaders, was able to develop a technique of reasoning with them in a scholarly fashion. Despite the many comprehensive conversations that Fertig was able to hold with Kuder and Bolt about the Moro problem, the major hurdle in bringing them into the movement was still the reality that there was not a common cultural element or grouping upon which to obtain agreement. In fact, there were 10 different Moro groups. The most prominent were the Maranao in the province of Lanao; the Maguindanao in Cotabato province; and the Sulu and Tau Sug in the Zamboanga peninsula and the Sulu archipelago. If there was a dominant trait of these four groupings it was separatism and non-integration with the Christian-dominated Filipino society.

While deliberating the pros and cons of Morgan's offer, particularly the implications of the Moro involvement in a guerrilla movement, Fertig traveled to the Baroy area and met with Charles Bolt, who was a master mechanic at the Kolambugan sawmill. He resided about five kilometers south of Baroy. As previously mentioned, Bolt was an acquaintance of Hedges and was friendly with Morgan in the Kapatagan valley. Moreover, Bolt employed Moros on his property and knew many of their leaders. Spending time with Bolt and his family would prove a most fruitful experience for Fertig in better understanding the Moros and how they could be brought into the guerrilla movement against the Japanese.

During this visit Fertig learned some interesting aspects of Morgan's military expertise. Morgan had established a perimeter defense protecting the approaches to the Kapatagan valley and had established some sea coast defenses consisting of strong points covering most of the likely landing places. It should be pointed out that at this time the troop strength of the Japanese in this area of Mindanao was minimal. They could not hold an area indefinitely. Their tactic was to invade an area, demonstrate their strength and then withdraw. Because of Morgan's conflict with the Moros, he was unable to adequately man the defenses he had planned.

Staying with the Bolts and investigating the area, Fertig gathered information on Morgan and Tait and their current operations.[11] It was not a clear and rosy picture. Their guerrilla type operations had prevented complete control of the area by the Japanese but had caused unnecessary bloodshed and loss of life among the Moros. Without Morgan's protection of the Christian Filipino farmers in the Kapatagan Valley, the Moros would have reasserted their authority over lands that had been considered theirs for centuries. Yet they had sold these lands to the Christians settlers from the northern part of the Philippines. With the Japanese occupation, the authority of the Philippine government and constabulary had in effect ceased to exist. Under these circumstances the Moros were working to take back their lands.

Fertig commented about this in his draft manuscript:

> This is not a criticism of the Moro, it is an explanation of his basic philosophy—only the strong are capable of holding what they have. Morgan was fighting what could be considered a losing battle—maintain control over lands in question and expending resources that could better be used fighting the Japanese.[12]

There was some information that the Japanese were encouraging this warfare because they may have thought the Moros would be successful in eliminating Morgan as a threat.

During the visit with Bolt, Fertig met with Moro people on his property and under his control. One such person was Datu Umpa, a former school teacher in the Kapatagan Valley who had been sent to a university in Manila. He belonged to the most powerful branch of the blueblood Moro people. Fertig later wrote in his draft manuscript, "Umpa impressed me with his quiet but forceful ways."[13] They spent hours discussing the Moro problems. From Fertig's point of view a solution to the Moro problem was necessary if a guerrilla movement were to be formed and remain viable. The movement could not fight both the Japanese and Moro people at the same time.

While staying with the Bolt family, Fertig had the impression that Morgan had him under observation

Colonel Wendell W. Fertig wearing a Moro hat (courtesy MacArthur Memorial Archives, Norfolk, Virginia).

and was gathering data on his activities. Fertig surmised that he was preparing himself for the ultimate meeting between the two on whether Fertig would accept command of Morgan's forces. Also, Fertig sensed that there was pressure from senior Filipino officers for Morgan to give up his command. Still trying to understand Morgan and his motivations, Fertig was conflicted as to the real Morgan personality. Was he a women chaser and a man after graft opportunities (as had been reported by some), or was there an element of redemption and idealism within Morgan that went beyond the current situation in how he was opposing the Japanese? Fertig was looking at the future of the Philippines; whether a person like Morgan could focus his leadership skills toward the postwar period where the results of his wartime efforts might catapult him toward regional or national leadership posts. If Fertig accepted Morgan's proposal of taking command of his forces, this then would commence a test period for Morgan regarding whether he can become a Filipino leader with national aspirations or whether he would continue his current interest in chasing women and making a fast buck. In any case the die was about to be cast.

As has been mentioned, Fertig had many walks and discussions with Bolt during his visit. Bolt, an old soldier of the 1903 American army, had learned much during his many years in the Philippines. He understood both the Filipino and the Moro. Bolt told Fertig, "I am certain that a resistance movement could be organized." He further commented that the Japanese had not won the favor of the Filipino people. He also sensed the unpopularity of the Japanese among Filipinos was growing.[14]

Prior to visiting with Bolt, Fertig had conversations with Catholic priests in Baroy. Their views bolstered what Bolt had said. In effect, the Filipinos were finding their life under the Japanese was not the picnic they had been led to believe by the propaganda coming from Manila. Discontent was common and this development would bode well for an emerging guerrilla movement.[15]

About September 1, 1942, Morgan and Tait made an official call at the Bolt residence. The conversation was general and covered the activities of the war since its inception. Morgan said that he now had a force of 600 riflemen and approximately 60,000 rounds of ammunition. He also had machine guns and automatic rifles. Morgan commented that some of the weapons were not working properly. Bolt offered to repair them. The meeting ended with nothing resolved.[16]

Days later, Datu Umpa, the Moro chief, invited Fertig for a meal. Charlie Hedges also attended. Datu Umpa had also included an older Moro Datu whose people were also being protected by Bolt. Fertig talked at great length with the old Datu about the actions of Morgan and Tait. The older Datu said that if an American was chosen as overall commander he was quite sure that Moro cooperation could be assured. This was of great interest in the meeting because he was a respected Datu in the area of Lake Lanao. He said his brother, the strongest Datu in the area, was ready to swear allegiance to the American commander—just has his father had sworn allegiance to Pershing.[17] Later, Bolt commented that the Moro people were sick of the endless fighting and killing with Morgan's troops. At this juncture Fertig believed that he had a solution to the Moro problem. The Moro leadership had to be dealt with on an individual basis, not as one group. Moreover, he came to the conclusion that the Moros would participate in the guerrilla movement if they were under an American commander.

A few days later Morgan and Tait returned to Bolt's residence. They now appeared ready for serious discussions with Fertig. Morgan said the situation was now beyond his control. The number of Moro people facing his troops was increasing, particularly as more were moving down from the Lake region. He was also worried about a Japanese attack from Misamis Occidental and Kolambugan against his region of Baroy. He also mentioned that Filipino officers were insistent that Morgan give up his command. The foregoing and the fact that Fertig was the senior American officer on the island now prompted Morgan to make the offer to Fertig. Fertig said he would take the matter under advisement and contact Morgan in a few days about his final decision.[18] Fertig also told Morgan that he was having a table of organization prepared and would formulate a suggested course of action for taking command. If these terms were acceptable to Morgan, discussions could then begin on how to transform the movement into a viable military organization rather than a ragtag gang of robbers. One can just imagine what effect these comments must have had on the stoic Morgan. He probably questioned in his mind as to what good a table of organization would do for the movement—the very thing he disliked being a part of; this was the reason he was offering the command to Fertig. The meeting was adjourned and a follow-on meeting was scheduled several days hence.

In the meantime Fertig began to review possible organization templates for a guerrilla force, using a 1935 military manual. Initially he decided to use a U.S. Army reserve division of 7,000 men as the template. While they did not yet have the personnel numbers for this, a reserve division would be the model for his initial organization, using the Philippine constabulary regional template as a tentative grouping of units to be organized. Fertig's plan was that he would assume the rank of division commander and Morgan would function as his chief of staff. Hedges would be named senior aide and personal adjutant. Tait would hold the position of commandant of headquarters troops.

Fertig's intention during the next meeting with Morgan and Tait was to include as many of Morgan's officers as possible. At this meeting he would announce his decision to assume command of Morgan's organization. He did not want to deal only with Morgan and then have his actions misstated when discussed with the junior officers. It was Fertig's objective when he took over the command to have the widest dissemination of the conditions for the formation of the new command. He did not want a situation where the troops could later claim that he had failed to state clearly his command position.

As Fertig approached the decision to assume command of Morgan's organization, he discussed his inner thoughts on this major step in his draft manuscript:

> It may sound egotistical, but at this interview (with Morgan) and the months that were to follow, I felt that I was indeed a man of destiny; that my course was chartered and that only success lay at the end of the trail. I did not at this time nor later envision failure although I recognized that our advance would be a series of ups and downs. It was obvious that with the odds against us we could not consistently win, and yet if we were to win only a part of the time and each time gain a little, we would in the end be successful.[19]

During the final meeting with Morgan and Tait at Bolt's house, Fertig outlined in concrete terms his ideas on how the guerrilla movement should proceed, particularly the cessation of armed actions against the Moro people.

While Fertig had been following very closely the growing hostility of the Filipino populace to the Japanese occupation, Tait had proposed a plan that would take advantage of this swelling resentment. Essentially he proposed that the movement launch an attack on the small Japanese presence in the province of Misamis Occidental, across Panguil Bay from their current location in Lanao. That area of Misamis Occidental had never been fully occupied and the Japanese strength was about 125 troops.

Tait further proposed that a small contingent of the newly reorganized guerrilla force make a raid on the province. If successful, a larger force would cross the bay with an announcement that a Brigadier General had arrived by submarine from MacArthur's headquarters and was prepared to take over the command of the guerrilla movement.[20]

Fertig believed that most aspects of this audacious proposal pointed to success. He interposed no objection to the concept and advised that the plan should continue. Once a probable date for the operation was set, Fertig would issue a proclamation in the name of the command saying the fight against the Japanese would now continue under the command of General MacArthur.

Later, Fertig talked with Charlie Bolt about his proposed plan with Morgan. Bolt told Fertig that Morgan should not be trusted and that Morgan would "barter his sister for a new woman." Moreover, he could not be relied upon as an honest leader and was extremely ambitious. Fertig acknowledged that he was aware of Morgan's weaknesses but recognized he was a leader and fighter. Fertig pointed out that prior to the surrender Morgan had kept his organization intact while more senior officers had given up and fled. In the aftermath his command had expanded and strengthened during a period when civilian rule was collapsing. While the follow-on actions of his organization against the Moro people were not justified, they came at a time when the local Christian population felt threatened. Now Morgan's organization was at a crossroads. It could continue as it had, but probably losing its effectiveness as its goals became detrimental to the local Filipino society at a time when the Japanese strength was increasing. If Fertig were to lead, the genesis of a reformed guerrilla movement would be established with increased organizational discipline. With these changes it now would be energized to launch a viable organization to confront the Japanese occupation. This was coming at a critical time when the local Filipino society had become increasingly hostile to the Japanese presence.

The day of assuming command had arrived. As requested, he met with the assembled officers of Morgan's organization. He was attired in a fresh uniform with newly minted stars of a brigadier general. His stature, his manner, the uniform and the stars of rank duly impressed the officers attending. On this occasion he would formally accept command of Morgan's organization. With an audacious act of promoting himself to a general officer he addressed Morgan's officers:

> "I have accepted command of this organization. Henceforth our designation will be the United States Forces in the Philippines. As of this date, you gentlemen are commissioned officers within the United States military establishment."[21]

At this meeting Fertig directed Tait, who had previously suggested taking over Misamis Occidental, to send an advance party to that province to verify the acceptable arrival of Fertig and Morgan in the province that was now scheduled for September 15, 1942. Fertig's leadership role in the new guerrilla movement would now make its first appearance.

3

Development of a
Guerrilla Movement

Based on reports from William Tait's operations group that there was a lack of a Japanese presence in the Misamis Occidental provincial area and that support of the local Filipinos for the guerrillas could be anticipated, Fertig and Morgan assembled a force of 200 guerrillas in Baroy, Lanao, and sailed across Panguil Bay to Tangub. At the same time the following proclamation, prepared by Fertig, was distributed in various parts of the province.

United States Army Forces In The Philippines
Office Of The Commanding General
In The Field Of Mindanao And Sulu

Proclamation

On September 18, 1942, our forces under Maj. L. L. Morgan completed the occupation of Misamis Occidental Province and Northern Zamboanga from the hands of the Japanese Military Government, and raised the American and Filipino flags therein.

In behalf of the United States of America, the Philippine Commonwealth Government is re-established in those regions under the Military Authorities. All civil laws and regulations will be followed except in those cases where they conflict with Military Laws. In such cases Military Laws will prevail.

This procedure shall continue to be enforced until such time when it shall be declared suspended, or terminated.

/s/ W. W. FERTIG

BRIGADIER GENERAL, USA
Commanding Mindanao & Sulu Force

It is interesting to note that Fertig wrote the draft of this proclamation on the back of an old court form that read "Notice of Delinquency in Payment of Real Property Tax."[1] Use of the reverse side of official and business forms and old documents was quite common as the war went on and paper became increasingly scarce. In reviewing Charles Hansen's papers many reports and memoranda between the guerrilla units were written on similar paper supplies. Furthermore, typewriters, ribbons and carbon paper were in extremely short supply, so duplicating and disseminating official documents usually involved copying the same document multiple times on different types of paper.

Leaving Tangub, Fertig's group headed up the coast to Misamis City. When they reached the city they were met by many enthusiastic people and a fiesta atmosphere enveloped their arrival. Thus far the landing in Misamis Occidental had been a major success.

It should be noted that there are interesting differences between Fertig's wartime diary and his draft manuscript, written after the war, regarding the time line of the guerrillas' capture of Misamis Occidental in September 1942. The diary entry for September 16 states that Tait (also known as Sambo) crossed over to Tangulo.[2] On September 17 the diary states guns were captured In Tangub and Sambo continued with the raid on Misamis City.[3] Entry for September 19 states Morgan proceeded to Misamis Occidental as Sambo had not returned.[4] Diary entry for September 24 mentions that Morgan and Sambo have been on the other side (Misamis Occidental) for eight days but no retaliation from the Japanese.[5]

In his diary, Fertig states on September 27:

> I have accepted command of the Mindanao force in the field. As I am in the district I had better command rather than be mere bystander.[6]

The October 4 entry mentions Fertig went to Baroy to meet Sambo who asked that they go to Tangub to start a tour of Misamis Occidental.[7] The dary notes on October 5 that Fertig and party arrived at Tangub to make an inspection of the province.[8]

In his letter to General Casey, dated July 1, 1943, Fertig stated that on October 1, 1942, Morgan asked him to take command of the movement.[9] This was just after Morgan and Tait had returned from Misamis Occidental.

A major question is why Fertig changed the dates of his arrival in Misamis Occidental, as noted in his diary, to those used in the draft manuscript. The manuscript was Fertig's written draft upon which Keats based his book about Fertig. It was written after the war. Both the manuscript and Keats' book use Tait's departure for Misamis Occidental as September 13 and the departure date for Fertig as September 15. By contrast the diary states Fertig and party arrived at Tangub on October 5. These changes in dates may have been made to have the arrival of Fertig in Misamis Occidental province track with the Proclamation of September 18. As mentioned, the changes of dates were made during the writing of the draft manuscript, perhaps to bring more consistency to what actually happened.

What possibly transpired in Fertig's situation may be similar to the circumstances surrounding the signing of the American Declaration of Independence. The document was not signed, as many believe, on July 4, 1776. The signing began on August 2 and continued through the year as absent delegates returned to Philadelphia. Again, no formal signing ceremony ever took place on July 4.

With the positive reception in Misamis Occidental behind him, Fertig now had to look ahead to the important steps of ensuring the forward momentum of the guerrilla movement. These included the following:

- Reaching out to other guerrilla units on Mindanao for inclusion into the movement
- Cultivating the business families of the province such as the Ozamis family
- Building relationships with the Catholic Church and missionaries in the area
- Commencement of contact with local judges and officials
- Establishment of a command headquarters at the old Spanish fort in Misamis City as a symbol and seat of authority—something that the local people could see and visit
- Modification of the movement's command structure to include regiments under one division that had been established

Looking beyond the provincial area of Misamis Occidental, Fertig now had to focus on other guerrilla groups on Mindanao that should logically come under his command, particularly since he had projected the impression that he was a general officer of the U.S. Army that had been sent to Mindanao from MacArthur's headquarters in Australia. Associated with this effort would be establishing radio contact with MacArthur's headquarters. Unfortunately Fertig did not have transmitters, or ones that he knew about, that could communicate with Australia.

In the meantime other American guerrilla leaders, already established and seeing or hearing of Fertig's proclamation, paid a visit to his headquarters to meet this general officer who had just arrived from Australia. Among these guerrilla leaders were Major Ernest McClish and Captain Clyde Childress. Both had been battalion commanders, assigned to the Philippine army from American units. Their respective battalions had participated in the initial defense of Mindanao. With their units unable to meet the Japanese onslaught and personnel dispersed, these two officers took to the hills a few hours before the surrender was effective. They remained in this mode even after the official American surrender. With the passing months they were able to establish units operating in the border areas of Misamis Oriental and Bukidnon provinces. The historical record is somewhat hazy as to what was discussed at these meetings. Fertig surely had to reveal his deception about being a brigadier general and coming from Australia. McClish and Childress probably understood the reason for this and accepted the command authority that was contained in his proclamation. These issues aside, Fertig promoted both officers to lieutenant colonel and major, respectively, and appointed them commander and deputy commander of the 110th Division. This command responsibility would include the provinces of Surigao, Davao, Agusan and portions of Misamis Oriental, where its first headquarters, in Balingasag, was located. (Due to the constant threat of Japanese discovery and attack, district and division headquarters had to be moved a number of times during the course of the war.)

It should be noted that the relationship between Fertig on the one hand and McClish and Childress on the other would have a difficult future. What was the basis of the future discord? Several factors may be involved, including personalities. First, Fertig was a reserve officer in the U.S. Army's Corps of Engineers while McClish and Childress were regular Army and combat arms officers. The latter two had battlefield experience and combat command while Fertig had not. While McClish and Childress would accept Fertig's rank, they probably thought it cheeky and audacious of him to have impersonated a general officer arriving from Australia. Nonetheless they probably respected his strategy in obtaining the Filipino backing for the guerrilla movement and bringing organization and discipline to the disparate opposition to the Japanese occupation. Certainly Fertig's poise as a general officer must have impressed them. Moreover, he provided inspiration to a greater view of the guerrilla movement than other American officers on the scene. Perhaps demand for paperwork and organizational detail were more than they could bear in the environment in which they were cast. Because of geographic distance between the 110th Division's headquarters in Balingasag, Misamis Oriental, and Fertig's headquarters in Misamis City, conflict between the two parties was mitigated. However, as the war progressed and logistical support from Australia became available, increasingly Fertig had a say in their ammunition supply and what battles against the Japanese would be justified in the expenditure of this scarce commodity. Also, there was the issue of intelligence and information on the Japanese that MacArthur's headquarters very much wanted and needed. Increasingly Fertig had to mediate the issue of attacking the Japanese as opposed to expanding intelligence collection. (This issue would promote distrust and dislike between the two parties but not on the scale that transpired when Fertig was forced to move his command to the Agusan River valley in the fall of 1943. With their two commands in closer proximity, animosity and conflict became more heated. The problems between the two parties would increase and grow. (Details on this are discussed in Chapter 9 of this book.)

Relative to bringing other guerrilla groups under his command, Fertig ordered Morgan to visit other areas on Mindanao to enlist personnel and groups into his movement. While Morgan was away Fertig was able to solidify his outreach to the Moros. He made an agreement with Datu Umpa, whom he had met while staying with Charles Bolt in late August. The agreement, while vague, articulated an understanding that the Fertig/Morgan force would end actions against the Moros in exchange for the Moros not attacking the guerrillas. Future cooperation against the Japanese was implied.[10]

It was during Morgan's recruiting effort that he met with Charles Hansen, then hiding out in the northern Surigao area. As Henry Hansen, his son, describes it, Morgan arrived in a large sailing banca. He had an outgoing demeanor but there was an almost arrogant nature about him. With a Tommy gun strapped across his chest, he projected a command authority as he stepped off the banca. Talking with Hansen, he described the guerrilla organization that he and Fertig were attempting to develop. He advised Hansen not to get involved in any guerrilla resistance until guidance was received from Fertig's command. Later, Hansen would receive an invitation from Lieutenant Colonel McClish, Commander, 110th Division, to join him in a formal meeting in Medina, Misamis Oriental. Hansen's two teenage sons, Rudyard and Henry, accompanied him to this meeting. At division headquarters Hansen was returned to active duty as a captain in the U.S. Army. His two sons were later inducted as infantrymen in the 114th Regiment of the 110th Division.

Vitally important to the guerrilla movement was the inclusion of family and governmental elites into the process of opposing the Japanese. While some may have cooperated initially with the Japanese occupiers, a majority were horrified by the godlessness and brutality of the Japanese. Fertig felt that having governmental officials, backed by the guerrillas, return to their offices to do the people's work was vitally important. Also important was the support of the general public for the guerrilla movement. Having worked in several provinces with the mining industry Fertig understood the importance of family elites and the Catholic Church. In the case of Misamis Occidental province, the major influential family was the Ozamis clan. The matriarch of this family was Doña Carmen and she wielded a great deal of persuasion among women of the province. Understanding the power of the Filipino women, Fertig put out a general order to his staff officers to attend Sunday Mass. The Filipino women, seeing the guerrilla leaders attending Mass on Sunday, would go home and brow-beat their husbands about supporting the movement. While these initiatives were somewhat inconsequential, when added up in the abstract they made a difference in the level of support that was afforded to the guerrilla movement.

Shortly after issuing the general order for headquarters staff to attend Mass, Fertig received via messenger an invitation to attend dinner at *Casa Ozamis*. Arriving at the residence in his best uniform, Fertig was impressed with the tastefully furnished *casa* of the Ozamis family and the gracious and personal reception that he was given by Doña Carmen. Others attending the dinner included Father Callanan, an Irish priest, and Doctor Contreras. In addition to the invited guests were Doña Carmen's five attractive sisters. The family treated their guests with the grace and hospitality of their Spanish heritage.[11]

During the dinner Fertig was given the opportunity to speak about the guerrilla movement. He underscored the need for unity in opposing the Japanese. This required the continued support by the people of their local civilian government that was a major player in upholding the laws which the military must always honor and protect.[12] After questions from Doña Carmen regarding Morgan, Fertig said that he was sending him on a mission to other guerrilla areas to bring them into the movement. Doña Carmen then asked Fertig if he wished her family to help, but then she changed course and with a smile said, "We, of course, will help!" She had given Fertig Misamis Occidental and Father Callanan had not objected in giving the guerrilla movement its due in a Caesar-like fashion.

Fertig at this juncture had secured the active support of the province's leading family and the passive approval of the Church. Later, Chick Parsons,

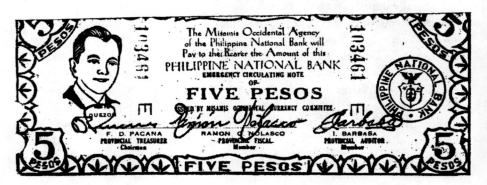

Emergency five peso note signed by F. D. Pacana, Misamis Occidental Provincial Treasurer (Thomas Mitsos, Guerrilla Radio—AGOM, American Guerrillas of Mindanao Records, AGOM Descendants Group, Falls Church, Virginia).

with his "padre kits" sent in with the submarine resupply missions, would affirm the U.S. support for the Church and the Filipino people.

In a symbolic move Fertig established his command headquarters in the old Spanish fort within Misamis City. Flying both the American and Philippine flags from its ramparts, it became an outward sign to the public that the guerrilla movement was behind the local government and the people in opposing the Japanese occupation.

In turning to the former Filipino ruling elite for inclusion in the movement, Fertig identified several in the region that would be most useful. One such person was Mr. F. D. Pacana. Fertig had met him through Jesus Montalvan, who had married into the Ozamis family. Prior to the war Pacana had been treasurer of the province but had been removed by the Japanese for noncooperation. It was Fertig's belief that such civil servants would be invaluable to the movement when the Japanese presence was displaced by the guerrillas. Their loyalty would qualify them for reinstatement in running vital governmental functions.[13]

Mr. Pacana had expressed to Fertig his concern on how the guerrilla movement would finance itself. He made his views known to Fertig early on in their discussions. He mentioned that when President Quezon visited the island, prior to his departure for Australia in March of 1942, he had appointed a Provisional Emergency Currency Board (PECB) for each province on Mindanao. Pacana was a member of the board for Misamis Occidental province. Members of the PECB were authorized to print money. In the case of Misamis Occidental the amount approved for printing was ₱3 million. Although plates for printing the money were not available, the amount authorized by President Quezon was still available. This was to be a godsend for Fertig and the movement. Later, Fertig would meet with the PECB for funding approvals for continued operation of the local government and the guerrilla organization. Guerrilla postage stamps were also introduced to facilitate mail service within guerrilla-controlled areas.

As a side note, in December 1942 Fertig received a letter from his brother, Claude, informing him that he and Laverne were safe on Panay and that he was serving

Two centavo guerrilla postal service stamp used in areas controlled by the Mindanao guerrillas (Thomas Mitsos, Guerrilla Radio— AGOM, American Guerrillas of Mindanao Records, AGOM Descendants Group, Falls Church, Virginia).

as the engineer for the guerrilla group led by Lieutenant Colonel Macario Peralta. In his reply Wendell indicated that he wished that Claude and Laverne would move to Mindanao, mentioning that the Ozamis family had extended an invitation for Laverne to stay at their home. He added that he needed a competent engineering officer in his command, especially one experienced in dealing with Filipinos.

The emissary from Panay also delivered a letter to Fertig from Peralta, in which he proposed merging their two commands. At this point MacArthur's staff had not yet established military district territorial boundaries and responsibilities. Prior to the surrender in May 1942, Colonel Albert Christie was commander of the USAFFE forces on Panay. These included the 61st Division (PA), two reconstituted infantry regiments and miscellaneous units—a total force of about 7,000 men. Peralta, a young Philippine army officer, was his Chief of Operations. As the situation on Bataan and then Corregidor became more and more untenable, Christie was prepared to withdraw his forces into the mountains and conduct guerrilla operations against the Japanese. Unfortunately, after the surrender of USAFFE forces on Luzon, all commanders in the various islands were ordered to surrender their forces, an order Christie reluctantly obeyed. However, only about ten percent of his forces surrendered; the remainder, including Peralta, did not. Peralta named himself commander and transitioned the remaining forces into a guerrilla organization.

Fertig's response to Peralta's proposal was cordial and positive. He sent an agreement stipulating that if Peralta's troops were placed under Fertig's command, "Peralta would be designated commanding officer of the Panay Division, with the rank of Colonel." As it turned out, MacArthur's staff in Australia developed a plan to split the Philippines into military districts and on February 13, 1943, advised both Fertig and Peralta of their command boundaries—Fertig's Tenth Military District would be limited to the islands of Mindanao and Sulu, and Peralta's Sixth Military District would be limited to the islands of Panay and Romblon. Both would report to MacArthur's headquarters. Fertig viewed this as one of the actions taken by "inexperienced staff officers in Australia" who were unfamiliar with conditions in the Philippines.[14]

As Fertig later expanded the guerrilla movement throughout Mindanao, he found it necessary to issue a proclamation revoking the authority of the PECB, replacing it with the Mindanao Emergency Currency Board (MECB) to print emergency notes for all of Mindanao. Fertig requested a new authorization for the printing of money and new appointments to the MECB. President Quezon raised the authorization for all of Mindanao to ₱20 million and approved the new members of MECB on April 10, 1943.[15] With this approval the submarine resupply missions would include plates and paper for the printing of notes. The MECB would oversee the printing of ₱20 million in notes and this currency was then used to pay for operational expenses of the Tenth Military District, as well as for provincial and municipal requirements. Later, Sam Wilson, a Manila businessman, would oversee the printing of all currency authorized by the Philippine president and the commander of the Tenth Military District. In this capacity Wilson would be the technical adviser to the MECB. He would keep detailed accountings for all expenditures and obligations on monies that had been authorized for printing.

Once Fertig had established himself in Misamis Occidental and the guerrilla organization was commencing to function as he had planned, he began to fine tune his command as an effective counter to the Japanese presence. While Fertig liked the idea of the division concept for each geographic region of Mindanao, the application of the Philippine constabulary template (districts, sectors and sub-sectors) was not working for the movement. Many of the commanders were inexperienced and were, at times, dictatorial toward the population for which they were expected to curry cooperation and respect. To correct this, Fertig decided to do away with the constabulary organization template and replace it with a regiment type organization under a regional division commander. Under this concept companies would be formed to cover several towns and would report to a battalion covering a larger area. The battalion would then report to a regiment which had responsibility for a regional area.

As the war progressed, these regiments then made up divisions that would all report to the Tenth Military District. Fertig, as the district commander, would be relieved of many details of administration so he might focus on the overall thrust of the war as it related to the entire island of Mindanao. Thus, the Tenth Military District, as designated by MacArthur's headquarters, represented a single command for Mindanao with Fertig as the commander. Later, in January 1944, after Fertig had moved his headquarters to the Agusan River area, he would establish "A" Corps with Robert V. Bowler commanding. Bowler would also function as deputy commander of the Tenth Military District and assume command should anything happen to Fertig. Eventually, six divisions would comprise and complete the Tenth Military District organization until the end of the war.

While finance was a major issue faced by the Mindanao guerrilla movement, there were other related economic problems that also had to be confronted by the command. To combat inflation which was becoming rampant, a Force Supply Administration (FSA) and a Trading Post Administration

(TPA) were established. The purpose of the FSA was to oversee the fair distribution of foodstuffs to the civilian population. Officers in the Tenth Military District would assist the FSA in police powers to insure compliance for fair food prices. The Trading Post concept was to create local municipal outlets for the distribution of rice and corn at a minimum profit.

Farm projects were also encouraged among the populace controlled by the guerrillas. This activity included community farms, victory gardens, poultry and hog raising projects sponsored by both the guerrillas and civil entities. Other home industries such as weaving were also encouraged. The production of salt, coconut oil and alcohol (from tuba) was promoted. The last commodity was a high priority for the guerrillas who needed the alcohol to power generators for communications and the few vehicles that they possessed.

During Chick Parsons' visit with Fertig in March 1943 the subject of civil government being reinstituted by the guerrillas was raised. Parsons indicated that there were some on MacArthur's headquarters staff that were concerned about this initiative, particularly since there was a Philippine government-in-exile. After the war people might be inclined to vote for those who remained instead of those who went into exile.[16] Nevertheless, following his instincts and knowledge gained from years of experience in the Philippines, Fertig believed that local governments supported by the guerrillas should be established throughout Mindanao so that foundations would be provided for the creation of civil authority. Directors of civil affairs were appointed for the operational divisions covering their respective geographic areas.

Captain Hansen was very much involved with civil affairs in the 110th Division. His assignments included liaison and food control officer for the province of Surigao as well as procurement officer for the division. In these capacities he had daily and in-depth contact with Filipino civilian officials. Hansen's personal papers, containing memorandums and reports about these conversations, reflect the concerns of the Filipinos in Surigao province regarding the Japanese methods to keep an important local commodity, *palay* (unhusked rice), from the guerrillas. This was a very crucial issue for Hansen, who had the responsibility for supplying more than 5,000 guerrillas in his division with sufficient supplies of food. When Japanese operations along the coast destroyed government civic buildings, churches or schools, Hansen was the first guerrilla official they called upon to document the wanton destruction the Japanese were inflicting upon the coastal towns of the province. The officials had trust in the guerrillas that this damage would be noted and recorded for claims against the Japanese government after the war. Again, civil affairs were a most important responsibility of the 110th Division, as well as other divisions in the Tenth Military District. Outreach to local and civil officials was a continuing and ongoing effort for guerrilla officers like Hansen—goodwill on both sides was essential for combating the common enemy. On a personal level, for Hansen this goodwill was critical for the safety of his wife and young daughters who were hiding out in his area of operations and were known by a number of Filipinos.[17]

4

Connectivity with Australia

Fertig continued to be stymied by his inability to establish communications with Australia. To remedy this he put together a small task force of personnel familiar with communications. Personnel vital to this task included both Filipino and American servicemen (American personnel were from the Army Air Corps that had been stationed at Del Monte airfield and radiomen from the Motor Torpedo Squadron 3 that had been stranded on Mindanao). While they were largely radio operators, none, unfortunately, were technicians. Robert Ball was designated as the officer in charge of this communications group which would later become known as the Force Radio Section (FRS) of the Tenth Military District. In early 1942 Ball was attached to the Army Air Corps as a radio operator with the 5th Air Base Group. Captured by the Japanese, he was interned at Keithley Barracks, Dansalan, Lanao province. On July 1, 1942, he escaped from the prison camp with William Johnson, William Knortz and James Smith. After joining the guerrillas he was commissioned a Second Lieutenant and was designated as commanding officer of an expanding signal detachment.

Under Ball, the FRS efforts to establish communications with MacArthur's headquarters were most enterprising. Amateur Filipino radio personnel would provide the early inputs to this project. These included Alfredo Bontuyan, Glicerio Lim and Gerardo and Eleno Almendras. This group had already begun recovering items that could be used in constructing a transmitter, e.g., discarded ham radio components, radio tubes and transformers, as well as equipment from local movie theaters. Before the war, Gerardo Almendras had taken radio courses from a U.S. correspondence school. Using diagrams from these courses, Almendras attempted to configure a potential transmitter. These efforts were supported by Florentino Opendo, a former Bureau of Aeronautics radio operator who had some previous experience in the construction of a transmitter. While unclear, in the end the achievement of constructing a crude transmitter probably resulted from the combined efforts of the Almendras brothers and Opendo.[1] As the group moved forward in the early testing of their equipment they were joined by Roy Bell, a former physics professor from Silliman University in Dumaguete, Negros Oriental. He was also a ham radio operator. At Fertig's invitation, he crossed the Mindanao Sea to Mindanao, landing at Dipolog in northern Zamboanga. From there he proceeded to join the fledgling FRS group in Bonifacio, Misamis Occidental, in late January 1943. Bonifacio was chosen as a second FRS operational site because its remoteness in the hills provided better security from the Japanese. It was located about 15 miles from Misamis City, site of Fertig's headquarters.[2]

In the meantime, the FRS commenced testing the crude transmitter they had assembled—at this point it was just an operational hum with no effective transmitting capability. After Bell's arrival, he solved their aerial problem but a crystal was still lacking. The makeshift crystal was devised using copper wire wound around a piece of bamboo. However, the crudeness of the device caused it to skip around the frequency spectrum. Despite the primitive state of this transmitter, it was nonetheless capable of sending out an erratic signal into the ether. Now the experienced American military radio operators could practice their dots and dashes in attempting to transmit a signal to an American station somewhere in the Pacific theater. The radio operators in this phase included William Johnson and William Konko from PT Boat Squadron 3 and Robert Ball and George Hall, U.S. Army Air Corps.[3]

Finally a signal from this FRS effort was received by KFS in San Francisco. Initially thought to be a Japanese hoax, the station decided to string the sending station on until its origin could be established, verified and some authentication developed. This latter effort was complex but luck played a role.

Several months earlier, in December 1942, Jordan A. "Ham" Hamner, Charles M. "Charlie" Smith and Athol Y. "Chick" Smith, mining friends of Fertig who had evacuated from Masbate, departed Mindanao for Australia in a 21-foot sailboat dubbed the *Or Else*. Their only navigational aids were a mining compass, a National Geographic map covering the Pacific Ocean from the Hawaiian Islands to the Philippines, India to Australia, and a ruler/protractor. With much luck the three, along with two Filipino crewmen, made it to the northern coast of Australia after a perilous thirty-day trip.[4] Prior to his departure, Charlie Smith and Fertig established a code that Smith would take with him to Australia—MSF. This meant Mindanao Smith Fertig. With reporting now going to Washington regarding Hamner and Smith's arrival in Australia, as well as information on Fertig and the guerrilla movement, the Navy and the Federal Bureau of Investigation commenced an investigation to establish Fertig's legitimacy. This included an interview with Fertig's wife, Mary, in Golden,

Colorado. In this interview she revealed the following: after Fertig's arrival in Mindanao he was able to write a letter to her saying, "Had pineapple for breakfast." Prior to the war Fertig often vacationed at the Del Monte Club on Mindanao, playing golf and eating fresh pineapple. To her this meant that he was now on Mindanao. Fertig was able to give his letter to one of the last officers departing for Australia and it was mailed to his wife as requested. With this information, Fertig's station was contacted by KFS using MSF in the call sign. It asked for the name of Fertig's oldest daughter and the place of residence. Fertig now knew that Charlie Smith had gotten through to Australia. Fertig supplied the information as requested. His authentication and that of his station was now established.

Unbeknown to Fertig, in February 1943 there was a parallel attempt to establish a communications system in Anakan, Misamis Oriental. Army Air Corps personnel Loyd Waters and Glyn Mitchell were working with Cecil Walter, an executive of the Anakan Lumber Company, in an effort to make a 250-watt transmitter operational. Prior to the outbreak of the war Walter had used the transmitter to communicate with both Manila and the U.S. After some weeks of effort, they, also, successfully communicated with KFS in San Francisco. During a visit to the Anakan site in May, Parsons brought instructions and codes from Fertig and communications were established between Walter's radio station and Fertig's FRS. Later, Waters and Mitchell joined the Tenth Military District's FRS operation in Agusan.[5]

Even so, time passed and Fertig became more impatient, particularly upon hearing through Roy Bell that Lieutenant Colonel Macario Peralta on Panay island had radio communications with MacArthur's headquarters. Fertig then had the FRS section send a radio message directly to the War Department via KFS that he had established a guerrilla command on Mindanao. KFS responded but said it had no traffic. Finally in early February KFS advised that Fertig's FRS would in the future receive communications directly from MacArthur's headquarters using a call sign of KAZ. (In following portions of this book MacArthur's headquarters in Australia will be referred to as General Headquarters Southwest Pacific Area [GHQ SWPA]). Later, KAZ sent the following message to Fertig directly from MacArthur: "XXX LT COL W FERTIG (CE) INF DESIGNATED TO COMMAND THE TENTH MILITARY DISTRICT (ISLANDS OF MINDANAO AND SULU) XXX HE WILL PERFECT INTELLIGENCE NET COVERING NINTH MIL DISTRICT (SAMAR-LEYTE) XXX NO OFFICER OF RANK OF GENERAL WILL BE DESIGNATED AT PRESENT XXX."[6]

Fertig was now once again Lieutenant Colonel Fertig. His command responsibilities had been laid out by MacArthur and they did not include waging a war against the Japanese. Intelligence was now the number one priority for GHQ SWPA.

FRS became a valuable component in the success of the Tenth Military District. Its connectivity within Mindanao and the outside world was vital to its operations. Survivability was a key element in its ability to service the guerrillas. It had to be relocated eight times before the Americans returned in October of 1944. FRS used the following locations for its operations:

Dates	*Station Locations*
January 1943–June 1943	Misamis Occidental
January 1943 to July 1943	Bonifacio, Misamis Occidental (FRS back-up station)
July 1943 to December 1943	Liangan, Lanao
December 1943 to March 1944	Esperanza, Agusan
March 1944 to June 1944	Talacogon, Agusan
June 1944 to August 1944	Waloe, Agusan
August 1944 to November 1944	Umayon River, Agusan
November 1944 to January 1945	La Paz, Agusan[7]

Another noteworthy member of the FRS was Beverly "Ben" Farrens, who served as a code officer. His military experience had not prepared him for this new assignment. Like many other U.S. military personnel, his life and career had been turned upside down after the invasion of the Japanese. Arriving in the Philippines in July 1941, Farrens, a Private First Class, was assigned to the 19th Bomb Group, 14th Squadron, U.S. Army Air Corps, at Clark Field. After the Japanese attack on December 8, which resulted in the destruction of the B-17s based there, members of his unit were sent to Mindanao by ship. Their mission was to repair, refuel and guard the remaining B-17s and other aircraft at the Del Monte airfield. In March 1942 he was assigned to a contingent providing protective security for President Quezon and his family as they transited Mindanao on their way to Australia. After their departure, Farrens was assigned to Lake Lanao to support Navy PBY seaplane operations there. Following the surrender, Farrens and 13 others took to the hills rather than turn themselves in to the Japanese. For a time they lived on meager rations among the indigenous people of the hill country. Meeting up with U.S. service personnel who had escaped from Keithley Barracks, they made their way to the Kapai Valley in Lanao province where they lived with the Moro people. In December 1942 the group proceeded to Misamis Occidental province where they joined Fertig's guerrillas. Commissioned a second lieutenant, Farrens was assigned as a code officer with the FRS.

As previously mentioned, FRS had to move many times between January 1943 and January 1945 due to vulnerability to Japanese attack. With the imminent threat to the station in Bonifacio in July 1943, Farrens led the successful evacuation of the facility, with all instruments and other equipment intact, to the new location in Liangan, Lanao province. For this exemplary achievement Farrens was awarded the Bronze Star.[8]

Lieutenant Beverly "Ben" Perry Farrens led the successful evacuation of the Force Radio Section from Bonifacio, Misamis Occidental, to Liangan, Lanao, in July 1943 (Beverly "Ben" Perry Farrens collection).

It should be noted that the FRS was off the air only once, and just for 36 hours during this move from Bonifacio to Liangan. Until the end of the war it was a 24 hours a day, seven days a week operation. During the final stages of the U.S. plan to liberate the Philippines the FRS was providing communications support for 32 coast watcher stations.

In the early part of this chapter the development of Fertig's connectivity with Australia was discussed and the creation of the Force Radio Section (FRS). After communications were established with MacArthur's headquarters the role of FRS increased dramatically as coast watcher stations were established and the resultant flow of intelligence to the U.S. command in Australia, particularly the U.S. Navy. As was pointed out earlier, FRS had to be relocated eight times because of the needs of Fertig's command and the periodic threat from Japanese military forces, both on the ground and from the air.

The following will discuss the daily operation of the FRS station as it met the difficulties of moving from one site to another. This narrative will begin with the FRS station at Liangan, Lanao. The personnel assigned there included:

> Kenneth L. Bayley, 19th Bomb Group
> Wilbur E. Dallenback, 19th Bomb Group
> James L. Garland, 19th Bomb Group
> William F. Konko, PT Boat Squadron 3
> Francis J. Napolillo, PT Boat Squadron 3
> Marvin H. DeVries, PT Boat Squadron 3
> Lowell G. Holder, 19th Bomb Group
> Harold D. Martin, 19th Bomb Group
> Thomas Mitsos, 19th Bomb Group
> Leonard R. LeCouvre, 19th Bomb Group
> Frederick Marston Taylor, 19th Bomb Group
> Beverly Perry Farrens, 19th Bomb Group
> Lincoln Hall DaPron, 19th Bomb Group
> Edward O. Chmielewski, Army Signal Corps
> Alma Bud Mills, 19th Bomb Group
> Sam J. Wilson, USN Intelligence

(The foregoing personnel were pioneers in the Force Radio Section. During the course of the war numerous other personnel would serve in various capacities in the FRS operations.)

The commanding officer of the radio station was Lieutenant Commander Wilson, USNR, with Harold Martin in charge of the code room. The station was in operation from July 1943 to December 1943. It was located three kilometers above the coastal town of Liangan, Lanao, on the north coast of Mindanao. To get there one had to walk alongside a small-gauged railway track that led to a ravine, which had to be crossed on the railroad ties. A second ravine had to be crossed before arriving at the station's location. These ravines varied in depth from 20 to 50 feet. The station personnel had access to a railroad hand car which was utilized for transporting diesel fuel, food and radio equipment. Rice, dried fish and vegetables had to be brought to the station to feed some 40 station and support personnel.[9]

Periodically the Japanese would utilize direction finding techniques to locate the source of the FRS radio transmissions, resulting in bombing raids on its site. During this period the station, if lucky, might go as long as 30 days without attacks from the air.

In September 1943 the U.S. Navy submarine the USS *Bowfin* arrived at the Liangan area with seven tons of radio equipment, arms, ammunition and medical supplies. Each new piece of radio equipment was transported to the station for survival testing in the jungle. Some of the radio transmitters were more susceptible to the high humidity of the jungle and would often short out. After some experimentation the station personnel learned that leaving the models on 24 hours a day would keep them from failing. The only problem was this 24-hour daily operation would consume twice as much fuel. Eventually the station received improved sets that would not short out.

During the early stages electricity for operating the station's radio equipment was a non-problem. Many lumber camps, plantations and affluent locals had their own diesel generating units and 200-gallon tanks of diesel fuel, which were all made available to the guerrillas to support the operation of the station. Fairbanks Morse was a common generator that was available for use by the station.

Every morning members of the station personnel would be awakened at dawn by the crowing of roosters, the chattering of monkeys and other early morning noises from birds and animals in the jungle surrounding the site of the station. The area around the station also had its share of roosters that would compete in cockfights, a favorite pastime organized by the locals on a regular basis. Many of the FRS personnel participated in the betting activity that went on during these cockfights.

As they prepared for the workday the station personnel would sit down for some "good ole-fashioned military chow." Breakfast would consist of rice or corn mush and rice coffee. Occasionally this meal would be supplemented with dried fish, vegetables or *camotes* (local sweet potatoes). Fruits, such as bananas, papayas, pineapples and pomelos (Chinese grapefruit) were available on the seacoast but were scarce in the remote location of the station.[10]

After breakfast the FRS personnel would start the daily routine of coding and decoding messages. The normal workday would be from dawn to dusk, between 10 and 12 hours per day, seven days a week. Their only time off was to eat and sleep; the only diversion was periodically betting on the cockfights.

The evening meal was usually served after dark. It consisted of rice, vegetables, *camotes* and an occasional piece of chicken or dried fish. After "dinner" the station personnel would relax, play cards, participate in their nightly bull sessions or attend periodic cockfights. The one advantage that the personnel had working at the headquarters radio station was that they were well informed of everything that happened around the islands and every night they would discuss important events that occurred that day. MacArthur's headquarters kept FRS personnel well informed about plans for the Leyte invasion and other attacks around the various islands. At approximately 10:00 p.m. the station personnel would head for their bunks for a night of rest from their very busy day.[11]

Initially, the only information provided to the families of most of the station personnel by their respective services was that they were missing in action. In time some were able to get letters out via the submarine missions and toward the end of the war return mail from families began to trickle in to the station personnel.[12]

Messages commenced coming as soon as the station went on the air. Coast watchers sent in messages containing information on Japanese activities,

Force Radio Section personnel at Liangan, Lanao. Left–right: Lowell Holder, Harold Martin, Thomas Mitsos, Leonard LeCouvre, Frederick Taylor, and Beverly "Ben" Perry Farrens (American Guerrillas of Mindanao Records, AGOM Descendants Group, Falls Church, Virginia).

especially those involving Japanese warships, freighters or aircraft operating in their respective areas. The messages received had to first be decoded and then sent to Fertig's headquarters for analysis. They would then be approved for decoding and transmission to GHQ SWPA in Australia. A normal day's work in the station would consist of handling 150–300 radio messages, or 4,500 to 9,000 messages per month.

With regard to the accuracy of the Japanese ship movement reporting from the coast watchers transmitted to GHQ SWPA, it should be noted that over a two year period three hundred ships were sunk, particularly between the Davao Gulf and Zamboanga city. With their kill ratio so high the U.S. Navy assigned several submarines on permanent duty around the island. While each of these submarines carried about 23 torpedoes, they would occasionally deplete their supply prior to running out of ships to sink. The Japanese losses around Mindanao were so high that their naval commanders resorted to cruising only after dark, which increased their travel time considerably.[13]

In October 1943 Fertig moved his headquarters to the Agusan River valley in the province of Agusan. This required also moving the FRS station to be collocated with his headquarters. Station personnel DaPron, Martin and Mitsos were sent to the Agusan River area to set up the station at its new location, arriving in Esperanza on December 4. All other personnel remained at the Liangan, Lanao site until the new station was established at Esperanza, close to the Agusan River. On December 22, the Japanese invaded Liangan and the station there was deactivated and all personnel moved to the new site in Esperanza.[14]

Relocation of the station to the Agusan River valley posed a food shortage problem for FRS personnel. Since the valley was flooded a good part of the year, planting a variety of crops was difficult, particularly rice. What was produced in the area was hardly enough for the local people. It required a full day to transport salted fish from the seacoast.[15]

The move of the FRS station to the Agusan River valley would be a far different experience for the FRS personnel. They were forced to move the station four times after relocating to Esperanza. This was primarily due to the Japanese military thrusts up the river against guerrilla positions. In January 1944 the station was moved up the river to Talacogon. In February Major James L. Evans, who had recently arrived by submarine, was put in command. Additional personnel also arrived at the station from Australia including four Navy radio operators and six Filipino operators. Reports from the various coast watcher stations and other intelligence information on the enemy situation were being sent in such a volume that going to a 24-hour operation daily became a necessity. In addition, two station components were assigned to process all of the incoming traffic. Another component was utilized to send flash messages to the Navy in Australia. A fourth component would process all of the message traffic containing intelligence reports to GHQ SWPA.

On March 15, 1944, a large Japanese force invaded Butuan, Agusan province, where the headquarters of the 110th Division was located. In addition, Japanese aircraft bombed every barrio along the river in an effort to destroy guerrilla radio installations and headquarters. These bombings continued for days. Over a two-day period Talacogon was bombed and strafed. Buildings housing the radio equipment, though not badly damaged, were riddled with bullet holes. One transmitter was hit but was able to be replaced immediately. As a contingency, a new facility was set up further up the river at Waloe. A team was dispatched to install generators and other support equipment there.[16]

On May 5 Japanese aircraft again bombed Talacogon. Immediate evacuation was ordered that day. That afternoon half of the radio station personnel went up the river to Waloe and arrived at the new site at around 8:00 p.m. They immediately began operating the radio equipment that had been set up by a team dispatched several weeks earlier. The personnel still at Talacogon dismantled all the remaining equipment and moved to Waloe that night. By dawn on May 6 the old facility had been completely evacuated and a major move had again been made by FRS without disrupting or missing any radio traffic. That morning six Japanese aircraft bombed Talacogon—the aerial attack was so relentless that not one building was left standing.[17]

Lieutenant Commander Montgomery Wheeler, who had arrived by submarine from Australia in March, was designated the new commander of FRS, relieving Evans. After taking over FRS operations at Waloe Wheeler introduced the following code system which was put into use with stations of the Tenth Military District and became a valuable addition to FRS operating procedures. "An aircraft warning system was then organized with all FRS stations using a special code that was to facilitate the transmittal of plane traffic so that each spotter station would send in a short message, not exceeding ten groups, to include type of aircraft, speed, direction, altitude and position of the aircraft sighted. Such info could be reported to a fighter command station within minutes. This system proved invaluable when American fighters and bombers began operating over the islands in September 1944. Plane sightings with this code system were being reported from watcher stations to FRS and then to Australia within minutes after sighting."[18]

July 1944 became a critical point for the guerrillas. It became evident that a specific aim of the Japanese was to track down Fertig's headquarters and locations of FRS operating sites. Fortunately, during that period the FRS station under "A" Corps in western Mindanao was functioning effectively under the leadership of Lieutenant John Simmons, USNR, who had arrived via submarine on June 5, 1944. With the enemy closing in, Fertig decided that "A" Corps and the FRS station in western Mindanao should be prepared to take over the entire net control for all of the Tenth Military District in the event that the Waloe station and Fertig's headquarters were forced to move and go off the air. Lieutenant Commander Sam Wilson, with a complete list of codes, key phrases and station records, left Waloe in July 1944 bound for "A" Corps in western Mindanao to deliver the foregoing material. With this accomplished, "A" Corps was prepared, at a moment's notice, to take over should the Waloe station be forced to go off the air. Thus, the large intelligence network of coast watcher stations could continue to function with the back-up communication system.[19]

With the Japanese troops threatening Waloe, Fertig decided to leave and move his headquarters to the interior area of Agusan province. Taking with them two diesel motors, radio equipment and a small amount of food, the advance group departed Waloe on August 5. The group included Fertig, four FRS personnel and a number of armed Filipino guerrillas. The new site would be near the Umayon River, close to the Davao border. Traveling by small *barotos* (dugout canoes), the trip took 10 hours. At the site the group was to expand the camp, set up the generator, install the communications equipment and be prepared to take over the net. Arriving at the site they found that no camp existed, contrary to the instructions previously given laborers that were sent to set up the camp. There were only two crude huts in an area hacked out of the jungle. All personnel in the advance group then began establishing the camp, with the radio operators readying the communications equipment for operations. A small battery-operated set maintained contact with Waloe. Reports indicated the Japanese were closing in on Waloe, causing a sense of urgency on getting the new site up and running. When Wheeler ordered the Waloe station off the air on August 10 three sets were ready and commenced operating that night. The changeover had been completed without missing any message traffic! The remaining personnel from Waloe then made the long and arduous trip to the new site.[20]

Scarcity of food at this remote location was a greater problem than in previous sites. Fertig's draft manuscript described the situation as follows:

> We found the food situation was extremely critical and there was only food for 10 days. Fuel was also a problem but if we can remain here we can operate for 32 days on the present supply. Our one chance of survival depended on the lack of aggressiveness of the Japs.[21]

In early September large formations of planes began flying over the area of the Umayon River. A few hours later messages started coming in from coast

A typical *nipa* and bamboo structure for guerrilla facilities in remote areas such as the FRS site near the Umayon River in Agusan and the weather station in Dimoroc Canyon, Zamboanga (courtesy MacArthur Memorial Archives, Norfolk, Virginia).

watcher stations confirming that these were U.S. aircraft. Many bombing raids were being mounted against Japanese targets all over Mindanao, including Davao and Cagayan, Misamis Oriental. From this point the sighing of American aircraft in large formations would become a daily occurrence.[22]

Later in September two of the diesel generators began acting up, probably due to the 24-hour schedule the station was on. Fortunately, a replacement was found on an abandoned motor launch in the barrio of La Paz, about a two-day trip down the river. Much to the relief of Fertig's command it was learned that Japanese troops were being evacuated from the Agusan River area. Later, in November 1944, La Paz would become the last FRS station in the Agusan River valley.

A second phase of Fertig's connectivity to MacArthur's headquarters was the March 1943 visit of Lieutenant Commander Charles "Chick" Parsons and Captain Charlie Smith. As previously mentioned, Smith had been with Fertig after the surrender but successfully reached Australia in a small boat with Hamner and "Chick" Smith. Smith was commissioned after his arrival in Australia and he returned to Mindanao to look after U.S. Army G-2 collection matters.

Both Chick Parsons and Charlie Smith were now on MacArthur's staff in Australia. Parsons, until the Japanese invasion, had been chief executive officer of Luzon Stevedoring Company. A long-time Manila resident, he was also the honorary Panamanian Consul. He had come to the Philippines in 1921 and had first served as secretary to General Leonard Wood, the Governor General of the Philippines. Later he was a manager in the Philippine Telephone Company and also held executive positions in trading, import and stevedoring. As a member of the Naval Reserve, he was called to active duty on December 14, 1941. The Japanese were not aware of his status other than he was a businessman and the honorary Panamanian consul in Manila. Though initially detained, he and his family were repatriated with other diplomats. The group boarded the Japanese hospital ship *Ural Maru* for Takao, Formosa. From there they were flown to Shanghai and boarded the diplomatic exchange vessel SS *Conte Verde*. The vessel then steamed to Lourenco Marques, Mozambique. Here Parsons and his family boarded the liner MS *Gripsholm* and reached New York on August 12, 1942. When Parsons reported to the Navy Department in Washington he was removed from the "Missing in Action" list and promoted to Lieutenant Commander. Though he was eventually ordered to MacArthur's staff in Australia as an action officer for the Philippines, there was some debate at the Joint Chiefs of Staff level as to whether a military officer escaping from an area controlled by the enemy should be allowed to return. Parsons signed a waiver and arrived at GHQ SWPA on January 5, 1943.

Of all of the officers on MacArthur's staff Parsons was the most knowledgeable on the geography, politics and people of the Philippines. As the action officer on the Philippine resistance, it was his responsibility to assess the capabilities of the various guerrilla groups in the Philippines.

Prior to leaving Australia for Mindanao aboard the USS *Tambor,* Parsons and Smith spent many hours deciding on the proper cargo mix for the guerrillas. Looking around the warehouse where the critical supplies were being packaged, they noted many items that would be high on the priority list for the guerrillas, such as radio transmitters, receivers, charging units, batteries, tools, wire and spare parts. Additional important items included side arms, ammunition and grenades. In another area were bundles of medical supplies, surgical kits, vaccines, etc. Tucked into every niche and cranny of sealed tins were copies of magazines, newspapers, bars of soap, sewing kits, cartons of cigarettes (or individual packs where cartons were too big to fit into the space), chocolate bars, socks, shirts and underwear. There was a set of Colonel's insignia to go with an official presentation to Fertig.[23]

Training and preparations now went into high gear with 18-hour days for both officers. Parsons' unique kind of foresight was registering things that would prove important, albeit out of proportion to their size. There was, for instance, his request for a sealed tin of buckwheat flour.

"But why?" he was asked. "There are fifteen million Filipinos up there, all hungry. What good can one tin do?"

"Fifteen million, right—and most of them Catholic. This is for communion biscuits. Spiritual food. Gotta get wine, too."[24]

There was also one major deficiency—the lack of Philippine peso notes needed by the guerrillas. These notes were as important as arms and medicines. Washington had approved shipment of a small fortune in Philippine pesos to Brisbane by air, labeled as "Finance Forms" for security reasons. A group from GHQ drove through the night in heavy rain to Amberley Field, about 30 miles away. They found the cases of "Finance Forms" in the morning, abandoned on a platform near the runway where they had been unceremoniously dumped the previous night by a weary and hungry crew anxious to taxi away in search of sandwiches and coffee. It took 15 hours for the determined GHQ group to count the peso notes and repackage and seal the cases for shipment on the submarine.[25]

Once underway the USS *Tambor* headed westward, bound for Pagadian Bay on the south coast of Mindanao. On board were Chick Parsons, Charlie Smith and three Moros, as well as four tons of equipment and miscellaneous cargo. The submarine surfaced and proceeded to Pagadian Bay on March 4. There had been an exchange of messages between GHQ and Fertig's command concerning the safety of Pagadian Bay as a landing spot. Upon arrival, Parsons and two Moros went ashore in a small inflatable boat, with the Moros paddling, while the submarine submerged to stay out of sight.

Nearing shore, several shots were fired from the beach and the Moros continued paddling hard until the small boat ran aground on the beach. Parsons observed a rifle protruding out of a mangrove thicket but noted that the holder was barefoot. Japanese soldiers wore boots! Greatly relieved, he yelled, "I come from General MacArthur. I bring letters, supplies—cigarettes. See!"[26]

Parsons was soon surrounded by a group of exuberant guerrillas, part of Fertig's organization. He indicated that there were several tons of supplies on board the submarine and asked about unloading the large amount of cargo. The local guerrilla leader led him to an inlet where a small lighter, complete with crane and winch, was anchored—"a present from the Japanese," according to the guerrilla. There was also a launch near the lighter. Parsons returned to the beach to send the appropriate signals to the submarine, which soon surfaced. The submarine's skipper gasped at the miniature navy around his submarine and marveled at the manner in which tons of cargo were offloaded so quickly and efficiently.

High on Parsons' agenda for this visit was emphasizing the importance of intelligence on the Japanese presence and the movement of their naval vessels through the various islands of the Philippines. This intelligence was vital to the U.S. Navy's submarine operations. A key element for this would be the establishment of guerrilla coast watcher stations.

It was Fertig's view, and confidentially confirmed by Smith, that Parsons was sent by MacArthur's staff to ascertain if Fertig was competent to command, particularly since he was a reservist and not a regular Army officer.[27]

Not long after the arrival of Parsons and Smith, Fertig began to note that the two visitors began to disagree on operational matters. According to Fertig, Smith had sent a message (using Fertig's communications) to Australia without clearing it with Fertig or Parsons. Fertig attributed this to Smith's affiliation with Army G-2 while Parsons had his loyalty to Naval Intelligence. Fertig attempted to mediate this by treating his visitors as representative of their respective services.[28]

In later conversations with Parsons and Smith about the nature of their visit, it was clear to Fertig that the driving force behind their mission was the development of accurate information regarding the situation on Mindanao, including reporting on the movement of Japanese shipping in and around the southern Philippines. Parsons bluntly told Fertig that promoting himself to general did not please either Australia or Washington. Fertig responded that

American guerrilla officers, from left: Sam Wilson, Clyde Childress, Wendell Fertig, and Charles "Chick" Parsons (courtesy MacArthur Memorial Archives, Norfolk, Virginia).

there were many bandits on Mindanao who were promoting themselves to field grade positions. Taking on the role of general and making the Filipinos believe he came from Australia made his job of organizing the resistance movement much easier if not clearer. Most important it gave the Philippine populace hope that "the Aid" and the Americans would soon return to liberate them.[29]

Fertig then shifted to the rationale for hit and run tactics against the Japanese. He stressed that the Filipinos needed victories to continue and sustain their efforts against the Japanese occupation.

Parsons now interrupted Fertig's rationale for the way he was fighting the Japanese and said, "These radios we brought you are for information. You are to establish a flash line of watcher stations along the coasts, and pass the word to us of Jap ship movements. We will have subs waiting for those ships."[30]

Parsons was in effect telling Fertig that while the guerrilla forces had the right of self-defense, these forces should not be seeking engagements with Japanese troops. Underscoring this argument, Parsons pointed out that the Japanese have had experience in combat and also have modern weapons and equipment. Moreover, the weapons (carbines and M-1s) that may be provided by the submarine resupply shipments will not be of sufficient quantities to replace the World War I weapons now used by the guerrillas.

Guerrilla leaders in action. Colonel Wendell Fertig (right) and Lieutenant Commander Charles "Chick" Parsons (courtesy MacArthur Memorial Archives, Norfolk, Virginia).

From this conversation with Parsons, Fertig realized that he was going to have to move ahead with the coast watcher program that Parsons and Australia desired, particularly if he wanted continued logistical support for the guerrillas. He did not buy completely Parsons' admonishment about not engaging the Japanese. He would now have another burden of command—to carefully balance operational opportunities against the Japanese presence as opposed to a strictly intelligence gathering effort that included information from both the guerrilla units and the coast watcher stations that were to be established.

After lengthy discussions with Fertig, the time came for Parsons and Smith to establish the coast watcher stations as approved by GHQ. The first station to be established was in the Surigao Strait region of northeast Mindanao. There, in October 1944, one of the great naval battles of all time would take place. The second station was to be established in the Davao area of southeast Mindanao. It was agreed that Parsons would go to the Surigao area, while Smith would set up the station in Davao.

Saying goodbye to Parsons, Fertig pointed to a 60-foot diesel motor launch and said that she was ready for a run to Medina, headquarters for Lt. Col. Ernest McClish's 110th Division. McClish had been a businessman in Manila and well-known to Parsons and their reunion was a warm one. Parsons was interested in the ability of the guerrillas to make a substitute for diesel fuel for the motor launch. This was accomplished by taking the unopened flower pouch of the coconut tree, extracting and collecting the sap and allowing it to ferment for several hours. The fermented beverage, called tubá, was distilled until it reached the alcohol state, then stored in 5-gallon tins.

McClish had armed the launch with a .50 cal. gun that had been taken from a smashed B-17 of the 19th Bomb Squadron. Equipped with rubber tubing from an old auto tire that would function as a recoil spring, it could be fired like a machine gun.

Saying good-bye to McClish, Parsons left his headquarters on the motor launch to establish a coast watcher station somewhere in the northeastern part of Mindanao. Intelligence from McClish had indicated the Japanese virtually had full control of the Surigao provincial area. Parsons wanted the station to be on Mindanao to have more direct land communication with Fertig and to insure it was within Fertig's administrative control.

After traveling all night on the motor launch Parsons and Truman Heminway, Fertig's candidate to run the new station, anchored at dawn on Panaon Island in the vicinity of Surigao. This well-concealed station began to operate immediately. Prior to parting, Parsons told Heminway, "This is one of the most important 'eyes' GHQ can have, and you are it!"[31]

Through the critical period of 1943–1944 this small station would feed Fertig's FRS important ship-movement information. However, at one point the Japanese landed on the island and Heminway had to move the station to Dinagat Island. Until the end of the war this station would provide valuable information on Japanese naval vessels passing through Surigao Strait. This information was passed on by the U.S. Navy to submarines on patrol in the area.

Though Fertig was unaware of its existence, there was a synergy developing between the U.S. Navy's submarine force and GHQ SWPA staff officers like Parsons who were working for more submarine transport to provide logistical support to the guerrillas. Once the submarine force began to receive and use guerrilla coast watcher information on Japanese ship movements in the Philippines, the more inclined it would be to making available attack submarines to support the logistical needs of the guerrillas.

A second resupply mission to Mindanao took place on September 3, 1943. These missions now had a code name of SPYRON (Spy Squadron). This SPYRON mission delivered a U.S. Navy 100-watt transmitter that could reach any place in the world. Also included in the shipment were navy codes as well as detailed instructions on forming a signal section within FRS to institute a flash line from Fertig's headquarters to Perth to the submarine command in Fremantle and Pearl Harbor for coast watcher reports. These reports could now be relayed to U.S. Navy submarines deployed in Philippine waters. This new communications support demonstrated the U.S. Navy's keenness to receive the intelligence that the guerrilla movement could provide.[32] The Navy's support for the program was further strengthened in March 1944 when it assigned Lieutenant Commander Montgomery Wheeler to Fertig's staff to oversee the Navy communications section in FRS. Early on Fertig was most impressed with Wheeler's performance. Within a few months he was designated chief of staff, replacing Commander Sam Wilson. Of course, Fertig was very mindful that appointing Wheeler to a key position on his staff would signal to the Navy his support for the joint effort in the guerrilla movement.[33]

FRS acquired and utilized a number of different radios in its operations after the SPYRON missions commenced. The initial mainstay for transmitting to Australia was the American HT-9. It was rigged with special heavy V-beam type antennas. As many as 12 personnel were required to move and service its many components including batteries, generator and gasoline. The Australian-made ATR-4 transceiver was used with the HT-9. The HT-9 transmitter was often inoperable because of the tropical humidity. It was later replaced with the Australian TW-12 that was more rugged and weather-friendly. It had been developed early in the war to support the Australian coast watcher program in New Guinea. Again, very important to the coast watcher program was equipment that was lightweight and that could withstand the high humidity of the tropics. Also critical were lightweight batteries that could be easily recharged from local sources or generators.

For connectivity within the Tenth Military District, Fertig's FRS used the 3BZ radio transmitter to communicate with its six geographic operational divisions and the growing coast watcher stations. In turn the receiving stations used the Australian ATR-4 transceiver. While this unit could be carried in a backpack, it weighed almost 20 pounds. The battery pack added another five pounds to be carried by the user.

Bob Stahl, a coast watcher brought in by a SPYRON mission in December 1943 to support Fertig's growing intelligence collection program, describes his experience with the ATR-4:

> The ATR-4 was a collection of resistors, condensers, vacuum tubes and wire packed as neatly as possible into a compact unit—about the size of a lunch bucket for a person with a big appetite. While the unit itself was quite portable, moving a whole station in a hurry was not easy. One problem was the power supply. The ATR-4 used a dry pack battery furnishing low voltage for the filaments of the vacuum tubes and higher voltage to push the signals out into the ether. The battery packs weren't large—they were smaller than the radio but weighed five pounds each. With a onetime life of about five transmission hours, the average watcher station would eat them up at a rate of one every ten days. A six-month supply was a ninety pound burden.
>
> An even bigger problem was the antenna. Before we left Mindanao, Larry Evans, our expert radio technician, gave us instructions on antenna installation. According to the latest theory, the most efficient signal output would be obtained by using half-wave antennas, that is, antennas cut to one-half of the wave length of our signals. Operating on five frequencies between 4,010 and 8,020 kilocycles would require five different antennas varying in length from 58 to 116 feet. Also, the desired height was at least thirty five feet off the ground, and the ideal orientation was perpendicular to the direction of the station being contacted.
>
> So much for theory. Our agents cut wire eighty feet long, strung between the two biggest trees they could find, regardless of the direction, and hoped for the best. Technical perfection was a luxury that was not ours.[34]

The expert radio technician Stahl referred to above was Captain James Lawrence "Larry" Evans, Jr., who arrived on the same submarine as Stahl. Evans was a medical doctor as well as a first class radio operator and his mission was to establish and maintain medical and communication facilities in the Tenth Military District. He brought with him five tons of medical supplies comprising of medications, dressings and surgical and other medical equipment, including one million quinine tablets, 800,000 Atabrine tablets and 500,000 therapeutic vitamin capsules. Fertig readily used his skills, appointing him to the position of Force Medical Officer and head of FRS, replacing Ball.

After the war Evans wrote a report on the subject: Observations on the Physical Conditions and Operational Environment Affecting American Service Personnel Engaged in Guerrilla Warfare, Philippines, 1943–45. Following is an excerpt from this report:

In Mindanao I found dispersed around the island approximately two hundred American service personnel from all arms of the service who had evaded capture when the American forces surrendered to the Japanese in May, 1942, and a few men who had escaped from Japanese POW camps. These troops, many of whom had been living in the field under wartime conditions since before the surrender, went into the hills for months of hiding after the fall of the islands to the Japanese. During this period they lived in very primitive and unsanitary conditions conducive to malnutrition and other disorders due to the tropical environment, unsanitary living conditions and unclean food. Among these were principally but not only the following:

- Epidemic malaria, including malignant and cerebral malaria
- Eroding tropical ulcers
- Malnutrition with avitaminosis, especially beri-beri
- Almost universal intestinal parasite infestations, particularly ascariasis
- Yaws (frambesia)
- Schistosomiasis (liver fluke)
- Various skin disorders, principally fungal
- Wounds due to enemy action
- Prolonged traumatic stress disorders
- Lack of dental care

By the time of my arrival in Mindanao in November of 1943, these men had organized themselves into a large, tightly controlled guerrilla force composed mostly of Filipino soldiers commanded by American officers. This organization had gained contact with General MacArthur's headquarters in Australia and was brought under control of his Southwest Pacific command and began receiving aid in the form of medicine, weapons, ammunition, radio equipment, etc., but little or no foodstuff. They were still dependent on the countryside for food, most of which was much different from that to which Americans were accustomed.

Despite the medical supplies being sent in, there were no other doctors and very little in the way of medical facilities for the remainder of the time up to 1945. The unsanitary and dangerous conditions of the tropical environment still remained. The American troops were still in jeopardy from the proximity of Japanese forces of suffering from wounds or other serious illnesses, without medical facilities to treat them.

It is my opinion from my observations as a medical officer during the period of time that these men suffered mental trauma and other physical ailments, such as those listed above, due to their long and dangerous service under tropical conditions with extremely limited medical attention which could possibly have a residual effect on them throughout their lifetime.

Their wartime service fighting guerrilla warfare was highly unusual from a medical viewpoint for American soldiers due to the prolonged involvement in combat conditions performed in a greatly undeveloped area of the world under severe tropical conditions without normal medical facilities, proper diet or any R and R relief. It is therefore my opinion from what I observed in Mindanao of the operations of the guerrilla forces, that the American service personnel participants are as prone to the same residual ailments as those, to which it is now accepted, the former prisoners of war are susceptible.[35]

While Australian radio equipment became the mainstay for Fertig's communications, Charlie Smith, during a trip to the U.S., found better American equipment. He was able to acquire two sets of suitcase radios developed by the Office of Strategic Services (OSS).

By way of background: MacArthur prohibited OSS from operating in SWPA. There have been various stories on this prohibition. It may go back to the rivalry between MacArthur and Major General William Donovan, head of OSS. During World War I both had seen action in France and had participated in the Meuse-Argonne offensive. MacArthur was a division commander and Donovan commanded a regiment. Both were recommended for the Congressional Medal of Honor. Donovan was awarded the medal for bravery. MacArthur, while decorated for his performance in this action, never became reconciled to the fact that Donovan and not he, the division commander in the offensive, had been awarded the medal. Moreover, it was probably difficult for him to accept the fact that a non–West Point officer and National Guardsman had been awarded the medal. According to Donovan supporters, MacArthur rejected the services of OSS in World War II for this slight, as well as believing that OSS was not a professional organization. If OSS was allowed to operate in SWPA it would not be under MacArthur's absolute control and authority. In other theaters of the war the OSS communicated directly with Washington with its own operational traffic. A situation where an in-theater organization could communicate with Washington without release of these messages by the commander was not acceptable to MacArthur. This prohibition of OSS (Central Intelligence Agency after 1947) in MacArthur's command would be in effect until the mid-point in the Korean War when CIA reporting became predominant in national intelligence relative to the intentions of Communist China in Korea.

The OSS radios that Smith brought back to Mindanao had been developed for agent operations prior to the invasion of Europe. They put out a 30-watt signal and operated on DC, AC or batteries. The battery could be charged from whatever power source was available. Overall these sets were more compact and field friendly than either the American or Australian radios. The OSS radio was tried in communications with Australia and presented no operational difficulties.[36]

5

Japanese Presence, Disposition and Tactics on Mindanao

The Japanese presence on Mindanao goes back to the early Japanese migration to the Philippines. According to a 1939 census by the Philippine Census Bureau the total population was reported to be 29,000. Over half of this number resided in the Davao province of Mindanao. This population had developed beginning in 1900 in a number of critical economic sectors to include shipping, fishing, lumber and mining. Early in the invasion planning for the Philippines the importance of Davao was recognized by Japanese military planners, particularly as it related to Japanese thrusts in Southeast Asia in 1941. As part of the Japanese invasion of the Philippines in December 1941, two Japanese 16th Army detachments, totaling 5,000 troops, were deployed to Davao. Moreover, the Japanese First Air Fleet Headquarters, along with the Japanese army's air regiment, were assigned to this area. In addition, one of the detachments deployed to Davao would later be deployed to take control of Jolo Island. This would become a base for future operations against Dutch Borneo.[1] Even so, Japanese military operations and occupation duties were restricted to the Davao area. As the Japanese were preparing to invade Mindanao in April 1942, Brigadier General Sharp, Commander of Vises-Mindanao force, estimated the total Japanese force invading the island at 43,700. This number would ebb and flow and be dependent on the operational and occupation needs of the Japanese army on Mindanao and other adjacent islands.[2]

After the surrender of the American forces in the Philippines in May 1942, the Japanese concentrated their occupation forces in Davao, Lake Lanao and the Cagayan-Iligan-Kolambugan areas with garrisons in 12 towns. For a time they had sent a small force to Misamis Occidental province but then withdrew it. Coincidentally, this is the province where Colonel Fertig first established his fledgling command in October 1942. Prior to June 1943 the Japanese military apparently believed that a show of force would be enough to limit guerrilla activities to a marginal or acceptable threat. To conserve the occupation forces, they would land or go into coastal towns for one or two days and then withdraw.

However, in the spring of 1943 the Japanese tolerance for guerrilla activity on Mindanao began to change. Japanese intelligence operations suggested a growing guerrilla presence throughout Mindanao. The Japanese Air Force began bombing guerrilla outposts in Lanao province. During the last week of May 1943 the Japanese military conducted a series of attacks along the sea coasts of Cotabato, Agusan, Surigao, Misamis Oriental and Lanao provinces. Moreover, they began retracing the land route from Davao northward toward Cagayan. While on the surface these operations appeared to be an effort to acquire sources of food for their occupation forces, it then became apparent that this was more than a food acquisition effort—it was aimed at locating and destroying the growing threat posed by Fertig and his growing guerrilla organizations. Japanese intelligence apparently had obtained information on the guerrillas being supplied by submarine and the recruitment efforts by Fertig to bring disparate guerrilla organizations under his command. Moreover, Japanese radio intercept capabilities were beginning to monitor the increase in radio traffic between guerrilla outposts and the command traffic between Fertig's command and Australia. All of this suggested to the Japanese that an immediate effort must be made to arrest the development of this guerrilla growth by hitting Fertig's command and his guerrillas operating in Misamis Occidental on June 26, 1943.

According to Fertig's assessment, 2,000 Japanese troops from Cebu and other parts of the Visayas had been brought into Mindanao to assist in this operation. They were aided in their efforts by 200 Bureau of Constabulary troops (a Japanese-recruited version of the Philippine constabulary), naval craft and air support. The first target was Fertig's headquarters in Misamis City. The Japanese began their operations north and south of the city. A combination of air attacks and amphibious landings caused most of the guerrillas to fade into the jungle rather than try to oppose the Japanese efforts. Fertig's major problem in meeting the intensified Japanese actions was lack of communication and information. Some radios that had been brought in during Parsons' visit in March had gone to support the coast watcher program rather than tactical units. Despite these setbacks the guerrilla movement began to stabilize by the second week of July as the Japanese penetrated further inland and they increasingly became the target of guerrilla attacks.[3]

With the JCS approval for MacArthur's forces to land at Leyte in October, an intensified bombing campaign was launched against priority Japanese targets on Mindanao and Leyte. This would begin to take its toll among the Japanese and relieve the pressure against the guerrillas.

Notwithstanding, in late 1943 Japanese maritime patrols began to curtail the ability of the guerrillas to use the coastal waterways to resupply the geographic divisions with food, as well as logistical support that had arrived by submarine from Australia. Now rivers and land routes would have to be utilized to move essential supplies.

The increased Japanese pressure on the guerrillas that commenced in Misamis Occidental province in June 1943 was spreading to other parts of Mindanao. In November 1943 the Japanese initiated a land and sea operation against the town of Claver in Surigao province. Robert Spielman, deputy commander of the 114th Infantry Regiment, 110th Division, recalled the incident in his thesis on the history of the 114th Infantry Regiment:

> This action by the Japanese was more impressive than usual. A Japanese cruiser and several small craft shelled the town and the surrounding hills. They sent landing craft with assault troops ashore and moved inland to a distance of about three miles. Only two of our men were killed but the administrative personnel had to move quickly in order to get back into the hills before being cut off. Our radio station on top of the hill was captured and some of the equipment destroyed. We could not understand what prompted the Japanese attack on Claver but after talking to our radio operator the cause was quite clear. Our radio operator had been in the Merchant Marine for several years before the war and was a radio ham. We had gathered parts from the radio station operated by the postal service before the war and had constructed a powerful radio transmitter. He had re-wired a hundred horsepower motor for his generator and had a Blackstone diesel engine for power. He and his assistants were happy and contented while building the set, but day by day operation was boring. To break the monotony they would get on one of the Japanese wave lengths and jam it. This was great fun but the Japanese took a fix on the radio station and sent force to destroy it. After this incident we took special pains to be sure that the radio operators made only necessary reports and kept them as short as possible.[4]

Despite the transgressions of the radio operator in causing the Japanese to target the radio station, the attack was part of the larger Japanese plan to increase pressure on the coastal towns of Surigao province.

The wife and two young daughters of Charles Hansen, Liaison and Procurement Officer of the 110th Division, were hiding out in Claver during this period. When heavy shelling commenced in the early morning hours of November 30 they fled to their hiding place (*bakwitan* in local vernacular) in the hills behind the town. Realizing that the *bakwitan* was too close to a heavily used trail, they ventured deeper into the interior and found refuge in a small *nipa* hut that had been abandoned by its occupants when the shelling began. Late in the afternoon they cautiously returned to the trail and from that vantage point they could see that the Japanese ships had departed from the bays around Claver. Ironically, their *bakwitan* was located a short distance downhill from the radio station and that same trail was used a few hours earlier by Japanese troops sent to destroy the radio facility.

After destroying much of the town along with the radio station during the naval bombardment and amphibious landing, the Japanese opted not to occupy the area but the fear remained that they could return at any time, causing the Hansen women to move southward. They repeatedly went through this process of fleeing the sporadic but continuing Japanese attacks on the various coastal towns where they were hiding out. This would continue until the arrival of American liberation forces in Zamboanga and the rest of Mindanao in March and April 1945.[5]

One of Hansen's major responsibilities was the procurement of food and other supplies for 5,000 guerrillas in the 110th Division. Rice, an important staple for the Filipino guerrillas, was also being procured by the Japanese for their troops. Hansen instructed the rice farmers in the Tandag-Tago area to store *palay* (unhusked rice) purchased for the guerrillas in bodegas deep in the interior until transportation could be developed for movement to deployed units. As the Japanese landed in key towns along the east coast of Surigao province their naval forces patrolled the coastal waters, cutting off this avenue for transporting cavans of *palay* (a cavan of *palay* is roughly equivalent to two U.S. bushels weighing over 100 pounds usually contained in a large jute sack). The Japanese also launched a campaign to purchase (on their terms) all available *palay* from the local farmers.

In reports to the commanders of the Tenth Military District and the 110th Division dated May 17 and June 4, 1944, Hansen described an attack on Tandag, an important town in the rice farming region of Mindanao. In the early morning of April 27, the Japanese landed about 500 troops from ships, motor launches and barges. As most of the residents fled to the nearby mountains when the Japanese entered Tandag, Hansen led a small group of guerrillas in repulsing the Japanese advance, inflicting scores of casualties before retreating from the superior numbers and firepower of the Japanese. Hansen, Lieutenant Bob Pease and another officer were initially trapped in town but subsequently escaped.

Units of the Japanese force were deployed to other towns farther south; the remainder stayed in Tandag for several weeks, initially offering to purchase *palay* and other supplies from local farmers. When they failed to win full cooperation they resorted to looting homes and bodegas and destroying property. A patrol sent to nearby Tago with the same mission was likewise unsuccessful, resulting in similar damage to that town. A follow-on contingent returned later with supplies and equipment in preparation for a long stay.

Ten days later more guerrillas arrived near Tandag commanded by Captain Marshall and Lieutenant Spielman. They attacked with trench mortars but failed to drive out the Japanese. Another guerrilla unit attacked the Japanese force occupying Tago, killing eight. Numerous Japanese patrols were sent deeper into the interior to fight the guerrillas while naval forces continued patrolling the waters east of Surigao province, sometimes anchoring near Bayabas south of Tago.

Hansen also reported that the guerrillas still had over two thousand cavans of *palay* stashed in different makeshift bodegas in the hills in the Tandag-Tago area. If the Japanese discovered these hiding places, he had issued standing orders for the guards to burn the bodegas rather than allow the *palay* to fall into Japanese hands.

Over the next several months Hansen devised plans to transport the *palay* overland but Japanese presence along the normal routes made such attempts impossible. Aware of the importance of getting this valuable commodity to guerrilla units badly in need of food, local Filipino officials marshaled a number of *cargadores* (bearers) to carry on their backs jute sacks weighing about 20–25 pounds over the Diuata Mountains to Agusan province, a difficult trek expected to last many days over extremely rough terrain. When news arrived that their destination area had been overrun by Japanese, the *cargadores* fled and the plan was abandoned. The *palay* was subsequently distributed to the guerrillas after the liberation of Mindanao.[6]

From early 1944 the Japanese pressure intensified and such coastal towns as Cagayan in Misamis Oriental were subjected to more frequent patrols and air raids. As it became increasingly apparent to the Japanese that the American liberation of the Philippines was on the horizon, Japanese land patrols now exceeded the 50 to 100 soldier level. With larger numbers their formations now moved away from the coastal areas to inland trails and roads. In some cases, more permanent inland outposts were established. Pressure on the guerrillas and Fertig's headquarters along the Agusan River increased. One air raid on the guerrilla headquarters destroyed a large amount of communications equipment. It was believed that the Japanese had increased their troop strength considerably in order to press these attacks in the 110th Division's operational area. These troops were a part of the Japanese army's 30th Division.

Regarding accurate figures on the Japanese troop dispositions on Mindanao, throughout their occupation of the island Japanese troops were constantly shifting, even in the Davao area. Prior to the American liberation of the southern Philippines in 1945, it was particularly important to know the number of Japanese troops being shifted to and from Mindanao against the American forces that may be landing to the north of Mindanao, or later on

Mindanao itself. The following message traffic going to GHQ SWPA from the Tenth Military District illustrates the shifting nature of the Japanese troop strengths:

January 1944   Misamis Oriental. 1,900 Japanese arrived in Cagayan.
February 1944   100 Japanese arrived in Zamboanga from the north.
April 1944   4 large transports unladed troops at Davao City; estimated 2,000 troops in this arrival.
May 1944   Elements of the Japanese 30th Division arrived from Cebu.
July 1944   Estimated 2,000 Japanese arrived in Davao from Palau for the month of June and first two weeks of July.
August 1944   Transports arriving Cagayan brought 3,000 troops. 1,000 of these troops immediately went south on the Sayre Highway. Indications show they came from Luzon and Visayas.[7]

Though the foregoing is but a small sample of the message traffic concerning Japanese troop arrivals and departures, it does indicate the shifting nature of the overall Japanese troop dispositions on Mindanao during the early months of 1944.

The following is the Tenth Military District's estimate of the Japanese troop strength on Mindanao as of October 30, 1944:

Agusan	350
Bukidnon	4,400
Cotabato	16,000
Davao	25,000
Lanao	500
Misamis Occidental	100
Misamis Oriental	3,500
Surigao	1,800
Zamboanga	5,700
Total	57,350[8]

On Mindanao, prior to the American invasion of Leyte in October 1944, the Japanese strength was estimated to be about 43,000. This was after two regiments were transferred to Leyte in November 1944.[9]

The overall Japanese presence for eastern Mindanao was broken down between two divisions. Under the leadership of Lieutenant General G. Morozumi the troop designations within his command were: 100th Infantry Division and the 32nd Naval Base in the Davao area; 74th Infantry Regiment and the 2nd Air Division at Malaybalay in the north center of the island; about half of the 30th Infantry Division (Lieutenant General Jiro Hirada) between Malaybalay and Cagayan on the north coast; and the 54th Independent Mixed Brigade at Zamboanga.[10]

Robert Ross Smith, author of *Triumph in the Philippines,* offers a very candid assessment of the 30th and 100th Japanese Divisions that were deployed to eastern Mindanao.

> The 30th and 100th Divisions were not in good shape to conduct delaying operations. Hopelessly isolated and short on artillery, small arms ammunition, transportation and communications equipment, they had no chance of obtaining supplies. Both divisions also faced serious personnel problems. Four of the 30th Division's nine infantry battalions had gone to Leyte and had been annihilated there. Garrison units, some of which had let to an easy life on Mindanao since early 1942, formed the nucleus of each of the 100th Division's eight independent infantry battalions. Not more than ten officers of the 100th Division were regular, and the quality of the division's junior officers and non-commissioned officers was poor. Moreover, about a third of the division's men were Korean, not noted for their enthusiastic adherence to the Japanese cause. Finally there could be little doubt the commanders and staffs of both division s had a defeatist attitude. They knew that once an invasion of eastern Mindanao began they would enter upon a battle they could not win, and they definitely had no relish for a defense to the death in place.[11]

The following is a breakdown of Japanese strength in the two divisions assigned to eastern Mindanao.

Japanese Strength in 100th Division Area

Army ground combatant and service elements	15,840
Army Air Force elements	2,900
Navy combat and service elements	6,165
Total	24,905

Japanese Strength in the 30th Division Area

Army ground combat and service elements	11,750
Army Air Force elements	5,150
Naval forces	300
Total	17,200
Total for both divisions	42,105

In addition to the foregoing, there were 12,580 Japanese civilians in eastern Mindanao.[12]

Japanese Occupation Policies

The Japanese had three phases to their occupation policy in the Philippines. The initial phase was in the early months of the war—December 1941 through May 1942. During this phase the Japanese exhibited military cruelty, irritation, puzzlement and impatience. That was caused by the unfriendly attitude of the Filipinos toward the Japanese invaders. The second phase began with the surrender of the Americans in May 1942 and lasted through August 1944. In this period the Japanese became more doctrinaire with their co-prosperity sphere concept and the establishment of a Filipino puppet government. Also, propaganda touting the Japanese liberation policies became more pronounced. The final phase began with the first American air attacks in the Philippines in the early fall of 1944. These attacks signaled very strongly the return of the American forces in the not too distant future. With the reality in the Japanese mindset their policies became more irrational and brutal.[13]

The Japanese economic exploitation of the Philippines began right after the invasion in December 1941. Schools, businesses and small shops were closed; transportation ceased and radio and newspapers were banned. In the heavy industry area mining equipment was dismantled and shipped to Japanese occupied areas in other parts of Asia. On the island of Mindanao grain and rice harvests were seized to supply the occupation forces. This was particularly damaging on the island because rice and similar crops could only be grown along the coastal regions or river basins. These areas were in many cases under the control of the occupations forces.

The foregoing economic disruption policies carried out by the Japanese occupation were creating critical economic problems for the Filipinos. The result of this was high unemployment and inflation. This in turn drove up the prices for all commodities.

Goods for daily living were just not available except through a growing black market. The production and importation of drugs were stopped with the arrival of the Japanese. This resulted in a growing incidence of malaria, pellagra, beriberi and typhus among Filipinos.[14]

Japanese Counter Guerrilla Tactics

The Japanese were generally aware of MacArthur's instructions to the guerrillas on organizing and gathering intelligence. They also understood the tactics being used by the guerrilla when engaging them. Even so, they were insulted in having to confront an enemy that would not give them an all-out fight. They were dealing with a foe that struck silently and quickly then disappeared into the jungle. This ran counter to Japanese training and code of honor.

The Japanese traditional tactic in dealing with a guerrilla threat was to deploy without delay to the area with mortars, machine guns and sufficient ammunition in the expectation that the guerrillas would meet the Japanese challenge. The guerrillas would bait the Japanese with enough fire to delay their advance. The guerrillas would then withdraw to favorable ground in the hope of baiting once more the Japanese into an unfavorable position. The Japanese commanders on Mindanao were charged with combating the guerrillas with an occupation force that did not recognize the political nature of guerrilla movement. When these tactical operations failed, they resorted to tactics of terror. However, such tactics would ultimately cause the people on Mindanao to move closer to the guerrilla movement.[15]

Japanese Casualties

Despite the shortages and sickness, the guerrillas, using hit and run/ambush tactics, were able to inflict a preponderance of casualties on the Japanese as compared to those on the guerrilla side. Records are not available on guerrilla casualties but beginning on January 1, 1944, to April 17, 1945 (when American forces landed in Parang) approximately 7,655 Japanese deaths were recorded in operational reports going to the Tenth Military District.[16] While is it certainly possible that the reporting on Japanese casualties going to the Tenth Military District may be on the high side, a review of the Significant Operational Encounters between Japanese and guerrilla units contained in Chapter 6 suggest the Japanese did sustain large casualty rates.

In reviewing the Japanese efforts to counter the threat posed by the Mindanao guerrillas, it is clear that the Japanese did not understand the threat that they were addressing. After the surrender of the Americans and prior to the build-up of the forces to meet an American invasion, they believed that a show of force would be enough to counter the guerrilla threat. They were content to control only the larger towns and leave the jungle to the guerrillas. However, in the first half of 1943 they changed their tactics somewhat in the face of the growing guerrilla threat. Even so, they embarked on tactics against the guerrillas that they had used against the guerrilla-type opposition in China. This included emphasis on rear area security and mopping up operations. The latter tactic was expanding the geographical area to be brought under control by using punitive expeditions and tactical concepts of encirclement.

These tactics that they had used in China would only bring failure. The local Japanese commanders did not recognize the political nature of guerrilla warfare in conducting these operations. More important, they did not under-stand the Filipinos. Again, this leads back to the overall occupation policies of the Japanese which were very damaging to the people of the Philippines. This caused the population of Mindanao to look to the guerrilla movement as a way to address the negative nature of the Japanese occupation.[17]

6

Guerrilla Organization, Strength, Disposition and Tactics

When Fertig assumed command of Morgan's organization its strength was about 500 men. Some were former USAFFE personnel who had fled to the hills or returned to their villages. Others, like Morgan, were former Philippine constabulary personnel who were in the same mode as the former Army personnel. But what about the USAFFE force that existed prior to the surrender? That force numbered about 35,000 Filipinos.[1] Of that number possibly 7,000 were interned by the Japanese. Like those in Morgan's force, roughly 28,000 had melted into the jungle or general population. Added to this number would be probably 8,000 Philippine constabulary troops who had been demobilized. Thus, Fertig had a manpower pool of about 36,000, some having military or paramilitary backgrounds, that could be recruited into the guerrilla movement. While a portion this manpower pool may not have been inclined to become guerrillas and fight the Japanese, there were undoubtedly probably many others who could, if inspired by an effective leader, join the fight against the common enemy. Many of these potential recruits would already have been exposed to some military discipline and training. Such skills, though rudimentary, would make the process of molding them into guerrilla fighters much easier. Though many lacked weapons, there were others with USAFFE service who may have kept their Springfield or Enfield rifles. With the proper leadership and logistical support the potential for an effective guerrilla force was close at hand.

Another factor working for Fertig in building a guerrilla force was the high literacy rate of the Filipinos and the use of the English language. Prior to 1940 the language of instruction in all grade levels had been English. Literacy and English language skills would be important factors in building a strong and cohesive movement.

Unlike the other islands, Mindanao had a large number of Americans who had not surrendered. Many of these had the necessary background to fill key leadership positions. Approximately 180 Americans were active in the Tenth Military District. Some were civilian, with previous military experience; others were commissioned officers with combat experience fighting the Japanese. However, the majority of the Americans were enlisted personnel from the Army, Army Air Corps and Navy components that had not surrendered or had escaped from POW camps, most of whom would later earn commissions and be given command responsibilities in the guerrilla organization. A large number of these enlisted personnel were members of the Army Air Corps that had served in support capacities at Clark Field, particularly from the 19th Bomb Group. Beginning on December 18, 1941, a number of aircraft specialists were moved southward toward Bataan. After waiting several days in the Mariveles area of Bataan most of the 19th Bomb Group boarded the inter-island steamer SS *Mayon*. Represented in the group were members of the Headquarters Squadron, 14th Squadron, 28th Squadron, 30th Squadron and 93rd Squadron. Again, these squadrons had supported aircraft that had been based at Clark Field. During the Japanese attacks on December 8 the U.S. Army Air Corps lost all its B-17 bomber aircraft; only six P-40 pursuit aircraft survived the Japanese attacks.

Without aircraft to service approximately 300 members of the 19th Bomb Group embarked on the *SS Mayon* but were not told of their destination—all they knew was that the ship's heading was in a southerly direction. Since the only field in the southern part of the Philippines capable of supporting B-17 bombers was Del Monte airfield on Mindanao, this became the favorite rumor concerning their destination among the personnel on board the ship.

After boarding the *Mayon* all personnel were directed to the main deck. A huge canvas cover tied to the mastheads provided protection from the sun and also some camouflage in the event they were spotted by Japanese aircraft. In the event of attack, personnel were advised not to fire at the aircraft and remain under cover. In addition, they were told not to jump in the water while being bombed or strafed—this could result in concussions and possible death if a bomb were to explode near the ship.

At about noon on December 30 a Japanese seaplane, similar to the U.S. Navy PBY, flew over the *Mayon*. The aircraft made additional passes attempting to discern what was under the canvas cover. After the third pass the plane climbed to a higher altitude for a bombing run. After four passes and four misses on the bombing runs, the aircraft made one more run. Prior to the last bomb being dropped, three of the personnel on deck jumped overboard and were swimming toward shore. When the last bomb exploded all three men suffered internal injuries from the concussion caused by the exploding bomb; one died. It was fortunate that the pilot did not strafe the area of the canvas cover on the main deck; otherwise, there would have been extensive casualties.

As the *Mayon* approached the island of Mindoro the decision was made to put the personnel ashore using the ship's lifeboats. The fear was that Japanese aircraft would return to bomb the ship. Just prior to dusk it was ascertained that there was minimal damage to the ship and it was still capable of steaming to its destination. All personnel on the lifeboats were taken back on board. The *Mayon* arrived at Bugo, Misamis Oriental province, without further air attacks. This was to be the assigned disposition of most members of the 19th Bomb Group. They were part of the defense of Mindanao force until the surrender on May 10, 1942. Upon arrival at Bugo they were issued either Springfield or Enfield rifles for their new defensive role. Whenever B-17s came to Del Monte airfield, either for bombing missions or to transport personnel to Australia, members of the 19th Bomb Group were assigned to service them. On March 25 12 B-25 bombers arrived at Del Monte, where they were serviced and loaded with bombs. After attacking targets around the Philippines the following day they returned to Del Monte where they were serviced for their return flight to Australia.

As a footnote to the movement of the 19th Bomb Group to Mindanao, the SS *Mayon* was sunk in February 1942 at Butuan, Agusan province, near the mouth of the Agusan River. Later, the guerrillas attempted to salvage as much fuel oil as possible from its tanks to support the vehicles and small boats they utilized in the Butuan area.[2]

As Fertig built his guerrilla organization he was mindful that leadership would be an important ingredient in making the movement a success. The manpower for potential leadership on Mindanao was greater than any other island in the Philippines—it was an extraordinary circumstance that allowed him to have such a pool of talent. Of particular note, there were a number of experienced businessmen on the island, most of whom had military experience in either World War I or during the period leading up to World War II. For the younger U.S. military, they were dubbed the "old timers." As the guerrilla movement matured they would serve as commanders in the six divisions that made up the Tenth Military District. The following "old timers" were most active in making this district the most effective guerrilla organization in the Philippines. Charles Hedges, a close colleague of Fertig, was a World War I veteran and lumber executive in the southern Philippines. Frank McGee, a West Point graduate (class of 1915) and highly decorated officer in World War

I, became a successful businessman in the Philippines after leaving the U.S. Army. James Grinstead, also a World War I veteran, had been an officer in the Philippine constabulary before going into business. Robert Bowler was a U.S. Army reserve officer who later became Fertig's second-in-command. Cecil Walter, manager of the Anakan Lumber Company on Mindanao and a civil engineer, brought area knowledge and technical expertise to the guerrilla movement. Sam Wilson, a World War I veteran and a Naval reserve officer, had an extensive financial background and was a millionaire. He would oversee the guerrilla money printing operation and maintain detailed accounting of expenditures.

There were other older civilians who operated businesses in the Philippines prior to World War II who also made valuable contributions to the guerrilla movement. Herbert Page, a Mindanao businessman, was well into his sixties when he accepted commands positions with the guerrillas. Fred Varney and Charles Hansen, who ran the East Mindanao Mining Company in northern Surigao province, were both in their fifties when they jointed the guerrillas. Hansen came to the Philippines in 1920, with the 27th Infantry Regiment. This regiment, along with 31st, had been sent from the Philippines to Vladivostok in the fall of 1918. It was part of the American Expeditionary Force (AEF) of 10,000 troops sent by President Wilson to secure the Trans-Siberian Railroad and ensure the safety of the Czech Legion that was moving along the railway from Western Russia to Vladivostok. While serving in Vladivistok with the AEF, Hansen transferred to the 27th Infantry Regiment and returned with it to Fort McKinley, near Manila, in 1920.[3]

Another group of American military that would add to the leadership pool were officers and NCOs that had escaped in April 1943 from the Davao Penal Colony. Though initially lost in the jungle after their escape, they were able were to make contact with guerrilla elements and then make their way to Fertig's command. Paul Marshall and Robert Spielman, the two NCOs from this group, would elect to remain in the Philippines and become impressive leaders in the 110th Division. Major Austin Shofner would for a while become chief of staff of the 110th Division. Captain Jack Hawkins during the same period would serve as the G-2 for the division. Both Marines, they were anxious to return to the Marine Corps and fight a conventional war. They were repatriated by submarine in November 1943.

Additional POW escapees from DAPECOL would join the guerrillas. On October 25, 1943, Sergeant Robert Pease and Private Oscar Brown successfully escaped from the prison camp. In March 1944 six POWs escaped and made it through to guerrilla lines. Included in this group were the following: Captain Mark Wohlfield, Lieutenant James McClure, Lieutenant James

East Mindanao Mining Company officials Fred Varney (left) and Charles Hansen (right) served as guerrilla officers. Here they are with Carl Gustafson, a mine employee who did not join the guerrilla organization and was evacuated by submarine in March 1944 (Virginia Hansen Holmes collection).

Haburne, Lieutenant Howard Watson, Lieutenant Andrew Bukovinsky and Lieutenant Marvin Campbell. Ensign Boone was killed in the attempt and four were recaptured and returned to DAPECOL for perhaps a fate worse than death—captains Wohler and Fansler, lieutenants Wight and Carmichael. In June 1944 Lieutenant Colonel John McGee and Major Donald Wills escaped from Japanese control by jumping overboard from the *Yashu Maru* as it passed near Coronado Point, Zamboanga.

The last group of potential leaders would come from Filipino members of USAFFE—both commissioned and non-commissioned officers. A number of Filipino officers would rise to command positions within the six divisions under the Tenth Military District. Many of these officers would fill most of the critical staff positions of the various regional divisions. It should be noted, however, that use of this leadership pool by Fertig involved delicate political decision-making. At the heart of this issue was the legacy of the American administration in the Philippines. Many Filipino officers would elect to serve under an American officer, either in a command or staff position, rather than take on the command role themselves. Many Filipinos felt troubled by seeing Americans working for a Filipino. This was a very difficult position for Fertig, particularly when he had to commission American NCOs who may not have had organizational or military experience.

In a letter to General Casey dated July 1, 1943, Fertig made a subjective comment that the American officer and enlisted manpower pool in the Mindanao guerrillas, serving in leadership positions, performed at a level superior to that of the U.S. military in the pre-surrender period. Looking back, Fertig was probably remembering his own experiences in Bataan and later in Mindanao as the U.S. military rapidly collapsed in the face the Japanese invasion.[4] Many of the commissioned NCOs remained in the military after the war and went on to serve as regular officers in either the U.S. Army or Air Force. In the Tenth Military District, when the American personnel did not perform or were discipline problems, Fertig dealt with them in an expeditious manner. The usual disposition was transfer to GHQ SWPA in Australia on the next available submarine. After liberation forces occupied Leyte, personnel with problems were sent there for reassignment. Of course, this could work both ways. An officer having personality conflicts with Fertig could ask for reassignment and the request was usually honored. Also, many officer personnel desired to return to their parent service and regular military duties.

While the foregoing has focused on the Americans and Filipinos relative to their contributions to the guerrilla movement, there were other nationalities that made vital contributions to the Tenth Military District. There was a group of eight Australians, captured by the Japanese and held on Berhala Island, Sandakan, North Borneo, who escaped and made their way to Tawi Tawi Island. Unfortunately, one of the escapees, Private Rex Butler, was killed by the Moros on that island. The remaining POWs made their way to Mindanao and joined the guerrillas. Lieutenant Charles Wagner of this group was killed during an engagement with the Japanese at Liangan in Lanao province on December 21, 1943. The remaining six Australians continued with Fertig's guerrilla movement. Major Leslie Gillon, Major Raymond Steele, Sergeant Walter Wallace and Private James Kennedy were evacuated by the USS *Narwhal* on March 2, 1944. However, the other POWs, Major Rex Blow and Captain "Jock" McLaren, remained with the guerrillas until April 1945, when the Australian government requested their return. Blow was awarded the American Silver Star medal for his service with the 105th Division operating in Lanao province.

A Syrian mining engineer, Major Khalil Khodr, played a major leadership role with the 110th Division when he commanded the 105th Infantry Regiment. Also active in that same division was a German named Waldo Neveling. At the outbreak of the war he was a mining engineer with the Mindanao Mother Lode mine. While initially interned by the Japanese, he was released because of his German nationality. Having built up a mistrust of the Japanese, he offered his services to the guerrillas and received a commission. His major contribution was operating his 50-foot boat, the *So What*. While his main task was to carry supplies for the guerrillas, he often engaged small Japanese craft. He had armored his boat with large, steel saw blades. Its armament also included a 20mm cannon and a .50 cal. machine gun.[5] After the war he returned to work at Mindanao Mother Lode. Later, he operated a boat repair business in Surigao, specializing in surplus U.S. Navy landing craft. During the post-war period, Rudy and Hank Hansen, then completing their high school education in Surigao, would often visit with Neveling in his boat yard. Because of his guerrilla service, he later received U.S. citizenship. He then retired in Arizona and died there of emphysema.[6]

Within Fertig's organization there was a generation gap. As previously mentioned, many of the young American military who refused to surrender or escaped from POW camps were non-commissioned officers. The inclusion of these young people would ultimately result in clashes with old-timers like Charles Hansen. While these generational differences were a part of the working dynamics in the guerrilla movement, it would seem that Fertig's organizational skills were able to tap into the capabilities of both groups. The old-timers provided experience, tested leadership and knowledge of the Philippines; the younger personnel brought vigor, daring and exuberance to the movement. They were risk takers who could excel in engagements with the Japanese. On the other hand, this risk taking, under some circumstances, could be counterproductive to the overall mission of the organization relative to collection of intelligence. It was a fine balance that Fertig constantly had to make.

William Knortz was an excellent example of the younger generation in the Mindanao guerrillas. An Army Air Force sergeant in 1942, he was among the USAFFE forces on Mindanao that were ordered to surrender and subsequently interned at Keithley Barracks in Dansalan, Lanao. Knortz was a former football player and physical fitness enthusiast who did not smoke or drink and would work out several times a day. He was also a black belt judo wrestler. While interned, he would challenge his prison guards, including officers, to matches.

In July 1942 Knortz, along with three other POWs, escaped from Keithley Barracks. Using cover of repairing disabled U.S. Army vehicles, the four POWs virtually walked past a Japanese guard (who was distracted by the presence of a comely young Filipina) and out to freedom. Joining the guerrillas, Knortz was assigned to Lieutenant Colonel McClish's regiment which later became the 110th Division. Working in the Cagayan-Bugo area, he was given a company to command. His attacks against the Japanese became legendary in the guerrilla movement. Even so, his actions also revealed a devil-may-care attitude. One day he decided that he wanted some canned pineapple. He proceeded to the Del Monte pineapple cannery in the Bugo area. Though heavily guarded by the Japanese, he was able to enter the facility and leave with several cases of pineapple. The question is why he went to such trouble when fresh pineapples were growing around the facility. Perhaps he just wanted to irritate the Japanese one more time.[7]

Knortz was tall and well built, blond haired and fair skinned. He had an angular frame, like John Wayne, and moved with a bit of a list. He was well schooled and had a commanding voice and the poise of a natural leader. When he walked into a roomful of people, everyone felt his presence. Even in the field, Knortz believed in keeping his body fit—on the trail he carried a Browning Automatic Rifle (BAR) and two belts of ammunition.

One of Knortz's initial missions after joining the guerrillas was to recruit Filipino military personnel for the movement. Captain Charles Hansen and his sons, Rudy and Hank, met Knortz while he was escorting a group of recruits to the 110th Division HQ for induction. Aged 17 and 16, respectively, the Hansen brothers were able to convince Knortz that they were older and volunteered to join the guerrilla organization. Upon arrival at division HQ they were sworn in by Knortz as privates in the USFIP and assigned to the

114th Infantry Regiment. When Knortz became its commander his charge from the 110th Division command was to unify the unit and overcome any separatist tendencies. His arrival caused a great deal of angst among the officers in the regiment, given Knortz's physical reputation and his successful encounters against the Japanese.

Hank (left) and Rudy Hansen prior to joining the guerrilla movement and serving with the 110th Division's Special Troops (Virginia Hansen Holmes collection).

In September 1943 Rudy and Hank Hansen were with Knortz when word came that a SPYRON mission submarine had landed off Lanao province with weapons and ammunition. These supplies were now with the guerrillas in the Liangan area of Lanao. Knortz told Rudy and Hank to remain in Claver while he took the *Albert McCarthy* (a launch that been designed for river work and had a low freeboard) and headed out to sea and then southward toward Lanao. After locating and loading the regiment's share of weapons and ammunition, the overloaded launch headed northward. Just off Cagayan City the launch was spotted and pursued by a Japanese patrol boat. Knortz headed toward Camiguin Island but encountered heavy seas and the boat capsized and sank. Knortz, confident of his ability to swim to the island to get help, set off in the direction of the island. Only three guerrillas of thirteen on the launch lived; they survived by clinging to debris that eventually reached land several days later. The remainder, including Knortz, were lost in this tragic incident.[8]

The gulf between the old-timers and the youthful members like Knortz did have trying moments. Captain Hansen had such an experience with Lieutenant Robert Spielman, deputy commander of the 114th Infantry Regiment. During the period October 4–10, 1943, the Japanese were landing in Placer, Surigao province—part of Hansen's area of operations as Liaison and Procurement Officer for the 110th Division. Hansen was attempting to establish the extent of the Japanese presence so a report could be sent to division headquarters. Needing input from Spielman, Hansen was unable to locate him until much later in the day. After discussions on the enemy, it was agreed that their number was much less than originally thought. At this point the two officers decided to attack the Japanese from two sides. After the operation commenced and shots were exchanged, Spielman's group retreated, leaving Hansen's group continuing to exchange fire with the Japanese. A runner arrived reporting that one of Spielman's guerrillas had been killed and the remaining guerrillas had fled. Later, Hansen and Spielman discussed the causalities which numbered one killed and three wounded. Hansen asked Spielman if he was sure that the man was dead. Spielman replied that his back and been torn open and that he had no pulse. He was left where he had fallen. The next day an ex-policeman from Placer found the guerrilla that was supposed to have been killed—he was only wounded and was taken to the town's hospital. In a report to headquarters Hansen expressed his concern about the incident, particularly since the local people did not respect the guerrillas for leaving one of their fallen on the battlefield.[9] After this incident Hansen met with Fertig at his headquarters in Amparo, Agusan, on October 20. In his draft manuscript Fertig described the meeting as follows:

There was also Captain Hanson [*sic*], an old time American, who had just arrived from Surigao with a story of the debacle that followed a battle at Placer at the upper end of Lake Mainit. As a result of this debacle, we had lost our outpost on the northern end of the lake and opened the road to the coast immediately north of the city of Butuan.[10]

As the war continued and the two groups shared hardship and difficulties, the gulf between the old timers and the youthful members became less important. Undoubtedly both groups realized that each side had skills that brought value to their common endeavor. Moreover, many of the younger personnel had received commissions and were being promoted into command positions because of the experience they had gained. Sergeant Paul Marshall, the POW escapee from DAPECOL, was an excellent example of this process. After joining the guerrillas, he received a commission and served in a number of leadership positions. This culminated in his being named commander of the 110th Division later in the war, succeeding McLish. Spielman would serve as his deputy and have a similar record of accomplishment.

Another problem faced by Fertig in the manpower/personnel arena on Mindanao was the diversity of USAFFE personnel sent to the island after the war commenced. Most of these were Philippine army personnel. Many of them came from other islands such as Luzon and the Visayas. Mindanao was not their home and they, like the Americans, were almost like fish out water. However, the Filipino soldier did have the cultural background and some language fluency that gave him an advantage in dealing with the adverse situation following the surrender, particularly if he fled to the hills.

Despite this diversity issue that transcended the whole island of Mindanao (from the Moro areas of southern Mindanao and Sulu to the Filipinos and Christians of the northeast), Fertig was able to sublimate these cultural and religious differences and bring many of these diverse groups into the movement. In the case of the Moros, it was insuring that they were commanded by American and Moro officers. Certainly Fertig's early mining experiences in the Philippines had given him background and sensitivity to the cultural and religious differences found in the various islands. Moreover, he had senior commanders such as Hedges and McGee who had extensive experience in dealing with the Moro population.

Once Fertig had established himself in Misamis Occidental and the guerrilla organization was commencing to function as he had planned, he began to fine-tune his command as an effective counter to the Japanese presence. While Fertig liked the idea of the division concept for each geographic region of Mindanao, the application of the Philippine constabulary template (districts, sectors and sub-sectors) was not working for the movement. Many of the commanders were inexperienced and were, at times, dictatorial toward the population from which they were expected to curry cooperation and respect. To correct this, Fertig decided to do away with the constabulary organization template and replace it with a regiment type organization under a regional division commander. Under this concept companies would be formed to cover several towns and would report to a battalion covering a larger area. The battalion would then report to a regiment which had responsibility for a regional area. As the war progressed, these regiments then made up divisions that would report to Fertig, the commander of the Tenth Military District.

From October 1942 until June 1943 the guerrilla movement, after its occupation of Misamis Occidental province, had a good deal of freedom to expand and develop a solid footing throughout Mindanao. Visitors to the province during this period would marvel at this island-like bastion of freedom surrounded by Japanese-dominated provinces in Mindanao, such as Zamboanga. Economic activity in the province had almost returned to its prewar level. Telephone, telegraph and electrical systems started functioning again. The civil government, supported by the guerrillas, began doing the people's work. Moreover, logistical support from Australia was starting to have an effect on the overall strength of the guerrilla movement

In early 1943 the Japanese had reporting suggesting that Fertig was making progress in expanding his guerrilla force and that it was receiving support from Australia via submarine. This threat prompted the Japanese to attack Fertig's headquarters and the guerrillas in Misamis Occidental by landing a major task force against this growing guerrilla presence. Fertig gave the following overview as to what happened to the movement in its first major encounter with the Japanese on June 26, 1943:

> To recapture in memory the happenings of that momentous period from June 26 to July 20, it is necessary to recapitulate briefly the happenings that had taken place. Prior to the 26th of June, little had actually been completed to assure the defense of my headquarters and the headquarters installation. Plans had been made but there had not been enough time for their implementation. Consequently, the Japanese attack had come at a time that disruption was easier than it would have been a few months later and yet it was the testing that we had expected and which must be survived if we were to continue our operations against them. The Japanese attack on June 26 had been well planned and was tactically successful, yet strategically it failed for they did not realize that they were not fighting in a static situation. They were in combat with a force as evanescent as drifting smoke. The initial impact of their attack disrupted lines of communication, destroyed complicated organization and apparently left my force a shambles, yet within a matter of days, my theory was vindicated. The small cohesive units had begun to coalesce into larger groups and by the end of the second week, these larger groups, not usually in excess of a company, were busily attacking the Japanese wherever they might be found.[11]

Although Fertig's guerrillas rebounded from this first major encounter with the Japanese, they would continue to be under sporadic pressure from them until the fall of 1944.

This reality, plus the focus of the Japanese on Misamis Occidental and Lanao provinces, would force Fertig to move his temporary headquarters from Lanao to the Agusan River valley in October 1943. The river would afford the movement of supplies to guerrilla units as well as providing his headquarters staff the means to avoid pursuit by Japanese forces.

October 1943 was a month of decision for Fertig. He was convinced that it would be unwise to continue bringing the SPYRON missions into the north coast of Lanao province for landing of cargo for the guerrillas. This area was within 15 miles of Japanese garrisons in almost every direction.

Fertig's headquarters had received word that the navy had agreed to assign a large submarine, the USS *Narwhal,* to the SPYRON program. This submarine had the capability of handling tonnages in excess of 100 tons. In order to take full advantage of this capability and reduce the problems associated with the smaller tonnages that had plagued the program from the beginning it was necessary for Fertig to move his headquarters to an area where the submarine rendezvous could be handled with a minimum threat from the Japanese presence.[12]

One might wonder why Fertig felt strongly that he had to move his headquarters to be close, geographically, to the area where future SPYRON submarine landings would be made. This was his rationale:

> I was convinced that unless I was present to look after all of the details, they would not be properly handled. This was not a reflection of my staff as individuals but as a group. They simply were not sufficiently well trained to handle a delicate matter of this kind without the possibility of a slipup. Therefore, it was inevitable that I move my headquarters to a more acceptable area.[13]

Fertig's attitude toward subordinates surfaced during the planning surrounding a SPYRON supply mission involving the USS *Narwhal* in November 1943. (See Chapter 9.) He indicated he did not like Colonel McClish's last minute preparations where the margin of error increased substantially. Fertig's concern was over a U.S. submarine landing at a pier under the noses of the Japanese. Moreover, besides the security of the submarine, he was worried about the safety of 32 American civilians awaiting evacuation to Australia by the *Narwhal.* His concern became exacerbated when he dwelled on the fact that President Roosevelt had to intervene to make the *Narwhal* available for the SPYRON program.

Following are some thoughts regarding Fertig's rationale for moving his headquarters and the selection of an appropriate site. Looking at a map of

Mindanao and considering the disposition of Japanese troops, it became apparent to Fertig that the northern end of that island, specifically the Agusan provincial area, was attractive for SPYRON missions and also the location of his new headquarters. The Agusan River flows northward from the area north of Davao through a large part of the island. This offered a venue for the movement of military cargo offloaded from SPYRON submarines landing in the vicinity of the city of Butuan, located at the mouth of the river. Small launches and boats could move quantities of the off-loaded cargo on the river to selected military sites. Though much of Butuan city had been destroyed, a small guerrilla presence would be in a position to block future Japanese incursions on the river.

Fertig gathered his senior staff members to discuss his proposal for a new headquarters location adjacent to an area suitable for SPYRON mission landings. Those participating in these discussions included Hedges, Walter and Bowler. Although McClish, commander of the 110th Division, was not consulted concerning locating the headquarters in his operational area, he had on previous occasions urged Fertig to move the headquarters to the Agusan River valley. All of Fertig's senior commanders agreed on his rationale for moving his command to the Agusan area and the move took on an urgency when it was decided that it should be completed in time for the arrival of the next SPYRON mission. The move commenced on October 15.[14]

Filipino guerrillas in the Agusan River Valley (courtesy MacArthur Memorial Archives, Norfolk, Virginia).

The *Athena*, a two-masted sailing vessel of the Mindanao guerrilla navy, captained by Vicente Zapanta (courtesy MacArthur Memorial Archives, Norfolk, Virginia).

On October 13 Zapanta arrived with his motor vessel *Athena*. He could hardly conceal his jubilation when Fertig informed him that his ship would be used to make the move to the Agusan area. Zapanta assured Fertig that with the help of the .50 caliber machine gun on board his troops could outfight and capture any Japanese launch that they might encounter on the trip northward on the Agusan River.

Radio equipment, headquarters staff and FRS personnel accompanied Fertig on this move. Upon their arrival FRS personnel established a radio station for relay to the reserve station in Hedges' operational area. Until the new station was fully established the FRS station in Lanao relayed all command traffic to Australia.[15]

Enroute to the new headquarters area the *Athena* stopped in Alubijid, near Cagayan city, where he spent the day with Bowler. While planning the move of his headquarters Fertig had considered establishing a subordinate headquarters in western Mindanao, to be designated as "A" Corps, which would function in the event Fertig's headquarters was attacked and destroyed. In Fertig's mind there were two possible candidates for this secondary command: Hedges and Bowler. Fertig preferred Hedges since he had known him for a number of years; however, Hedges was essential in the Lanao area, particularly in dealing with the Moros. Fertig was impressed with Bowler's back-

American and Moro guerrilla leaders. Left–right: Lieutenant Colonel Robert Bowler, Datu Salipada Pendatun and Lieutenant Commander "Chick" Parsons (courtesy MacArthur Memorial Archives, Norfolk, Virginia).

ground and capabilities and after the meeting made the decision to appoint him his second-in-command. He waited until his new headquarters was established before officially naming Bowler as the commander of "A" Corps.[16]

With the arrival of a new year on January 1, 1944, it might be well to review the accomplishments of Fertig's organization as of that date. To put this into perspective one should reflect on where the guerrilla movement was in October 1942. It had a force of about 500 poorly armed personnel and no organization. Since that time an organization had been developed which covered most of Mindanao. Coast watcher stations had been established. Moreover, the guerrillas had been able to contain the activities of the Japanese to the main port cities on the island. In 1943 the Japanese had been forced to realize the threat to their rear areas posed by the guerrillas. It would be only a matter of time before they confronted this threat.[17]

In the meantime, the guerrilla movement would continue to grow and expand. This was assisted in two ways: development of the capability within the organization to communicate with GHQ SWPA and the resultant visit from Chick Parsons, who became the major coordinator of support to the guerrillas in MacArthur's headquarters. Arriving via submarine, Parsons brought four tons of logistical support matériel. As a result of this visit the SPYRON program was created and seven additional submarine missions to Mindanao would be successfully completed in 1943. Three of these missions would be by the USS *Narwhal*—with a cargo capacity of 100 tons, this was a major improvement over the 5–10 ton capability of the regular submarines used initially to support the guerrillas. The support matériel included arms, ammunition, medical supplies and communications equipment. The communications support was vital to the capability of the guerrillas to relay intelligence information being reported by the growing number of coast watcher stations to GHQ SWPA.

Fertig's guerrilla organization had about eight months of uninterrupted growth with logistical support continuing to flow in with the SPYRON missions. This ended on June 26, 1943. When a large Japanese force landed in Misamis Occidental. At that point it became apparent the ability of the guerrillas to operate in that provincial area was coming to an end, causing them to regroup in Lanao province, along the north coast of Mindanao. This was only a stopgap measure and Fertig began assessing where his headquarters and the FRS communications operation should be located. His decision was to move his headquarters to eastern Mindanao where the coastline there offered opportunities for more frequent SPYRON mission landings without detection by Japanese garrisons.[18]

Fertig established his headquarters in the Agusan River area initially in Esperanza. Talacogon would shortly be the next site due to Japanese activity in the area. In 1944 he anticipated additional moves south on the river by launch or native canoes. The mobility offered by the river was beneficial to his operations since the personnel, both staff and FRS elements, could move over long distances but still have a degree of security. This was of utmost importance as the radio net grew to handle the expanded intelligence flow coming from an increasing number of coast watcher stations.

In chapter 4 the many relocations of Fertig's headquarters and his FRS communications facilities were discussed in detail, particularly the site on the Umayon River. At this location Fertig's guerrillas were very close to the Agusan/Davao provincial border. Due to the military thrusts of Japanese forces up the Agusan River, the guerrillas had run out of space in which to maneuver within the Agusan River basin. Although the situation was somewhat dire for Fertig at this point, there was some hope nonetheless. The bombing of Japanese military targets in Mindanao by American aircraft became an almost daily occurrence. This was in preparation for the planned invasion of Leyte in October 1944. By early September these constant bombing raids were causing the Japanese to curtail their operations on the Agusan River. Fertig expressed his thoughts on this development as follows:

> Although still unconfirmed, we believe the Japanese had withdrawn from the Agusan River. Certainly they had withdrawn their outposts and we were awaiting word from our patrols as to conditions further down the river. It is difficult for one who had not spent the poverty-stricken years with us to understand the feeling of elation that came with the turn of the tide. The fleet headed by Admiral Nimitz had hit Palau with a carrier task force and it appeared certain that the Americans would move toward the Philippines in the near future. Since we had spent nearly three weary years of war, it was a real relief to know that although the tide may not have yet turned, it had reached the flood. I still wanted to be back in Colorado when the aspens turned. Optimism grows easily in the fertile soil of hope.[19]

Shortly after noon on September 9 Fertig's headquarters began to receive messages describing the attack by the U.S. Navy against a Japanese convoy headed south along the east coast of Mindanao. Admiral Halsey's leading task force had trapped a Japanese convoy of 49 merchant ships and light escort vessels. As the U.S. Navy's surface ships entered the battle Japanese ships attempted to flee but in the narrow channel many ran aground on the widespread coral reefs that are prevalent on the east coast of Surigao province.

The flights of American aircraft continued on September 10. One coast watcher reported, "There are so many American planes over my station that they can't be counted." For the guerrillas, they had gone from famine to feast in a few days. They now had the strong feeling that the ability of the Japanese to resist had been broken in the raids of the past two days.[20]

On the evening of September 10 Fertig's headquarters had reports from many areas and it appeared that Japanese aircraft on Mindanao and Negros had been effectively destroyed. The changes to the Japanese order of battle on

Mindanao were impressive. Many of the Japanese troops had been withdrawn from Surigao province. The east coast was now clear from Lianga southward. However, the Japanese intended to defend the Davao, Cagayan and Cotabato defense triangle. In addition, they still maintained a strong garrison in the city of Misamis but had removed troops from the rest of Misamis Occidental. Commander Sam Wilson was now back in that province printing money full-time which would greatly assist the guerrillas with their daily operations.

On September 22 a SPYRON mission conducted by the USS *Narwhal* landed at Kiamba, Cotabato. The cargo included special radio equipment to establish a weather control station. In addition, five Filipino radio operators were landed with their communications equipment and 30 tons of supplies were also landed for Colonel Frank McGee's headquarters in Cotabato. This was a good month for SPYRON support. After Kiamba, the *Narwhal* proceeded to Alubijid in Misamis Oriental where it discharged 35 tons of equipment, including eight tons of food.[21]

On September 27 a second SPYRON submarine, the USS *Nautilus*, discharged cargo at Caraga on the east coast of Mindanao, just north of Davao. Cargo included 30 tons of radio equipment and eight tons of food. These items were all destined for Fertig's headquarters and FRS and were expeditiously transported overland.[22]

The extensive physical damage inflicted by the U.S. bombings in September had a negative effect on the morale of the Japanese troops. The Japanese then ordered the movement of their troops from the Surigao area into Cagayan and the Del Monte district in Bukidnon province.

In early September the tempo of U.S. bombing operations increased. Davao was hit with a heavy raid by American B-24 aircraft from New Guinea. The main targets were Japanese airfields in the Davao area. Unfortunately, the weather prevented fighter aircraft, part of the protective initiative for the B-24s, from also attacking their targets. However, Japanese air defense was unusually light—only three aircraft opposed the B-24 raid. In this attack the American bombers dropped 100 tons of bombs, destroying 34 aircraft and killing about 100 Japanese personnel. At this point MacArthur and his staff believed that the Japanese were conserving their aircraft in order to use as many as possible against anticipated U.S. landing operations.[23]

During the period September 9–14 Admiral Marc Mitscher launched large, carrier-based air attacks in the Philippines in order to protect the Palau and Morotai landings. On September 9 carrier aircraft attacked Japanese airfields and installations throughout Mindanao, destroying 60 aircraft on the ground and eight in the air. On September 12 another carrier-based attack was directed against the Visayan Islands. Of the estimated strength of 225 aircraft in the area 125 were destroyed on the ground and 81 in the air. During the night of September 12 the Japanese flew in reinforcements from Luzon. A strike by Third Fleet aircraft on September 13 against this reinforced Japanese aircraft defense destroyed approximately 135 aircraft on the ground and 81 in the air. The air strength which the Japanese had conserved for U.S. landing attacks, and which MacArthur had feared, was almost eliminated. Some 500 Japanese aircraft, or about 57 percent of the 884 Japanese aircraft believed to be in all of the Philippines, had been destroyed or made inoperable. This success, largely made possible by American carrier-based aircraft strength in the Philippines, was an important factor in speeding up the landings in Leyte.[24]

The carrier-based aircraft from the Third Fleet also made effective strikes against Japanese shipping in the southern area of the Philippines. It was estimated that during the period September 1–15, 105 merchant ships were sunk by a combination of American carrier-based aircraft, surface ships and submarines. While precise information is not available, it is believed that 50 percent of Japanese shipping in the southern part of the Philippines was eliminated.[25]

On October 14 Fertig received a somewhat cryptic message from Chick Parsons saying he was in Leyte and would see him in a short time. With Parsons' message and the relentless bombings of Japanese facilities on Mindanao it became clear to Fertig that the first American landings would be on the island of Leyte. After the American landings at Tacloban, the capital of Leyte, on October 20 Fertig received another message from Parsons saying that Tacloban would be the major base in the Philippines to support the coming landings on Luzon, adding that Mindanao would be on its own for the present time.[26]

MacArthur later sent a message saying that Fertig's guerrillas should do everything possible to prevent the Japanese from moving additional troops toward Surigao. He further instructed that the guerrillas should commence an initial offensive against all Japanese garrisons and that supplies to support these attacks would be provided by the middle of November.[27]

The province of Lanao was free of the Japanese for the first time in months and Hedges had established his headquarters in Dansalan. Across the bay in Misamis Occidental all the Japanese had been withdrawn except for those in Misamis City. Fertig ordered his guerrillas to increase the pressure on that Japanese garrison to remove their presence as quickly as possible. Although Mindanao had been bypassed by American liberation forces for the present, Fertig's command believed that they would be totally free of the Japanese threat in the not too distant future.[28]

With the much-awaited liberation of the Philippines commencing with the American landings on Leyte in October 1944, it would be appropriate at this time to include a discussion about the historic Battle of Leyte Gulf. Although this would only have an indirect relationship with Mindanao and the efforts of Fertig's guerrilla organization there, it is important for the reader to understand the implications of these four epic sea battles on the American sustainability of the final major landings of U.S. forces in Leyte.

The Battle of Leyte Gulf

The Japanese reaction to the American invasion of Leyte on October 20, 1944, was the mounting of major sea actions by the Japanese Imperial Navy. This endeavor on the part of the Japanese resulted in the Battle of Leyte Gulf (also known as the Battle for Leyte Gulf). The Battle of Leyte Gulf consisted of four separate engagements between the U.S. and Japanese naval forces: the Battle of the Sibuyan Sea, the Battle of Surigao Strait, the Battle of Cape Engaño and the Battle off Samar.

The Japanese objective was to engage the American forces after they had landed on Leyte. For this purpose the Japanese fleet was divided into three major forces. The first was the Central Force, which included two large battleships. This force would approach the Philippines from Borneo in the south. The plan for the movement was to enter the center of the Philippines and transit the San Bernardino Strait between Samar and Luzon and then emerge into the Philippine Sea. From this point it would head southward toward Leyte.

The second force, known as the Southern Force, would steam northward from Borneo toward the Philippines through the Sulu and Mindanao Seas. It would enter the Leyte Gulf through the Surigao Strait, forming a pincer movement with the Central Force coming southward from the San Bernardino Strait. The two forces would then engage the American Seventh Fleet supporting the Sixth Army elements that had already landed.

A third force, known as the Northern Force, had sailed from Japan and included four aircraft carriers, 11 light cruisers and destroyers. The function of this force was to lure the American Third Fleet carriers away from Leyte Gulf.[29]

On October 24 search planes from the USS *Intrepid* found the Central Force steaming through the Sibuyan Sea toward the San Bernardino Strait. The American Third Fleet under the command of Admiral William Halsey would launch its carrier group aircraft against this force. One battleship was sunk; two cruisers and two other battleships were damaged. With this damage, the Central Force reversed course. It would delay until later its movement through the San Bernardino Strait. At this point Halsey assumed that the Central Force was not longer a threat. He now regarded the Northern Force, now 300 miles northward to the north of the San Bernardino Strait, as the major threat. This decision by Halsey would later become a major error. The San Bernardino Strait was now unguarded by any U.S. Navy ships.[30]

At this point the battered Central Force reversed course and began working its way once more through the San Bernardino Strait. At the same time the Southern Force was approaching the Surigao Strait. Aircraft and coast watchers under the guerrilla Tenth Military District had kept the Seventh Fleet informed as to the movement of the Southern Force.

The Japanese Southern Force was met by Vice Admiral Jesse Oldendorf's task force consisting of six battleships, eight destroyers and 39 PT boats. As the Japanese force steamed in a single file formation it was met by American PT boats. While torpedoes were fired, none damaged the Japanese ships. A few miles further into the strait the Southern Force was attacked by the American destroyers steaming on each side of the Japanese ships. These attacks by the destroyers firing their torpedoes were very effective. One Japanese battleship was blown up. Two other battleships were hit and two destroyers sunk.[31]

As the Japanese force continued northward, Oldendorf's six battleships came into play. Using the classic maneuver of crossing the enemy's "T" the American battleships cut in front of the Japanese column of ships. This allowed every American ship in the battle formation to fire broadside at the Japanese column. At a range of 15,000 yards the order to fire was given. In 18 minutes the six American battleships fired 270 rounds and the accompanying cruisers fired 4,000 rounds with their smaller guns. After these major salvos the American destroyers again went into action against the damaged Japanese ships. Most of the Southern Force ships were out of action; only a destroyer survived. Throughout this major engagement only one American destroyer was badly damaged.[32]

To the north of the foregoing action the Central Force was taking advantage of the American blunder that left the San Bernardino Strait without any monitoring force. The Japanese Central Force was now steaming at 20 knots through the narrow channel of the strait.

In the meantime Admiral Halsey and his Third Fleet steamed northward toward the area off Cape Engaño and the Northern Force. On October 25 Halsey's aircraft attacked the Northern Force. The result was one carrier sunk and the remaining three damaged. At this point Halsey received a message from Vice Admiral Thomas Kincaid reporting on the attack of a task group of six escort carriers by the Central Force off of Samar island after it had exited the San Bernardino Strait. Halsey replied that he was engaging the enemy carriers of the Northern Force and that his Third Fleet was too far out of proximity to be of much help.

Rear Admiral Clinton Sprague wasted no time in engaging his task group of escort carriers against the Central Force now off Samar. He launched all available aircraft and instructed all ships to make smoke screens and alerted his three destroyers and four destroyer escorts to prepare for possible attack. The counter attack by his aircraft and seven fighting ships was so fierce and concentrated that the Japanese believed they were fighting a much bigger force. They finally retired and made their way to the San Bernardino Strait before they could be intercepted. The battle for Leyte Gulf was over.[33] The U.S. now controlled the seas around the island of Leyte. The Sixth Army was safely ashore and would continue to fight the Japanese for total control of the island until May 1945.

The battle for Leyte Gulf had resulted in victory for the Americans. By the time of the battle, Japan had fewer aircraft than the Allied forces had sea vessels, demonstrating the difference in power of the two sides at this point of the war. It was also the first battle in which Japanese aircraft carried out organized *kamikaze* attacks. The losses of one light carrier, two escort carriers, two destroyers and one destroyer escort were small when compared with those of the Japanese, who lost three battleships, one large carrier, three light carriers, six heavy cruisers, four light cruisers and nine destroyers. The Sixth Army commander, Lieutenant General Walter Krueger, made the following comment:

> Had the Japanese plan succeeded, the effect on the Allied troops on Leyte in all likelihood would have been calamitous, for these troops would have been isolated and their situation would have been precarious indeed.[34]

While the American campaign on Leyte was going was going slower than expected, in early November 1944 Fertig moved his headquarters to La Paz, Agusan province. This would be the last location of his headquarters in the Agusan River valley. Also, at this stage in the liberation of the Philippines the U.S. had achieved complete air control over all of Mindanao. Furthermore, the pattern of U.S. bombing raids had changed. The American bombers were now concentrating on airfields in Negros while carrier-based aircraft were hitting targets in Manila and other parts of Luzon. Japanese aircraft operations in the Leyte-Mindanao area had ceased and U.S. aircraft were flying without any opposition from the Japanese.

At long last supplies of food and communications equipment began to arrive—in such quantities as to be in excess of the needs of the guerrilla units. This allowed individual guerrillas to be issued more than five rounds of ammunition. The extra supply of communications equipment allowed stations to be issued reserve/standby transmitters and receivers.

The Leyte campaign continued to be a slow slog with the Japanese contesting every mile of attacks by the U.S. Sixth Army. By late November they were still holding the west coast of Leyte, forcing the U.S. to launch an amphibious landing on that coast. At the same time the Japanese attempted to reinforce their units. A hard-fought battle resulted with the Japanese taking many casualties.

During late November Major Rosenquist, G-2 for Fertig's staff, went to Leyte to brief Lieutenant General Walter Krueger on the Tenth Military District's guerrilla activities. Returning, Rosenquist brought with him a personal letter from the general, which said:

> I have the utmost confidence in your ability to protect my flank. No troops of the Sixth Army will be utilized to land on Mindanao but you will be supplied with ammunition and rations as needed.[35]

Rosenquist also had verbal and specific assurances from General Charles Stivers, G-1, in response to a query made by Fertig to Krueger. The assurance was that all officers presently serving with Fertig were assured of rank and privileges in the grade under orders from Fertig's headquarters. Moreover, they would continue serving with equal rank in the Army of the United States as long as their services were needed. This was announced at a Thanksgiving dinner held at Fertig's headquarters. Items on the Thanksgiving menu had been brought back from Leyte by Rosenquist, consisting of canned turkey, cranberry sauce, plum pudding, some fresh apples and oranges, and candy and nuts. In addition, Rosenquist had brought in a supply of whiskey. Much to everyone's surprise, 26 American officers got somewhat drunk on less than two quarts of whiskey. The rich American food that Rosenquist brought back from Leyte was too much for some of the officers, who had lived all those months on a bland Filipino diet.[36]

In December it became necessary to destroy the Japanese radar facility that was located at the Mindanao Mother Lode mine in neighboring Surigao province. This radar capability could detect and report on U.S. ships passing through the Surigao Strait. The Sixth Army was advised that the guerrillas would require sufficient air support to effectively destroy the site. Rosenquist, who was still in Leyte at the time, was able to arrange for an attack of the site by P-51 fighters using 500 lb. bombs. Colonel Marshall's 110th Division troops, which had established a perimeter around the mine, attacked immediately after the bombing. However, because the heart of the radar equipment was underground in concrete revetments, it could not be destroyed. A second and larger bombing raid was arranged for the following day. This time 50 aircraft took part, using napalm and bombs, and after this attack Marshall's troops successfully overran the position. With the radar site destroyed the Japanese had no observation capability over Surigao Strait and this opened the way for American ships to transit the strait on their way to Luzon.[37]

On December 16 American forces landed on the island of Mindoro. This would be the next invasion before landing on Luzon. The landing was in large part unopposed except for some limited air strikes that cost the Japanese the loss of their aircraft.

On January 14 three C-46 transport planes landed on the Labo airstrip in Misamis Occidental, bringing 15,000 pounds of supplies. Chick Parsons came with these aircraft. He indicated that he was instituting a regular supply system for the guerrilla forces on Mindanao, utilizing both surface ships and aircraft for this purpose. He also stated that as of February 15 U.S. Navy submarines would no longer be available for supply missions to the guerrillas.[38]

In early February Fertig was invited to Leyte to visit the various military commanders, including staff from GHQ SWPA. The first stop on his visit was Major General Courtney Whitney's section, meeting with his various staff members. Later, he met with Major General Charles Willoughby, G-2, who announced that the Eighth Army was now assigned responsibility for Mindanao and that Fertig's Tenth Military District would come under that command.

Fertig's next meeting was with Major General Stephen Chamberlain, the G-3 for MacArthur's staff. A good deal of their discussions focused on methods that could be used to integrate the guerrillas into combat roles when the Americans landed on Mindanao. Fertig also met with Major General Clovis Byers, Chief of Staff, Eighth Army, and his various staff officers. Fertig gave a talk on his guerrilla organization and answered many questions from the staff officers.[39]

Prior to returning to Mindanao Fertig participated in planning meetings regarding the forthcoming invasion of Zamboanga. He arranged for Donald LeCouvre, the guerrilla commander in the Zamboanga area, to meet with the Eighth Army planner. Later, Fertig met with Lieutenant General Robert Eichelberger, Eighth Army Commanding General, who expressed interest in establishing an advance command post in Mindanao as soon as possible. Fertig returned temporarily to Mindanao, specifically Claver in Surigao province, loaded with 200 tons of supplies for the 110th Division, including a Jeep. Returning to Leyte, Fertig then met with Major General Jens Doe of the 41st

Division, task force commander for the invasion of Zamboanga. Fertig was provided with the exact date and beachheads to be utilized in the invasion.[40]

This concludes a review of Fertig's staff activities as the 41st Division, Eighth Army, prepared for its invasion of Zamboanga, followed by further landings in eastern Zamboanga. Details on these actions and the role of Fertig's Tenth Military District guerrillas are contained in Chapter 11.

Guerrilla Strength and Organization

After the Japanese attempt to destroy Fertig's guerrilla organization in Misamis Occidental in June 1943, the organization was reconstituted in Lanao province and Fertig's command temporarily located there. At this time the estimated guerrilla strength was about 8,000. By the summer of 1944 the organization had expanded to about 25,000 men. It should be noted that there are differing views as to the actual numbers of guerrillas in the Tenth Military District. Fertig claims that he had 35,000 but GHQ SWPA felt the number was much lower. Samuel Eliot Morison disagrees with Fertig's number and cites 25,000 as the probable strength of the Mindanao guerrillas, which the author tends to share.[41]

The following narrative describes the structure and history of the Tenth Military District and each of the six divisions, namely 105th, 106th, 107th, 108th, 109th and 110th. The overall command of these divisions rests with Headquarters, Tenth Military District, which was established in February 1943 by a message from General MacArthur. It specifically designated Fertig to command the district which included the islands of Mindanao and Sulu. He was charged with establishing an intelligence net cover in Mindanao as well as the Ninth Military District, to include Samar and Leyte. See Chapter 8 on intelligence collection by the guerrillas.

Later, after moving his headquarters from Lanao to the Agusan River area, he established "A Corps" in western Mindanao to include all divisions in Zamboanga and western Mindanao. Fertig would continue as Commander, Tenth Military District with the 107th and 110th Divisions under his immediate control. All of the Divisions in western Mindanao reported to Fertig through the "A Corps" commander, Lieutenant Colonel Robert Bowler.

105th Division

This division garrisoned the area of Lanao province from Kolambugan to Panguil Bay to the Zamboanga boundary; the southern part of the province of Misamis Occidental and that part of the province of Zamboanga lying north and east of Dipolog River; and all the northern and southern municipalities of Zamboanga province to the vicinity of the city of Zamboanga.

The division was activated on January 28, 1943, and consisted of the 105th, 106th, 107th and the 115th Infantry Regiments. The division was commanded by Colonel Hipolito Garma (former chief of the Philippine constabulary under Brigadier General Sharp). Personnel consisted of 324 officers and 4,270 enlisted.

106th Division

This division garrisoned the province of Cotabato and that portion of Davao south of Digos. It consisted of the 116th, 118th and 119th Infantry Regiments. The division was activated in October 7, 1943, and commanded by Lieutenant Colonel Frank McGee. He graduated from West Point in 1915 and served in Europe during World War I. Division personnel consisted of 298 officers and 3,595.

107th Division

Division responsibility included the area of the Agusan River, south of the east-west line through Lianga, and included the province of Davao extending to Davao City. The division was activated on May 1, 1944, and consisted of the 111th and 112th Infantry Battalions and the 130th Infantry Regiment. The division was commanded by Lieutenant Colonel Clyde C. Childress, formerly the Deputy Commander of the 110th Division. Division personnel consisted of 141 officers and 2,308 enlisted.

108th Division

This division garrisoned the province of Lanao. It was activated on December 14, 1942. It consisted of the 105th, 108th and 120th Infantry Regiments and the Maranao Militia Force (Moro troops). The division commander was Lieutenant Colonel Charles W. Hedges. His business experience before the war made him familiar with the local people in the Lanao area, particularly the Moros. The division personnel consisted of 974 officers and 13,012 enlisted.

109th Division

This division garrisoned a portion of Misamis Oriental west of the Tagoloan River and the province of Bukidnon. It was activated on March 14,

Moro troops of the 108th Division under the command of Lieutenant Colonel Charles Hedges (center with wide-brim hat) (courtesy MacArthur Memorial Archives, Norfolk, Virginia).

1943, and consisted of the 109th, 111th, 112th and 117th Infantry Regiments. The division commander was Lieutenant Colonel James Grinstead, a retired U.S. Army officer with service in Mexico and World War I (twice wounded and recipient of the DSC), who had also served as Philippine constabulary officer in Moro campaigns. The division personnel consisted of 321 officers and 3,987 enlisted.

110th Division

This division garrisoned portions of Misamis Oriental province east of the Tagoloan River, the provinces of Agusan, Surigao and Davao. The division was activated in November 20, 1942, and consisted of the 110th, 113th, 114th, and 30th infantry regiments. The division was commanded by Lieutenant Colonel Ernest E. McClish. Prior to joining Fertig in the guerrilla movement, he had organized one of the first guerrilla units in August 1942. After hearing of Fertig's organization, he went to Misamis Occidental to meet with Fertig. After the meeting Fertig decided to incorporate the organized guerrilla units in northeast Mindanao and named McClish as the division commander for the 110th Division. Division personnel consisted of 317 officers and 5,086 enlisted.

(The total personnel in the Tenth Military District's six divisions consisted of 2,523 officers and 33,056 enlisted. The foregoing information on the six divisions is contained in the "History of the Mindanao Guerrillas."[42])

Operational Employment of the Mindanao Guerrillas

The most important mission that GHQ SWPA had given to the Mindanao guerrillas was that of gathering intelligence information, particularly the movement of Japanese shipping in the waters around the island. (See Chapter 8.) In this regard, there were orders from General MacArthur to avoid combat with the Japanese. However, in the case of self-defense or attractive Japanese targets, the guerrilla leaders would violate GHQ SWPA's standing orders. As a rule pitch battles between Japanese and the guerrillas were avoided because of the modern weapons available to the Japanese compared to older weapons and limited ammunition available to the guerrillas from limited supplies arriving by submarine.

Prior to moving his headquarters to the Agusan River area in October 1943, Fertig issued orders clearly defining the mission of the Tenth Military District. The primary mission was to collect and transmit intelligence to GHQ SWPA. The District's second mission was to defeat the Japanese military forces on Mindanao by the use of guerrilla warfare. While this did not reflect the spirit of MacArthur's order to the guerrillas, Fertig believed that without active guerrilla operations the movement would not be able to maintain public support. Without public support intelligence collection would be somewhat tenuous.[43]

Guerrilla Tactics

As a tactic in countering the offensive operations of the Japanese, Fertig developed a concept of the "pillow defense." The guerrillas, he said, are like a pillow covering the land. When the Japanese conduct their operations they are really only making a dent. But as soon as they withdraw the place of the dent can no longer be found. Moreover, when the Japanese soldier makes a step he loses all that he had. Fertig instructed his guerrillas that when they made contact with the Japanese the guerrillas must be sure of the direction of the Japanese before surrendering ground. He further told them to remember that one shot would pin down a Japanese patrol for a few minutes while they tried to figure out where they were, what they had run into, and what they

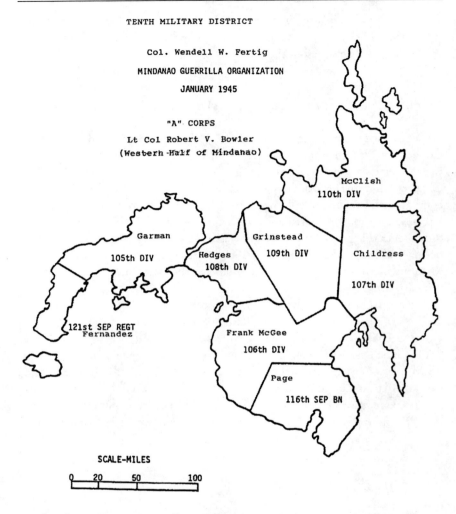

TENTH MILITARY DISTRICT

Col. Wendell W. Fertig

MINDANAO GUERRILLA ORGANIZATION

JANUARY 1945

"A" CORPS

Lt Col Robert V. Bowler

(Western Half of Mindanao)

McClish
110th DIV

Garman

105th DIV

Grinstead
109th DIV

Hedges
108th DIV

Childress

107th DIV

121st SEP REGT
Fernandez

Frank McGee

106th DIV

Page

116th SEP BN

SCALE-MILES

0   20   50   100

Tenth Military District Guerrilla Organization—1945 (Larry S. Schmidt, "American Involvement in the Filipino Resistance Movement on Mindanao During the Japanese Occupation, 1942–1945," MA thesis, U.S. Army Command and General Staff College, Fort Leavenworth, Kansas, 1982).

would do about it. He advised that "when you see what they will do, then hit them fast and then get out and run like hell." In this disengagement the guerrillas would run different routes to an assembly area some five hundred meters from the ambush. He further cautioned that the assembly area should be on the flank, because as soon as the Japanese had been ambushed they would attempt to envelop the guerrillas. Fertig envisioned a guerrilla action in which the Japanese wander into a hopeless morass of endless small-arms skirmishes in which the guerrillas would gladly trade territory for advantage of movement and surprise attacks. They would then wipe out small Japanese patrols, delay the larger patrols and melt away in the presence of Japanese forces in excess of company strength. Fertig had no thoughts of winning a decisive victory, but rather exhausting the Japanese to the point where they would concentrate in fortified camps.[44]

Guerrilla Navy

The Mindanao guerrillas had a small naval capability consisting of an odd assortment of craft. The largest was probably the captured 60-foot Japanese-made diesel motor launch called the *Nara Maru*. Having only small quantities of diesel fuel available it was converted to run on coconut oil. This craft was armed with a .50 caliber gun that was taken from a damaged B-17 bomber from the 19th Bombardment Squadron. The gun had a recoil mechanism made from rubber tubing.

Filipino guerrillas training with automatic weapons (courtesy MacArthur Memorial Archives, Norfolk, Virginia).

Another craft, the *Athena*, was a two-masted sailing ship. Its captain was Vicente Zapanta, the legend of the Agusan River. Thought to be a U.S. Navy veteran of World War I, he volunteered not only his service but also his large sailing vessel. The ship had a muzzle loader fashioned from a four-inch pipe which fired balls that had been cast from melted fishing weights. The crew consisted of 150 men armed with 20 automatic rifles. The *Athena* also had a 20 mm cannon. It is reported that the ship brought down a Japanese medium-size bomber with this weapon.[45]

The *Athena* had a small one-cylinder diesel auxiliary engine. FRS personnel boarded the *Athena* in December 1943 for a trip to the Agusan River Valley. On the lower deck they found about 100 sacks of rice that would function as their beds. The *Athena's* major role during the war was to transport rice and other supplies to the various guerrilla-controlled towns. It also transported troops from one point of Mindanao to another. Zapanta was particularly helpful in delivering radio equipment to some of the coast watcher stations. Another mission was to bring evacuees to the next expected rendezvous with submarines such as the USS *Narwhal*.[46]

A very different ship in the guerrilla navy was a ship called the *So What*. It was a 50-foot boat developed by Waldo Neveling, a German citizen who had been a mining engineer at the Mindanao Mother Lode mine in Surigao province. Initially interned and then released by the Japanese because of his German nationality, he became a "soldier of fortune" and joined Fertig's guerrilla organization, where he was commissioned a Captain in the U.S. Army. The *So What* had been fitted with circular saw blades on its gunnels. This provided armor for the boat. Its primary mission was to transport supplies to the guerrillas, raid Japanese shipping and protect the mouth of the Agusan River.[47]

Another vessel in the Mindanao naval fleet was the *Bastard*, a 26-foot whaleboat. Its skipper was Robert K. "Jock" McLaren, a captain in the royal Australian army who was part of a group of POWs that escaped from a Japanese concentration camp in Sandakan, Borneo, made its way to Mindanao and served in the Tenth Military District in various capacities until the end of the war. McLaren's boat had a 20-millimeter cannon mounted in the bow, twin 30-inch guns amidships and a .50 caliber gun in the after part of the craft. Another unique feature was an 82-millimeter mortar in the craft's stern. The boat would sail into Japanese-controlled ports in daylight hours, direct its automatic fire at the piers and fire its mortar at Japanese boats. It is said that its crew would even challenge the Japanese by sending them invitations. This craft was also effective against Japanese aircraft.[48]

A last addition to the guerrilla navy was a group of small, fast sailboats and escort launches that had machine guns or .20- or .30-millimeter cannons. These small craft would protect the delivery of supplies that had been brought in by submarine.[49]

Significant Encounters of the Mindanao Guerrillas with Japanese Military Units

The first resistance by the guerrillas against the Japanese began in September 1942. Many hundreds of operations were carried out by the guerrillas until the liberation in 1945. While most of these encounters were defensive, there were a few that were offensive. The Tenth Military District records indicate a total of 2,894 encounters until liberation. Most of these encounters were minor clashes with Japanese patrols and represented the norm of these operations. Though the tactical operations of each guerrilla division varied, there were several factors that affected the tactics of the entire organization:

• Shortage of ammunition and weapons. Very few units were adequately equipped with mortars, machine guns automatic weapons, hand grenades and ammunition, unlike the Japanese units which had these items in abundance. These shortages constrained the guerrillas in conducting large-scale offensive operations. Instead, their operations were typically guerrilla in nature and included hit and run and ambush tactics. Many operational reports of these encounters would state that the reason for terminating the contact was shortage or low availability of ammunition.

• Lack of medicine and food. Malaria was the predominate affliction among the guerrillas with up to twenty percent of a unit on the sick list because of malaria. This problem was met with the arrival of thousands of Atabrine tablets by submarine shipments. Lack of food affected some units and their families because of Japanese disruption by Japanese actions. These shortages were usually temporary.[50]

Significant Operational Encounters

The following contains a selected number of guerrilla operations against the Japanese presence. These cover the entire island and range from 1943 until 1945. Most of the six guerrilla divisions are represented in these encounters. Several were a part of the invasion of eastern Mindanao by the American forces in 1945.[51]

The Kabacan Siege
October 25, 1942

Kabacan, in the heart of Cotabato, was garrisoned by the Japanese in 1942. Early on the morning of October 25 the Japanese coming out of the garrison were ambushed by one company of guerrillas. The siege continued for fourteen days, with 68 of the 76 Japanese in the garrison killed. The garrison was about to fall when Japanese reinforcements arrived. With their ammunition supply diminished, the guerrillas were forced to withdraw.

The Butuan Siege
March 3–10, 1943

During the period of March 3–10 1943 forces of the 110th Division launched an attack against a Japanese stronghold at Butuan. Over 2,000 guerrillas were involved in this operation against the garrison which lasted for seven days. More than half of the town was burned in the battle. The Japanese remnants were finally driven to a school building where they entrenched themselves and were about to surrender when Japanese aircraft attacked the guerrillas. This was followed by Japanese reinforcement of 200 troops. Japanese casualties in this battle were estimated at approximately 100. Twenty guerrillas were lost during this action. This offensive operation was among the very few large scale operations attempted by the guerrillas to dislodge the Japanese from a stronghold. With a continuing lack of equipment and ammunition, this experience tempered the guerrilla against launching major operations as opposed to conducting low key attacks on Japanese patrols.

The Invasion of Glan
May 2, 1943

On May 2, 1943, Glan, in Cotabato province, was invaded by a contingent of 100 Japanese soldiers and 70 pro–Japanese Moros. Several launches and a one gunboat, supported by aircraft, were used to land the Japanese troops at two points. The beach encounters were fiercely fought by the guerrillas and caused many Japanese casualties. No casualties were suffered by the guerrillas. However, being outnumbered and under-armed, the guerrillas retreated to the Tubal Mountains. This allowed the Japanese to occupy the town without further opposition.

The Labo Attack
June 30, 1943

Labo is a barrio six kilometers away from Misamis City, Misamis Occidental. It was garrisoned by approximately 100 Japanese after the invasion on June 26, 1943. The headquarters of the 106th Division had been located here but evacuated with the Japanese attack. To the guerrillas Labo had importance and the guerrillas wanted it back. Under cover of darkness on June 30 a guerrilla group of 67 personnel closed in on the four buildings housing the Japanese. Early on July 1 the guerrillas directed their fire on the occupied buildings. Taken by surprise the Japanese did not return their fire for about 30minutes. However, by that time reinforcements arrived in two trucks and saved the garrison from annihilation. In this encounter the guerrillas suffered no casualties but the Japanese lost 30 personnel.

Guerrillas Ambushed Near Kilometer 4
on the Surigao Road July 12, 1943

On July 12, 1943, the combat company of the 114th Infantry Regiment of the 110th Division, led by Lieutenants Thomas Baxter and Albert McCarthy, was ambushed by the Japanese at Kilometer 4 of the Surigao National Road. McCarthy was killed in the attack while Baxter was wounded. Even so, Baxter, using his .45 automatic from a prone body position, was able to kill four Japanese soldiers. Two additional guerrillas were killed and two wounded in the encounter. The enemy suffered 18 dead and six wounded.

The Macalibre Ambush
September 7, 1943

The clash with Japanese troops at Macalibre, Misamis Occidental province on September 7, 1943, was considered the most notable encounter during the year in the operational area of the 107th Infantry Regiment.

On the morning of September 4 the Japanese garrison at Dipolog, Zamboanga (having been there since June 26, 1943) evacuated eastward to Misamis Occidental. The strength of the Japanese unit was 120 soldiers. The 107th Infantry Regiment quickly organized a company of 47 guerrillas to intercept the Japanese unit with an ambush. To do this required them to overtake the Japanese unit and pick a good site ahead of them. At a horseshoe shape in the road before the Macalibre bridge a site was selected. At 1730 hours the Japanese unit was sighted moving toward the bridge in a mass formation. The guerrillas opened fire with rifles, one BAR and ten shotguns. Approximately 39 Japanese were killed and many wounded. The guerrilla casualties were one dead and three wounded. With their ammunition almost expended, the guerrillas withdrew from the ambush area.

The Japanese Attack on Liangan
December 19, 1943

The Liangan attack by the Japanese was a threat directed at the headquarters of the 108th Division which had the responsibility for Lanao province. The headquarters was located about four kilometers from the coast of Iligan Bay.

A Japanese force of 600 men, using landing craft and barges, landed at a point southwest of Liangan. One guerrilla company defending the area could only offer a slight resistance against the larger Japanese force. At 0200 hours another force landed at a point 12 kilometers southwest of Liangan. The guerrillas offered stiff resistance but after 30 minutes withdrew. At 1000 hours the guerrillas came back at the Japanese using rifles, mortars and BARs. Japanese casualties were 20 killed. One guerrilla was killed. At 1100 hours another attack was mounted by the Japanese but repulsed by the guerrillas. A Japanese unit with 50 soldiers attacked again at 1300 hours. They were driven back with casualties numbering 18. One guerrilla was wounded. Even so, the Japanese force, unopposed, occupied Liangan at 1500 hours on December 21. The guerrillas had crossed a creek from Liangan earlier in the day before the Japanese had arrived. Also, supplies, arms and ammunition had been removed from the division headquarters. During this period the Japanese and guerrillas had exchanged fire and Lieutenant Wagner was killed. By 1700 hours the Japanese had broken through the defenses and were in complete control of the division headquarters.

On December 22 at 0400 the Japanese landed at three more points in the Liangan area. They clashed with guerrilla forces and suffered 20 dead. The guerrillas had one casualty. On December 23 and 24 the Japanese withdrew from all areas of Liangan using landing craft and barges. All points previously held by the Japanese were immediately re-occupied by the 108th Division guerrillas.

The Talakag Operation
June 18, 1944

A regiment of the 109th Division guerrillas garrisoned a portion of Misamis Oriental province between the Cagayan and Tagoloan rivers and the northern portion of the province of Bukidnon. This regiment came under pressure from a Japanese force of approximately 900 men. This force attacked various guerrilla units during this period of June 18–29.

At one point in these attacks the Japanese penetrated to Talakag, Bukidnon province, site of the 109th Division headquarters. On the morning of June 20, the enemy deployed near Bayanga but did not advance. A brief clash developed between a guerrilla patrol and a Japanese outpost. At the same time four Japanese dive bombers strafed the area for about one hour. While they did no damage, they did affect the morale of the poorly equipped guerrillas. Still, the guerrillas attacked repeatedly without any results.

In the Talakag area the 112th Infantry Regiment made contact with the Japanese units but both sides withdrew. Later three Japanese dive bombers, supporting the Japanese ground attack, arrived and the Japanese force then moved toward Talakag on the main highway and entered the town at noon.

Earlier that day the division commander, Lieutenant Colonel James Grinstead, had ordered his headquarters in the town burned and relocated his guerrillas to Balagon.

On June 28 the Japanese retired all of its units toward the area of Cagayan. In the following days the guerrillas re-occupied their old positions and headquarters in Talakag. It should be noted that the Japanese force in this major attack against the Talakag were mostly Korean troops with Japanese officers totaling 500 personnel.

In this operation against the guerrillas at Talakag it was estimated that 14 Korean/Japanese were killed and 13 wounded. In spite of the bombing and ammunition expended by the Japanese the number of guerrillas were three killed and three wounded. Throughout the entire engagement the guerrillas were short of ammunition.

The Battle of Baga
August 24, 1944

Eight men from the 106th Infantry Battalion set up an ambush in the Tangub area of Misamis Occidental on August 24. On signal the guerrillas let loose with a barrage fire on an element of a Japanese patrol killing approximately 20. The remainder of the patrol pushed to the area of the ambush. In the meantime, the guerrillas had withdrawn some distance from the first encounter. When the patrol came closer the guerrillas threw a hand grenade at the approaching Japanese. Ten more were killed in this second encounter. Then a fire fight developed between the guerrillas and the Japanese. After one hour the guerrillas withdrew because of lack of ammunition. The total number of Japanese killed was estimated at 50. Guerrilla casualties were one killed and one wounded.

The Pagadian Operation
November 5, 1944

The attack on the coastal town of Pagadian, Zamboanga province (the town is situated on Illana Bay) was undertaken to disperse some 80–100 Japanese entrenched in the heart of the town, specifically the municipal building, plaza and a radio station. The Japanese were heavily armed with .50 Cal machine guns, BARs, mortars and rifles. The attacking guerrillas were deployed as mobile units to different houses 150–500 meters away from the municipal plaza in such a manner that a semi-circle was formed with the Japanese troops imprisoned within. Commencing on November 5, the operation lasted 20 days with daily encounters throughout the period.

On November 13 the municipal building was abandoned by the Japanese and then occupied by the guerrillas. On November 16 the Japanese burned the radio station.

On November 25 two guerrilla speed boats, which had been involved in unloading an American submarine at Tukuran Bay and armed with 22 mm cannons, strafed the Japanese on the eastern side of the town. A total of 180 rounds were expended. This action was unique in a sense that the Japanese were being attacked from all directions.

During the 20 days of the attacks on the Japanese in Pagadian, they suffered 16 dead and an undetermined number wounded. None were killed on the guerrilla side—only one wounded.

The Mina-Ano Encounter
January 17, 1945

Mina-ano is in Agusan province, between Cabadbaran and Butuan towns. This was a noteworthy encounter with the Japanese because it was a valiant effort by the 110th Division's Special Troops to prevent the Japanese from Surigao reinforcing their garrison in the Butuan region. Since October 1944 the Japanese, sensing likelihood of the U.S. invasion, were reinforcing their garrisons in places that might be objectives of amphibious assaults.

On January 17, 1945, at 0630 hours contact was made by the division's Special Troops with a Japanese force of 200–250 men which marched along the national highway from Cabadbaran and Butuan. Rudy and Hank Hansen were members of the Special Troops and participated in this operation. The guerrillas had formed a defensive line about 300 yards to the right of the road. They were armed with .50 cal machine guns, bazookas and automatic rifles. These weapons simultaneously fired at the Japanese unit and 50–60 Japanese fell from the fusillade.

The Japanese fought desperately to exchange fire. This lasted over three hours. Then, the Japanese were forced to retreat. However, 30 minutes later Japanese reinforcements arrived with a force the same size as the original. Three times the new force drove an assault toward the guerrillas but was thwarted. Since the supply of ammunition for the guerrillas could not be replenished, an order of withdrawal was given. The Special Troops used rounds from the bazooka to cover the exit from the encounter. Casualties for the Japanese were estimated to be from 110–160 killed or wounded. One guerrilla was wounded.[52]

The "Mountain Gun" Battle
March 1945

On March 3 some civilians reported seeing a large contingent of Japanese troops hiking along Route 1, the main road between Butuan and Buenavista in Agusan province. Captain Dongallo, CO of the 110th Division's Special Troops, assembled members of Company "A" (Rudy and Hank Hansen's unit) to brief them on a plan to ambush the Japanese at a juncture midway through a horseshoe-shaped bend in the road. Fifty foxholes were dug 10 feet apart around the bottom of the "U" about 300 feet from the road. Hank Hansen's foxhole was closest to the midpoint of the U and he was designated to fire a shot as soon as the Japanese contingent reached his position. The guerrillas held their positions until roughly 2100 or 2200 hours when three Filipino guides holding coconut frond torches approached, followed by four or five uniformed Japanese soldiers. This was apparently a scouting party and was allowed to proceed without challenge. A short while later the night was filled with loud creaking noises and Japanese guttural voices as the main Japanese force approached. When Hank Hansen determined that the Japanese were halfway around the bend he fired his signal and all members of Company "A" opened fire with everything they had—machine guns, BARs, carbines, etc., with tracer bullets illuminating the action. The Japanese took cover in the ditch on the opposite side of the road and returned fire. After about 30 minutes they ceased firing and the sound of a bugle pierced the air. Following a period of silence Rudy, Hank and three other guerrillas, each with five hand grenades, ventured out of their foxholes and crawled on their bellies toward the road. On signal all five threw their grenades at the opposite side of the road, repeating this action every 10 feet until they reached the ditch on their side of the road. There was no activity from the ditch on the opposite side so they climbed onto the road where they stumbled upon a piece of artillery called a "mountain gun"—gun barrel about three feet long, mounted on a two-wheeled carriage harnessed to a horse that had been killed in the crossfire. At first light the guerrillas confirmed the departure of the Japanese during the night, leaving behind three supply carts pulled by *carabaos* in addition to the mountain gun. These carts carried sacks of rice, canned meat, tea and other food items, but the Japanese had taken their ammunition and a machine gun, leaving the tripod. The gun carriage and carts explained the creaking noises that heralded the approach of the Japanese the previous night. The guerrillas unharnessed the horse from the gun carriage, freed the weapon, rolled it down an embankment and dragged it through a cornfield to headquarters for display as a trophy.

Fully expecting the Japanese to return, Company "A" once again took up positions guarding the highway from their foxholes. About three weeks later, before dawn, about 200 Japanese soldiers attacked their positions from three sides—left, right and center. The Hansen brothers, part of the group with heavy weapons covering the right flank, sprang into action, raking machinegun fire from right to left nonstop until the muzzles of their machineguns became too hot to touch. Just before daybreak Dongallo, realizing that his troops were badly outnumbered, ordered them to retreat to a nearby river which they crossed and reached the opposite bank before daybreak. Japanese casualties were unknown as they opted not to pursue the guerrillas across the river and returned to their base, bringing with them their wounded and dead. On the guerrilla side, the only casualty was Hank Hansen's knapsack—a fellow trooper pointed out a hole in the upper area where a Japanese bullet had bored straight through, just inches from his neck.[53]

The Attack on the Vit-us Line
March 16, 1945

The Vit-us line was established by the guerrillas eight miles up the Agusan River to prevent possible Japanese infiltration into the La Paz area in which both the headquarters of 110th Division and the Tenth Military District were located. The Japanese made two attempts to break through this line; the first on March 16 and the second on March 17, 1945.

On March 16, an estimated 250 Japanese troops from Butuan advanced to attack the Vit-us line. Strong resistance to the advance was made by a battalion of the 113th Infantry Regiment. The Japanese succeeded in breaking through the line. However, in the afternoon the guerrillas attacked the Japanese and re-captured their former positions.

On March 17, the Japanese attempted again to breach the line and forced again the withdrawal of the guerrillas. However, with the aid of a 37mm gun the Japanese were driven from their position that they had previously gained and returned to Butuan. The Japanese causalities from the action were unknown; the guerrillas had none.

The Talisayan Operation
March 22, 1945

A significant guerrilla role was played out in an amphibious operation against the Japanese presence in Talisayan. The enemy garrison was selected as a target of an amphibious operation because of its value as a barge-staging area midway between Cagayan and the Mindanao Sea. This offensive operation included the participation of 350 guerrillas of the 110th Infantry Regiment of the 110th Division under the leadership Lieutenant Colonel Paul Marshall. Working with the U.S. Navy, this guerrilla force was trained for 10 days in amphibious operations. They were then embarked aboard Navy amphibious ships and made a landing against the Japanese garrison at Talisayan on March 22, 1945. The operation achieved its objectives and 138 Japanese were killed. There were no U.S. Navy or guerrilla casualties.

The Guerrillas Break Through
the Cabadbaran Line
March 31, 1945

In the last days of March 1945 orders were issued to move the location of 110th Division headquarters from Las Nieves, Agusan province to Gingoog, Misamis Oriental province. During this period the entire area of Agusan province was populated with Japanese troops, particularly along the roads and trails of the area. Under the leadership of the Division Chief of Staff, Major Juan Rivera, all records and headquarters personnel were moved successfully through this high threat area. To do this required an attack on the Japanese garrison at Cabadbaran. Some 30 Japanese were at the garrison. With Major Rivera in this attack were ten enlisted. The attack lasted about one hour during a heavy rainstorm. With 12 Japanese dead from the attack, the remaining men in the garrison fled. Guerrillas suffered one wounded.

The Bugo Operation
April 27, 1945

In order to support an American amphibious landing in the Macajalar Bay on May 10, 1945, the Tenth Military District was authorized by the American Tenth Corps to perform a reconnaissance of the Bugo beach area and attack Japanese elements in the area. The mission was assigned to the 110th Infantry Regiment of the 110th Division. Major Rosenquist, the division intelligence officer, was in charge of this intensive intelligence collection effort prior to the landings in the Bugo area of Macajalar Bay. The collection element, which included Rudy and Hank Hansen, would carry out beach reconnaissance and scouting in the area of the proposed landings. A U.S. Navy LST transported the guerrillas to the beach near the Del Monte pineapple cannery. Using two small Navy launches, the group divided into two elements. Major Rosenquist in one boat would do depth soundings off shore. The other boat, with Major Spielman of the 114th Infantry Regiment in charge, would land on the beach, providing cover for Rosenquist's mission. Rudy and Hank were on the beach with Spielman's group. Once on shore a burst of fire from a concealed Japanese machine gun hit Rosenquist's boat and one guerrilla on board was wounded. The boat then moved out to open waters. In the meantime Major Spielman's group located and returned fire against the fortified sniper position, located high above ground on a platform suspended between two coconut trees. Eventually the guerrillas prevailed and four Japanese were killed. Even so, one guerrilla was wounded in the back and was carried by Rudy and Hank back to the pick-up point. Fortunately they had Sulfanilamide packs and Hank applied the medication and bandaged the wound. The group then returned safely to their launch base. The following morning the reconnaissance group looked out into the bay and observed the 108th Regimental Combat Team arriving in landing craft. This was the beginning of the end for the estimated 15,000 Japanese troops that had occupied this area of Mindanao.[54]

The Carmen Operation
May 9, 1945

In May 1945 about 650 Japanese were garrisoned in the town of Carmen, Cagayan, Misamis Oriental. A guerrilla operation was mounted using three battalions from the 108th Division. This was being done in coordination with the American landing in Cagayan on May 10.

On May 9 the guerrilla offensive began. Only a slight resistance was offered by the Japanese garrison except at the Iponan Bridge. Even so, the guerrillas managed to reach the Cagayan River but had to withdraw because of potential friendly casualties from the imminent American invasion. After the American landings the guerrillas launched an offensive and crossed the Iponan River. Also, another guerrilla battalion advanced to the west of the Cagayan River.

The operation lasted four days. The Japanese suffered an estimated 100 killed or wounded. One guerrilla was wounded.

7

Logistical Support for the Mindanao Guerrillas

Initially, with no hope for "the Aid" arriving from the U.S. or Australia, Fertig's guerrilla forces were faced with the grim reality of using only the weapons and ammunition they had on hand. Stores of these, both USAFFE and Philippine constabulary, which had not been seized or surrendered to the Japanese, were available on a haphazard basis. When Hansen and his two sons joined McClish's 110th Division at Medina, they carried with them one .38 caliber revolver, a shotgun and hunting rifle. While this may not be representative of arms available, it is an example of what was available to civilians. Much of it could not be supported by U.S. military ammunition stocks. Members of USAFFE that had not surrendered would probably have had Springfield and Enfield rifles. These weapons could be supported from limited U.S. military stocks that had been hidden from the Japanese.

After Rudyard and Henry Hansen had been inducted into the guerrillas they were issued Springfield and Enfield rifles, probably because the ammunition for these weapons was more readily available than would have been the case for non-military weapons.[1]

To build up an inventory of weapons, Fertig initiated an appeal to the civilian population to turn in weapons to the guerrillas. For these weapons the civilians were issued receipts. Those that were turned in would have been a mixed bag of military and civilian weapons. Nonetheless, it was an earnest effort to bring more weapons into the guerrilla inventory despite the difficulty of supporting such weapons. When ammunition was not available, brass curtain rods and explosive material from captured Japanese mines were used to fabricate cartridges.[2]

While it is not exactly clear when GHQ SWPA decided to provide token aid to the guerrillas on Mindanao, it was probably between the first message sent by McArthur to Fertig in early February and the departure of Chick Parsons and Charlie Smith for Mindanao via the submarine USS *Tambor*. This aid to the guerrillas was approved directly by MacArthur who felt it was so important and symbolic to sustain the guerrillas and give them hope in the return of the Americans. Accordingly, four tons of support accompanied this visit by Parsons and Smith in March 1943. Items carried by the submarine included communications equipment, arms, ammunition, medicine, clothing, U.S. dollar currency and wheat flour for communion wafers. The inclusion of wheat flour in the shipment may seem odd, but Parsons, a longtime resident of the Philippines, was sensitive to the importance of the Catholic religion in the lives of the Filipinos and the shortage of wheat flour for communion wafers was being felt in the various parishes throughout the islands. Though this was a token shipment, one of Fertig's first questions to Parsons was the frequency of logistical support by submarine that could be expected. Parsons pointed out that this first shipment came at the specific direction of General MacArthur who was concerned about the Filipino guerrillas. Parsons further pointed out that there was little support at the War Department for the Filipino guerrilla program. Parsons at this point probably wanted to be more upbeat on future logistical support but the program was just evolving. Moreover, Parsons was on an exploratory mission to evaluate the capabilities of the various guerrilla groups, including Fertig's, and reinforce with them the importance to MacArthur's headquarters on the collection of information and intelligence by the guerrillas as opposed to conducting warfare against Japanese units. Of particular note was interest in the movement of Japanese shipping through the Philippine archipelago. In this regard, Parsons stressed to Fertig the importance of setting up coast watcher stations at or near strategic maritime passages where the movement of Japanese ships could be observed and reported to Fertig's staff for evaluation. Once processed, this information would then be relayed by his Force Radio Section (FRS) to action commands such as the Commander, Submarines, Southwest Pacific (ComSubSoWesPac) in Fremantle, Australia. During Parsons' visit the first coast watch station was established in the vicinity of Davao. This accomplishment would be a selling point for Parsons in his talks with the Navy in Fremantle after his return to Australia.

The use of submarines for resupply to the guerrillas became the best initial option. In the minds of MacArthur and his staff it was a proven operational concept because of submarine support to Corregidor during the early days of the war.[3] There had been some thought about resupply from the air, particularly as the U.S. forces got closer to the Philippines in their advance across the Pacific. During the April 1943 timeframe Fertig actually received a message from GHQ SWPA requesting that his command investigate the conditions of airstrips on Mindanao.[4] This led Fertig to believe that some logistical support may in the near future come from airlift. Later, William Dyess, an aviator POW who had escaped from the Davao Penal Colony, spent some time with Fertig's command. Dyess believed that aerial resupply was feasible. At a later date Fertig had several American and Filipino guerrillas commence work on the construction of airfields that could be hidden from Japanese observation planes. It will be recalled that Fertig's initial engineering responsibilities early in the war included the upgrade of airfields. Thus, building resupply airfields was very much on his mind. His term for such fields was "farm projects." These so-called "farm projects" constructed by the guerrillas were covered with topsoil and growing crops that could be readily removed by a bulldozer or tractor to expose the prepared runways when needed. Aircraft could even land at night with torches outlining the strip at the sides and ends.

One guerrilla, John Tuggle, was intimately involved for two years in "Farm Project #2." Tuggle was the engineer on PT Boat 41, the boat on which MacArthur made the trip from Corregidor to Mindanao in March 1942. As a crewmember on this evacuation mission he was personally awarded the Silver Star by MacArthur. He served with PT Boat 41 on its various missions until it was sent to Iligan for overland transport to Lake Lanao. Refusing to surrender, he went into hiding and in December 1942 joined Fertig's guerrilla group in Misamis City, Misamis Occidental. He was commissioned a Second Lieutenant in the USFIP and assigned to the 108th Division.

Later Tuggle was assigned to work with Captain Chandler Thomas (a P-40 pilot who had joined Fertig's guerrilla group in November 1942) on one of the longest farm projects undertaken by the guerrillas. Farm Project #2 was located in northern Zamboanga province near Domingog. The airfield, with a length of 7,000 feet, was carved out of the jungle. Father Edward Haggerty, former volunteer chaplain of the Visayan-Mindanao Force, visited the site with Colonel Bowler in early April 1944. He described the state of Farm Project #2 as follows:

> The strip seemed cornfields, sugar cane fields, banana groves, all separated by fences with a house in each plot. Stretches of forest even continued to separate one clearing from another. We looked in vain for a field but it was waiting for a final assault by workers to lay bare a giant seven thousand foot runway, level as a table, baked hard as concrete by the sun.[5]

According to Tuggle, 20 guerrillas and about 250 Subanons worked on the project, using shovels, some 200 wheelbarrows and one tractor. The work had gone on since early 1943.[6]

During Father Haggerty's visit to the farm project Thomas and Tuggle were advised that the field must be operational by April 20. Lieutenant Colonel Jose Cabili, the "A" Corps quartermaster, accompanied Haggerty on the visit. He was told by Bowler to bring the village leaders together and indicate to them the importance of the field being ready, hastening the day of liberation. If they could get possibly 1,500 workers and persuade them to stay three days they could finish the project. Two days later long lines of men began streaming toward the site with provisions on their backs and tools in their hands. Work shifts were arranged. Cabili had not only recruited the men but also large supplies of food for the new volunteer workers.

The week passed quickly and with the felling of the last trees blocking completion of the project the landing field became a reality. The evening of April 19 was spent waiting for confirmation of impending use of the landing field. The message that was subsequently received indicated that the flight had been canceled, but the field was to be kept in readiness.[7]

The airfields constructed by the guerrillas would have dual purposes— resupply and emergency landing fields for damaged allied aircraft. In reality, aerial resupply to the guerrillas was only used after the landings on Leyte. Even then, U.S Navy amphibious ships were used for the most part to provide the bulk of the logistical support to the guerrillas vice aerial resupply. LST-type vessels, with a beach landing capability, could carry far more than a C-47.

With Parsons' first trip to Mindanao via submarine behind him, it was now possible to develop a coherent program for supplying the guerrillas in the Philippines. As previously mentioned, this program was given the code name of "SPYRON" or "Spy Squadron" and be closely held by all who participated in the program. Even the civilians who were evacuated from the Philippines had to be debriefed on their evacuation by submarine. To make SPYRON work, Parsons established a special mission unit to facilitate the clandestine movement by submarine of supplies to the guerrillas. While the program lasted only two years, it did more than just carry supplies; intelligence, weather and communications specialists were also landed. On their outward bound trips the submarines carried a number of evacuees that included POWs and American civilians that had been stranded by the war. Some 41 submarine resupply missions were conducted by the SPYRON program. Of these, sixteen missions were made to the island of Mindanao. (A listing of the more significant missions to Mindanao follows.) During the two year history of the program a total of 1,325 tons of supplies were landed. In addition, 331 specialists were landed for special missions and 472 persons were transported to Australia.[8]

Significant Spyron Missions to Mindanao

Date	Submarine/Place	Mission
March 5, 1943	*Tambor*/Pagadian Bay	Delivered four tons of supplies; landed 50 personnel including Chick Parsons and Charlie Smith.

Date	Submarine/Place	Mission
		This first shipment contained the following:
		• 50,000 rounds of .30 cal
		• 20,000 rounds of .45 cal
		• radio equipment/parts
		• medicine/medical equipment
		• food, clothing, cigarettes
		• flour for communion wafers
June 12, 1943	*Trout*/Pagadian Bay	Landed Jordan Hamner, five personnel and communications gear
July 9, 1943	*Trout*/Dumanquilas Bay	Evacuated Chick Parsons and Charlie Smith as well as DAPECOL escapees Mellnik, McCoy and Dyess
Sept. 3, 1943	*Bowfin*/Iligan Bay	Landed seven tons of radio equipment and miscellaneous supplies
Sept. 29, 1943	*Bowfin*/Iligan Bay	Evacuated military personnel including Lt. Col. Morgan and DAPECOL escapee Grashio
Nov. 15, 1943	*Narwhal*/Nasipit	Landed 46 tons of supplies and Chick Parsons; evacuated 32 civilians and DAPECOL escapees Shofner, Hawkins and Dobervich
Dec. 2, 1943	*Narwhal*/Cabadbaran	Landed 90 tons of ammunition, Larry Evans and Bob Stahl; evacuated eight personnel, including Chick Parsons
Dec. 5, 1943	*Narwhal*/Macajalar Bay	Landed cargo and evacuated nine civilians
March 2, 1944	*Narwhal*/Butuan Bay	Landed 70 tons of ammunition and stores and Wheeler and Silva; evacuated 28 people, including Australian ex–POWs Leslie Gillon, James Kennedy, Raymond Steele and Walter Wallace
June 5, 1944	*Nautilus*/Pagadian Bay	Landed 25 tons of weather equipment and supplies; 16 personnel, including Luke Campeau and Harold Rosenquist
Sept. 22, 1944	*Narwhal*/Kiamba	Landed radio party, weather unit and 30 tons of supplies
Sept. 22, 1944	*Narwhal*/Alubijid	Landed 35 tons of cargo
Sept. 27, 1944	*Nautilus*/Caraga	Landed 30 tons of supplies
Sept. 29, 1944	*Narwhal*/Siari	Evacuated 81 POW's from "Hellship" *Shinyo Maru* sunk off Sindangan Point

Date	Submarine/Place	Mission
Jan. 20, 1945	*Nautilus*	Landed 45 tons on east coast of Mindanao; evacuated one Army officer
Jan. 23, 1945	*Nautilus*	Landed 45 tons on east coast of Mindanao

Following are hull numbers for several submarines used in the resupply effort:

USS *Tambor*, SS-198
USS *Trout*, SS-202
USS *Bowfin*, SS-287
USS *Narwhal*, SS-167
USS *Nautilus*, SS-168

Although Parsons was the principal staff officer for support to the guerrillas in the Philippines, he had more senior staff officers with whom he had to consult. His technical superior was colonel (later major general) Courtney Whitney in the Philippine Regional Section (PRS) of the Allied Intelligence Bureau. He came to the PRS on the recommendation of General Richard Sutherland, MacArthur's chief of staff. Whitney had been a lawyer in Manila for 15 years and had a number of contacts among the Filipino elite. Prior to Whitney's arrival Colonel Allison Ind had headed PRS. He now became Whitney's adviser and Deputy Comptroller of AIB.

It should be noted that there was friction between Whitney and General Charles Willoughby, MacArthur's G-2. It was Willoughby's contention that resistance organizations, like the one Fertig had formed, did not exist. Moreover, such organizations would not be formed in the future. That said, he did not support sending arms and ammunition to the Philippines.[9] While Willoughby's view may have some relevance on Luzon, it had less validity as one looked at what was happening in the southern Philippines on such islands as Leyte, Panay and Mindanao. In fact, Willoughby's views on guerrillas in the Philippines ran counter to those held by MacArthur. Prior to his departure from Corregidor, MacArthur had formulated concepts on a guerrilla movement surviving or taking over after the USAFFE surrender.[10] Despite Willoughby's negative views on the guerrillas, Whitney had MacArthur's ear on providing support to Fertig's guerrillas, particularly after Parsons' first trip to Mindanao.

Returning to Australia, Parsons went all out to establish the development of the SPYRON resupply concept. In this regard, he coordinated with Captain Arthur H. McCollum, the Seventh Fleet staff officer, on the submarine resupply requirements and coast watcher operations. He also went to Fremantle and discussed his requirements for submarine support with the U.S. submarine command. Moreover, he related his submarine requirement with the resultant benefit of coast watcher reporting to submarine operations in Philippine waters. Parsons undoubtedly came to the early conclusion that there was the potential of a synergy between the Navy support for resupply of the guerrillas and the intelligence that could be derived for submarine attacks against Japanese shipping moving through Philippine waters. As the intelligence flow increased to the Navy, so would the availability of submarines for resupplying the guerrillas.

In the initial stages of the submarine resupply effort to the guerrillas, attack submarines were assigned. This meant that these submarines would have their attack capability reduced by carrying cargo/passengers rather than the maximum number of torpedoes. At first the submarine command was not too enthusiastic with the diversion of their attack capability. However, as coast watcher intelligence information on Japanese shipping became available the Navy could see the cost/benefit of the SPYRON program to their attack capability. Thus, the programs became a win-win situation for both the Navy and the guerrillas. It is doubtful if Fertig was aware or understood the dynamics of this relationship. He mentally put his resupply requirements in one box and the tasking from MacArthur's staff for coast watcher intelligence information in another.

Though patrol submarines were initially assigned to the SPYRON program, their cargo capacity was limited—5 to 10 tons. In October 1943 a larger cargo submarine, the USS *Narwhal*, was assigned to the program. The following year a similar class submarine, the USS *Nautilus*, was also assigned to the program. Both of these submarines had been built in 1930 when the Navy was thinking about operating larger submarines. The length of these two boats was 371 feet and had a displacement of 2,780 tons. This was almost 1,000 tons more than the standard attack submarine used in the 1940s. Their beam was 33.3 feet. Because of their much larger displacements, greater cargo capacity could be accommodated. Between 50 and 100 tons of cargo could be carried by these boats. Even so, because of their age, the engines were increasingly prone to breakdowns.[11]

Making these two large submarines available to SPYRON in 1943 became a difficult task even though Admiral Chester Nimitz, Commander in Chief, Pacific, had promised MacArthur to have them made available for the program. Manuel Quezon, president of the Philippines and an enthusiastic supporter of the guerrilla program, went directly to President Roosevelt to plead for the assignment of the larger submarines. Intrigued about the program after being briefed by Quezon, the president ordered at least one of the large submarines immediately assigned to Brisbane and the SPYRON program. The *Narwhal* arrived at Brisbane in October 1943 under the command of Lieutenant Commander Frank Latta. Later the *Nautilus* would join the program. On the *Nar-*

The USS *Narwhal,* SS-167, made seven SPYRON missions to support the Mindanao guerrillas between November 1943 and September 1944 (courtesy MacArthur Memorial Archives, Norfolk, Virginia).

whal's first mission she carried 92 tons of equipment which was split between Fertig's guerrillas and guerrillas on Mindoro.[12] With the larger submarines the problem of quickly unloading the cargo became greater. The first SPYRON mission (USS *Tambor*) had little difficulty in unloading the cargo in about one hour, even though the cargo had to be moved through hatches 23 inches in diameter. Even so, the guerrillas did have local craft similar to lighters to handle all of the shipments, but the use of these larger submarines required detailed planning by Fertig's staff. *Cargadores* had to be assembled to transfer the cargo to the lighters and large *bancas*. A large number of *cargadores* would also have to be staged on shore to move the supplies quickly inland. All of this activity had to be carried out in secrecy to avoid attracting the attention of the Japanese. It goes without saying that the problems multiplied with the use of the larger submarines, but the end result more than justified the extra effort.

After Parsons' first trip to Mindanao he wrote an extensive report for Whitney on the conditions among the guerrillas and the general population, particularly as to essential items that might be included in future cargo shipments carried aboard the SPYRON submarines. While drugs to fight malaria were essential, Parsons broadened the list to include items that most military supply specialists would not have considered. Sewing machine needles was one such item. Most barrios had at least one machine. With the shortage of clothing material, the Filipinos were turning to the use of material woven from abaca fibers (known as Manila hemp) for clothing. Unfortunately, the coarseness of the fibers caused accelerated wear on sewing machine needles. Charles Hansen's daughter, Virginia Hansen Holmes, vividly recalls the stiff and itchy abaca dresses that she and her mother and sister wore during that period. These were made by local seamstresses with the help of their stalwart sewing machines. Such clothing was all that was available during the latter part of the war. Thus, sewing machine needles became a priority item for SPY-RON missions.[13]

Supplies brought in by the SPYRON missions took time to move down to the fighting units. Even so, the guerrillas had an effective system for distribution. By early December 1943 Charles Hansen was a recipient of this support. In his papers was a copy of receipt number 159, dated December 8, 1943, for the items he received from the 110th Division Quartermaster. Items received included the following:

1 Carbine M1 Cal. 30. ser. No. 3245164	2 pair of socks
100 rounds of Ammo Cal. 30 M1	1 pair of Jungle boots
1 Jungle pack	1 Molle shaving cream
1 Musette bag with strap	1 Razor with blades
1 Field jacket	1 Towel
1 each shirt and pants	6 bags of Duke's tobacco
1 Jungle medical kit	1 carton of Camels cigarettes
2 each under shorts and underpants	1 can of gun oil
1 Match box compass	1 Sewing kit
1 Sweater	1 pair of Leggings, canvas
1 Jungle suit	

There is an old military saying, "Rank hath its privileges." By no means did all guerrillas receive such items. As privates, Hansen's two sons, Rudy and Hank, received new weapons and ammunition delivered by early SPYRON missions, but would not receive boots and other uniform items until late 1944.[14]

Parsons was most sensitive to the spiritual needs of the Filipinos. After his return to Australia he contacted the Catholic Church regarding the assembly of "padre kits" that would be transported on the SPYRON missions and then distributed to Catholic priests such as Father Edward Haggerty on Mindanao, the unofficial chaplain for the Tenth Military District. These padre kits were assembled and packed in five-gallon kerosene tins. Each tin contained flour for communion wafers and small containers of Mass wine. Also, included in the kit were religious medals, candles, rosaries and holy pictures. It was Parsons' view that the padre kits would perform a vital function by allowing priests to administer to the religious needs of Filipinos, thereby maintaining morale and loyalty of the population to the Commonwealth and the U.S. government.

Other unusual items contained in the cargo shipments included small copper stills for making *tuba* (fermented coconut sap) in order to produce fuel for generators that powered the radio transmitters that were crucial in passing intelligence to Australia. While unusual, counterfeit Japanese currency was also contained in the shipments. The goal here was to depreciate the currency. By the same token, plates and paper to print Philippine currency were also included.

Items associated with psychological warfare were also contained in the SPYRON cargo. These included packets of candy and fruit imprinted with the historic MacArthur slogan "I SHALL RETURN." This slogan was also included on matchbook covers that were widely distributed. These efforts tied into the once-a-day news broadcast into the Philippines from Australia. The program would start with a recording of General MacArthur saying "I shall return" and followed by the playing of the Philippine national anthem. In order to influence the Mindanao Moro population in supporting the guerrilla movement, copies of *Life Magazine,* dated May 31, 1943, were part of the SPYRON cargo. These magazines contained an article and pictures featuring King Ibn Saud of Saudi Arabia. The article carried comments from the King in his expressions of friendship for the United States. Providing these magazines to Moro leaders made it easier for them to support an American-led guerrilla movement.

The foregoing comments about the cargo carried by the SPYRON missions underscore the precise planning and care exercised by Parsons in making the program successful. Parsons had lived many years in the Philippines and had a comprehensive understanding of the country and the people. His frequent trips into the Philippines from Australia gave him an accurate measure of what was needed to maximize U.S. efforts in support of the guerrillas and pave the way for the coming invasion. The important element in this trajectory would be making the guerrilla operations and the coast watcher system viable and expanding sources of intelligence on the Japanese presence both on land and sea in the period leading up to the liberation.

One of the more interesting SPYRON missions was the movement of a weather forecasting team to Mindanao. This was the initial effort to set up a chain of weather forecasting stations throughout the Philippines prior to the invasion of the Philippines in the fall of 1944. The team was formed from the weather squadron located at Amberley Field in Ipswich, Queensland, Australia. The team of six was led by Lucien "Luke" Campeau.

Prior to deployment, Campeau's team was trained in radio, weather, demolition, rubber boat landings and commando tactics. They were allowed just 5,000 pounds for all their specialized equipment. This included no food for they were expected to live off the land as did the guerrillas to whom they would be assigned. Arriving in Darwin, Campeau's team was joined by other specialized teams also being inserted by submarine. Among the group was Captain Rosenquist, whose mission was to explore the possibility of a POW rescue operation at the Davao Penal Colony (DAPECOL).

The specialized team embarked on the submarine USS *Narwhal* on 15 April 1944. They reached the Philippines after a 15-day voyage, interrupted by an attack by the *Narwhal* on a Japanese convoy. Four torpedoes were fired, with two successful hits. Part of the group, including Rosenquist, had been destined for the east coast of Mindanao but, because of a navigational error, had to continue on with the rest to Illana Bay on the south coast of Zamboanga. This was far from their original destination and it required them to go overland for a distance of 180 miles. The submarine rendezvoused with the Mindanao guerrillas at Pagadian City, Zamboanga province. Seventy tons of supplies, including the weather team's specialized gear, were off-loaded from the submarine in record time. The final destination for Campeau and his men was the Dimoroc Canyon area which was located in northern Zamboanga province at an elevation of 4,000 feet. The team's equipment had to be carried up to the site using *carabao* mud sleds. This site would be the team's home for most of their assignment.

The station at Dimoroc had a complement of Filipino soldiers assigned there. A diesel generator provided power for the station. The Filipinos built a *nipa* shack on stilts with bamboo floors. It had two bedrooms and a covered porch which housed the team's weather instruments. These included an aneroid barometer, rain gauge, anemometer, wet and dry thermometers, weather balloons and a hydrogen generator. The hydrogen was used to fill the balloons. When released the balloons ascended at a known rate and the balloons position was then measured with a theodite. A balloon was released every six hours during the day. Weather observations were made every hour and wind readings aloft every six hours. All of this information was transmitted to Australia for further dissemination to various weather users.

Living conditions were less than ideal and Campeau suffered from a number of physical ailments, such as a painfully infected molar, bouts of malaria and dysentery. With no medical facilities close by, recovery was slow. But he and his team persevered and provided a steady flow of weather information to the planners of the upcoming landings of U.S forces in the Philippines.

When the 41st Division, X Corps, Eighth Army, landed at Zamboanga City on 13 March 1945, there was little else for the weather team to do on Mindanao. Campeau was ordered to the weather detachment in Manila. Later, he returned to Australia where he received orders for his return to the States.

8

Intelligence Collection

The intelligence collection responsibilities for the guerrillas on Mindanao were clearly outlined by MacArthur in his message to Fertig in February 1943. In moving ahead with GHQ SWPA's desire for intelligence and information collection against Japanese forces on Mindanao, Fertig had the responsibility to balance the establishment of the coast watcher station programs with the demands of guerrilla operations against the Japanese. It was the desire of GHQ SWPA to minimize the latter. While Australia was quite ready to supply weapons and ammunition via submarine, they did not want the guerrillas to become actively engaged with operations against the Japanese occupation forces. This policy from Australia would make Fertig's overall responsibilities more difficult. Moreover, if Fertig's forces were to continue receiving logistical support via submarine, intelligence collection operations would have to be initiated and maintained, responding to the needs of GHQ SWPA. During this first trip of Parsons, Fertig provided support to both Parsons and Smith in establishing the first coast watcher stations. American personnel from Fertig's guerrilla force would man the initial stations.

The first coast watcher station was established on the coast of Davao. This station functioned until the liberation of the Philippines in 1945 when it was overrun by advancing American troops of the 24th Infantry Division as they pushed toward the city of Davao from Digos, approximately 20 miles southeast of the city. While research has not located the precise location of this station, it would seem to have been located in the high terrain below the mountain of Boribing (elevation 1,275 feet). This mountain range overlooks Route 1 and the Gulf of Davao between Davao City and Digos. In this location the coast watcher station would have had a viewpoint whereby it could visually monitor the entrance to the Gulf of Davao and the Japanese ships that were being deployed to and from the Gulf.[1] The information provided by this station was most valuable to the U.S. Navy and its submarines operating in the waters around Mindanao. Sighting information would be sent by radio to Fertig's headquarters for evaluation and then retransmitted to Fremantle, Australia for possible action by U.S. submarines.

Bill Johnson, former Navy radio operator on motor torpedo boat 35, was sent to Davao in March 1943. He was in Lieutenant Bulkeley's PT boat group that transported General MacArthur, his family and staff from Corregidor to Mindanao. After Johnson's boat had been damaged, he was assigned to Lake Lanao to support Navy PBY operations on the lake. With the surrender of U.S. forces in May 1942, he was interned at Keithley Barracks. However, along with Bill Knortz, James Smith and Robert Ball, he escaped from the POW camp and joined the guerrillas. After Parsons' arrival in March 1943, Johnson was sent to Davao to establish the first coast watcher station. His initial understanding was that the assignment would be for only six months but it lasted a total of twenty seven months. Early in the assignment his shack housing the radio equipment burned down but he was able to retrieve most of the equipment and keep the collection site in operation. Even so, he suffered third degree burns on his leg and foot. Since the Davao Gulf had a very large Japanese naval presence, this station generated numerous ship sightings that were transmitted to the U.S. Navy in Fremantle for possible action by Navy submarines operating in the area. Because of the growing number of sinkings of Japanese ships, based on reports from coast watcher stations, the route between Davao and Zamboanga City became known as "torpedo alley."

The second coast watcher station was established in the area of Dinagat Island north of Surigao province which had an overview of the strategic Surigao Strait. Chick Parsons was personally involved in setting up this station with Truman Heminway. Because Parsons deemed Dinagat too hot with Japanese, he selected instead the nearby island to the west called Panaon. Later, Heminway would have to relocate his station to Dinagat to maintain his reporting on Japanese shipping passing through Surigao Strait. The information on Japanese shipping passing through this strait, like Davao, was of great value to the U.S. Navy. Parsons boasted to Heminway, "This is one of the most important 'eyes' GHQ can have."[2]

The Force Radio Section of Fertig's command played a vital role in assisting in the establishment of other coast watcher stations, particularly after the Davao and Dinagat stations were in operation. Expansion of this vital intelligence-gathering network was made possible by the arrival of two major SPYRON re-supply missions, one at Nasipit on November 15 and the other at Cabadbaran, Agusan province, on December 2, 1943. Included in these shipments were many radio sets, enabling the FRS to assist in establishing more coast watcher stations throughout Mindanao.[3]

With various strategic sites identified, Lieutenant Willard Money was dispatched to establish a coast station at Mambajao, on Camiguin Island. When this was accomplished, Money proceeded to Liangan where another station was established. Then Money moved on to the province of Cotabato to establish another station, overlooking the Moro Gulf.[4]

Eventually 30 stations would be established, completely covering the island of Mindanao. Many of these stations were manned by FRS personnel. As part of the Tenth Military District's overall intelligence responsibility, two coast watcher stations were also established on the island of Samar. Prior to the return of the American forces, 32 coast watcher stations had been established by Fertig's command on both Mindanao and Samar. At times command and control of the coast watchers was not always clear. For example, in early April 1944 Gerald Chapman moved his station from Samar across the San Bernardino Strait to Luzon for better observation and security reasons.

Intelligence collection in the Tenth Military District expanded greatly in 1943. As additional divisions were created, G-2 sections in these organizations were actively involved in expanding intelligence collection operations for their specific geographic areas. At midpoint in the war some 1,500 assets were employed in the effort. Reporting from these operations was forwarded to Fertig's headquarters for evaluation and then dissemination to GHQ SWPA. Targets covered by this reporting included Japanese military installations, Japanese troop dispositions, airfield activity, road and trail intelligence and bomb damage assessment of raids conducted by U.S. aircraft. By 1944 the intelligence flow in message traffic handled by FRS was between 8,000 and 10,000 messages per month.[5]

Targets covered by this reporting included Japanese shipping information, military installations, troop dispositions, airfield activity, road/trail intelligence and bomb damage assessment of raids conducted by U.S. aircraft. The following are examples of this reporting, by target[6]:

Shipping Information from Coast Watcher Stations
1943

December 15

A CONVOY OF 11 ENEMY SHIPS WAS SIGHTED AT 0420 GMT, POSITION 10 DEGREES 17 MINUTES NORTH, 124 DEGREES 14 MINUTES EAST. HEADING SOUTHWEST AT MEDIUM SPEED.

1944

January 7

28 SHIPS WERE SIGHTED IN SURIGAO STRAIT TO EAST OF ESPERANZA AT 1725 HEADING SOUTHWARD

January 15

34 UNIDENTIFIED VESSELS COMING FROM CEBU WERE SIGHTED AT 0315Z SLOWLY HEADING TO SOUTHEAST. POSITION WAS GIVEN AS 0572415.

February 12

20 COASTAL MOTOR VESSELS THAT CAME FROM THE DAVAO DIRECTION WERE LYING OFF SACOL ISLAND AT 1300.

February 15

A BIG CONVOY OF 20 UNIDENTIFIED SHIPS WAS SIGHTED AT 0900 MOVING SOUTHEAST CELEBES SEA AT A REGULAR SPEED.

April 8

AT 1115 ONE HEAVY CRUISER APPROACHING TICTUAN ISLAND FROM ZAMBOANGA ON AN EASTERLY DIRECTION. AT 1305 SAME HEAVY CRUISER REPORTED FOLLOWED ANOTHER CRUISER OF THE SAME CLASS FROM ZAMBOANGA GOING WESTWARD TO TICTUAN ISLAND.

April 8

AT 0830 ONE SHIP INSIDE LIANGA BAY WITH A DESTROYER BEING TOWED. AFTER HALF AN HOUR STOP, IT PROCEEDED NEXT TO SURIGAO.

April 19

TWO TRANSPORTS ESCORTED BY ONE DESTROYER SIGHTED AT 1730, 10 MILES OFF LEBAK COAST, COTABATO, GOING NORTH AT MEDIUM SPEED.

June 1

JAPANESE TASK FORCE IN DAVAO GULF—ONE BIG AIRCRAFT CARRIER, 5 BATTLESHIPS, 6 DESTROYERS, 15 SUBMARINES, 9 TRANSPORTS AND 15 SMALLER SHIPS.

July 18

SIX SHIPS FROM ZAMBOANGA PROCEEDING EAST WITH 1 DESTROYER LEADING, FOLLOWED BY 1 SUB CHASER, 2 LARGE MERCHANT SHIPS, 1 DESTROYER AND 1 FREIGHT TRANSPORT.

August 1

ONE CRUISER AND ONE MERCHANT VESSEL ENTERED SARANGANI BAY HEADING AT FAST SPEED TOWARD DADIANGAS.

September 19

NINE VESSELS, LARGE APPROXIMATELY 500 TONS, ENTERING CAGAYAN HARBOR FROM WEST. 8 MERCHANT VESSELS REPORT ARRIVED CAGAYAN PORT FROM NORTHEAST EARLY IN MORNING.

October

DURING MONTH OF OCTOBER 1944 A TOTAL OF 405 SHIPS WERE SIGHED BY COAST WATCHER STATIONS IN THE VISAYAS AND MINDANAO AND REPORTED THROUGH FRS TENTH MILITARY DISTRICT HEADQUARTERS TO THE U.S. NAVY.

Military Installation Information

This type of information made a significant contribution to the overall intelligence collection on Mindanao. Most of it was collected by low-level sources that worked on the Japanese installations. Following are examples of information reports:

1944

November 24

ENEMY AIR SPOTTER AND RADIO STATION LOCATOR ON TOP OF SA AVEDRA HILL, LOCATED ONE MILE WEST OF TAPUNDO POINT ON SOUTHEAST CORNER OF MINDANAO

December 1

FOUR LARGE CANNONS ARE LOCATED ABOUT 400 METERS NORTHWEST OF MATINA RESERVOIR. AT POINT 100 METERS WEST OF MATINA RUNWAY AND ONE KILOMETER SOUTH OF NATIONAL HIGHWAY ARE FOUR AA GUNS. FOUR MORE GUNS ARE LOCATED 300 METERS WEST OF SOUTH END OF MATINA RUNWAY.

1945

March 10

GUN EMPLACEMENTS: PINPOINTED IN DAVAO SHEET NR 4732-II: ONE AT 377–572 ONE AT 285–570.

March 14

REF DAVAO SHEET NR 4752-II: FOOD DEPOT AT 536–655.2. REVETMENT 3 METERS THICK AND 50 METERS LONG CAMOUFLAGED WITH GRASSY SOD LOCATED AT 345.6–320. REF BUNAWAN SHEET NR 4732-I. FOOD DEPOT IN 3 BUILDINGS AT 318–687. GAS DRUMS SCATTERED IN PILES AROUND THESE BUILDINGS.

April 2

LARGE TUNNEL WITH 16 OUTLETS LOCATED 25 METERS EAST OF DAVAO RIVER AND WEST OF KILOMETER 15–5 LAPANDAY ROAD. ELECTRIC MACHINERY IN TUNNEL WORKING DAY AND NIGHT.

April 15

TROOPS ARE LOCATED AT POSITION 194–221. ARTILLERY PIECES HIDDEN UNDER FRUIT AND BANANA TREES AT NURSERY. RECOMMEND BOMBING AND STRAFING WITH RADIUS OF 600 METERS OF POINT INCLUDING FOREST AREA SOUTH OF NURSERY. TARGETS ARE ON KORONDAL HIGHWAY.

April 19

CARMEN FERRY: REF PIKIT SHEET NR 4532-III. CULVERT ON ROAD AT 36.4–64.28 USED AS AIR RAID SHELTER. MOTOR POOL WITH 33 TRUCKS AT 38.57–61.5. 30 JAPANESE OCCUPY HOUSE AT 38.8–65.1. GAS DUMP AT 38.53–64.19.

June 13

JAPANESE IN ABTALEL AREA HAVE CONSTRUCTED TRENCHES. 18 TRUCKS AND MANY DRUMS OF GASOLINE AT MOTOR POOL WHICH IS NOW LOCATED IN WOODED AREA SOUTHWEST OF BASE OF NUFOL HILL.

Enemy Troop Disposition

The Japanese troops on Mindanao were constantly shifting, even in the heavily garrisoned area of Davao. Road conditions did not facilitate travel, making reporting of troop movements somewhat easier. Guerrilla agents with radios were located near the Japanese garrisons to facilitate reporting of troop movement by either land or water. It was particularly important in late 1944 and early 1945 to report Japanese efforts to relocate troops to counter U.S. campaigns on Mindanao or adjacent islands.

The volume of reporting on Japanese troop movements represented a major portion of messages handled by FRS. The following are just a few representative messages covering Japanese troop dispositions:

1944

January 11

MISAMIS ORIENTAL. 1,900 JAPANESE TROOPS ARRIVED IN CAGAYAN FROM ILOILO.

February 11

1,000 JAPANESE ARRIVED ZAMBOANGA FROM THE NORTH

April 7

DAVAO. 4 LARGTE TRANSPORTS UNLOADED TROOPS AT DAVAO CITY. ESTIMATED AT 2,000.

May 16

SURIGAO. ELEMENTS OF JAPANESES 30th DIVISION ARRIVED SURIGAO FROM CEBU.

July 15

ESTIMATED 2,000 JAPANESE TROOPS ARRIVED DAVAO FROM PALAU FOR MONTH OF JUNE AND FIRST TWO WEEKS OF JULY.

September 1

MISAMIS ORIENTAL. FROM 15 TO 30 AUGUST ESTIMATED 6,000 JAPANESE TROOPS ARRIVED CAGAYAN FROM VISAYAS AND LUZON. TROOPS APPEAR TO BE FROM SOUTHWEST PACIFIC AREA BUT HAVE RESTED IN NORTH.

September 19

SURIG AO. ESTIMATE 2,000 JAPANESE TROOPS MOVED FROM NASIPIT TO TAGOLOAN . UNKNOWN NUMBER LEFT ON 6 BARGES WITH SUPPLIES.

October 27

4 SHIPS WITH ESTIMATED 5OO JAPANESE LEFT CAGAYAN FOR LEYTE. ADDITIONAL 600 JAPANESE BELIEVED FROM BUGO TAGOLOAN AREA LEFT CAGAYAN ON SHIPS FOR SAME DESTINATION.

November 17

MISAMIS ORIENTAL. ESTIMATED 2,200 JAPANESE LEFT CAGAYAN FOR NORTH, BELIEVE LEYTE. ALMOST NIGHTLY DEPARTURES OBSERVED SINCE NIGHT OF NOV 6. USUALLY ABOUT 500 EACH NIGHT USING LAUNCHES AND BARGES.

December 14

BUKIDNON. MORE THAN 1,000 JAPANESE TROOPS FROM BUKIDNON PASSING BUGASAN ENROUTE TO BUTUAN, COTABATO.

1945

January 30

200 JAPANESE TROOPS SHIFTED FROM CAGAYAN AREA AND A SMALL NUMBER WENT SOUTH FROM MALUKO-DALWANGAN.

February 18

COTABATO. APPROXIMATELY 1,000 JAPANESE ARRIVED PARANG FROM COTABATO CITY AREA. THEY ARE LOCATED SOUTH OF WATER TOWER IN BARRACKS AND A SCHOOL BUILDING.

March 25

BUKIDNON. TROOPS ALONG SAYRE HIGHWAY ARE MOVING SOUTH. SINCE MARCH 15 APPROXIMATELY 2,500 JAPANESE HAVE GONE SOUTH FROM IMPASUGONG AREA.

Airfield and Japanese Arrival Activity

The Japanese utilized Filipino laborers, mechanics and other technical personnel to work on their airfields. The guerrillas took advantage of these opportunities to place agents in these positions. For example, at Licanan Airfield an agent worked as a surveyor. He drew most of the plans for the airfield and these were smuggled through another guerrilla asset for delivery to Fertig's headquarters for transmittal by FRS to Australia. Following are examples of messages containing this type of interaction going to GHQ SWPA:

1944

July 18

MALABANG HAS 80 PLANE SHELTERS LOCATED OUTSIDE OF RUNWAYS NEAR SEA EXTENDING NORTH.

November 24

JAPANESE PLANE ASSEMBLY AT BATUTITIK. OVER 90 PLANES ASSEMBLED THERE; HIDDEN AND DISPERSED AS FAR AS 2 KILOMETERS FROM FIELD. FIELD LOCATED 2 KILOMETERS WEST OF BATUTITIK BARRIO.

1945

February 10

NO AIRCRAFT ASSEMBLY SHOP AT LICANAN AIRFIELD. PLANES ARRIVE ALREADY IN FLYING CONDITION. SMALL PORTABLE REPAIR SHOP COMPOSED OF 3 LATHES. 2 SMALL HAND BLOWERS FOR BLACKSMITH AND IRON WORK. REPAIR DONE IN HANGAR OR ON RUNWAY WHERE NEEDED.

March 2

27 PLANES AT LICANAN AIRFIELD DAVAO AND 82 AT MATINA AIRFIELD.

Aircraft Activity

1944

May 23

FLIGHTS OF 6 TO 9 BOMBERS FROM PATAG AIRFIELD PATROLLING MACAJALAR BAY FOR LAST 3 DAYS.

April 1

FLIGHT OF 11 HEAVY BOMBERS, ALL TWIN ENGINES, AND 4 SINGLE MOTOR FIGHTERS PASSED MALITA HEADING TOWARD DAVAO.

Road and Trail Activity

Only two highways on Mindanao offered suitable road surfaces for mechanical units—the Sayre and National Highways. Accordingly, it was not difficult for guerrilla assets to monitor Japanese military traffic on these roads.

1944

October 25

18 TRUCKS WENT NORTH AND 12 WENT SOUTH. CARGO UNIDENTIFIED.

1945

April 28
ENEMY TRUCK TRAFFIC CONTINUES. FOR PERIOD OF THREE DAYS A TOTAL OF 42 TRUCKS WENT NORTH AND 101 TRUCKS WENT SOUTH. OF THOSE 68 MOVED BY DAY AND 75 BY NIGHT. TRUCKS GOING NORTH USUALLY EMPTY WHILE THOSE GOING SOUTH ALL LOADED WITH TROOPS.

Trails

The Japanese undertook construction of trails to augment the scarcity of good roads, particularly to the interior. This was to a large extent in the Davao area. Following are a few intelligence messages concerning new trails:

1944

October
JAPANESE IN CAGAYAN IMPROVING BACK TRAILS THROUGH LIBONA, MAMPAYAG AND DALWANGAN AS POSSIBLE MEANS OF RETREAT.

1945

February 26
NEW ROUTES OF WITHDRAWAL FOR JAPANESE TROOPS SOUTH DAVAO AREA. INFORMATION CONCERNS WIDENED TRAILS ABOUT 6 METERS WIDE. ONE FROM MATINA SECTOR (KM 2.6) GOING NORTH TO CATALUNAN GRANDE THEN TO MINTAL, COMPLETE ABOUT 31 JANUARY. SECOND TRAIL FROM SIBULAN (KM 30 SOUTH HIGHWAY) PASSED END OF INAWAYON, EAST OF CATIGAN DIRECT TO BAYABAS THEN TO MANUEL PLANTATION (ABOUT 4 KMS WEST OF NAMING).

Bomb Damage Assessment

The first U.S. bombing in the Philippines was on August 6, 1944, when two bombs were dropped in the Davao area. From that point onward there were increasing bombing missions in all areas of Mindanao. There grew a need for intelligence reporting on bombing and strafing results. The following are a few messages concerning the effectiveness of these bombing missions:

1944

September 10
AMERICAN BOMBERS HIT AND STRAFED LANDING FIELD AND TRUCKS ALONG THE NATIONAL HIGHWAY SURIGAO. 19 TRUCKS DISABLED ON

HIGHWAY. BOXES OF AMMUNITION, FOOD, GASOLINE DRUMS AND SOME
FIELD GUNS AT WHARF.

September 14–15

PILOTS QUARTERS, MOTOR POOL, TWO LARGE WAREHOUSES, TWO FUEL
TANKS UNDER ACACIA TREES ALL IN ZAMBOANGA, DESTROYED BY AMER-
ICAN BOMBING.

September 27

THREE TRANSPORTS SUNK BETWEEN BONGO ISLAND AND COTABATO
CITY, 600 DEAD BUT 200 SURVIVED.

Much of the improvement in intelligence collection in the 1944–1945
period was due in no small measure to the efforts of Fertig's G-2, Major Harold
Rosenquist. After improving the intelligence coverage in the Davao area,
Rosenquist was sent by Fertig to the 110th Division to assist Major Paul Marshall in the development of intelligence capabilities in Surigao province.
Apparently Fertig had not been happy with the collection effort there as well
as the entire north coast of the province.[7]

A history-making contribution by the coast watcher program was made
by the station that observed and monitored the San Bernardino Strait between
Samar and Luzon. This station was manned by Gerald "Gerry" Chapman.
Chapman came to the Philippines as a young Army Air Corps Staff Sergeant
prior to the war and was assigned to the 440th Ordnance Company (Aviation
Bomb) at Clark Field, which was moved to the Del Monte airfield in early
December 1941. After the Japanese invasion of Cagayan City in May 1942,
Chapman was involved in moving equipment inland away from the airfield.
While working with several other Army Air Corps personnel they chanced to
encounter a courier who indicated all U.S. personnel would be ordered to surrender the next day. Chapman and his colleagues decided that they would flee
the area for Agusan province. During the course of his journey Chapman came
down with malaria and beri-beri and was cared for by several Filipino families
for over eight months. In early 1943 he met with other American military personnel that had not surrendered and joined the guerrillas led by Fertig. He
was soon promoted to second lieutenant. His first major duty was escorting
some of the American POWs that had escaped from the Davao Penal Colony
in April 1943 to the 110th Division headquarters. Following this assignment
Chapman volunteered to replace James Schoen, a coast watcher on Leyte who
was stricken with a serious illness and evacuated to Mindanao. About two
months later he was moved to the northwestern tip of Samar, overlooking the
San Bernardino Strait. In April 1944 Chapman moved that station from Samar
across the strait to the southern tip of Luzon, near the town of Santa Mag-

dalena. This location had an improved view of the strait though security threat from the Japanese was greater. Bob Stahl, another coast watcher on Samar, was in frequent contact with Chapman. During the late afternoon of June 15 Stahl monitored Chapman's communications and noticed that he was attempting to send a priority message to Fertig's command. Unfortunately he was being jammed by the Japanese. Through the jamming Stahl was eventually able to copy Chapman's urgent communication. Moving to a higher frequency Stahl attempted to contact GHQ SWPA without success. He now attempted contact with KFS, the Mackay Radio station in San Francisco. They received his message and relayed it to GHQ SWPA and Fertig's headquarters. The message that Chapman was attempting to send read as follows:

"GOING EAST, TWO SMALL PATROL BOATS, TEN CRUISERS, THREE BATTLESHIPS, ELEVEN DESTROYERS AND NINE AIRCRAFT CARRIERS."[8]

Chapman had spotted a Japanese task force moving through the San Bernardino Strait toward the Philippine Sea. This information would later have great significance to the war in the Pacific. At the time of Chapman's sighting the Fifth Fleet was engaged in an amphibious assault on Saipan. The fleet and Admiral Raymond A. Spruance's Task Force 58 were not aware of an approaching Japanese task force exiting the San Bernardino Strait. With the information supplied by Chapman, Spruance had time to deploy his ships to the west and engage the Japanese task force. This was the first battle of the Philippine Sea and what later became known as the "Marianas Turkey Shoot" on June 20. In this major engagement the U.S. Navy did major damage to the Japanese Navy, particularly its air capability. The Japanese lost over 400 aircraft and three aircraft carriers in this air battle. It is an interesting footnote to history that George H. W. Bush, our 41st president, participated as a pilot in these tactical air encounters.[9]

Though Chapman had technically moved his station out of the Tenth Military District when he moved across the San Bernardino Strait to southern Luzon, his command and control remained under Fertig.

9

Critique of Fertig's Leadership

Much of the criticism of Fertig as leader was generated long after the publication of a book about his wartime experience as a guerrilla leader. Written by John Keats and published in 1963, it was titled *They Fought Alone*. The form of the book was somewhat unusual in that it had the style of a novel and contained fictitious portions dealing with the Japanese side of the war in Mindanao (i.e., what they would have thought and their planned tactics against the guerrillas). The preface of the book states that "parts of the book are based on diaries and manuscripts of several Americans and Filipinos who served with the guerrilla movement on Mindanao." The book contains no footnotes, bibliography or index. Prior to writing the book, Keats had access to Fertig's draft manuscript and also traveled with him to the Philippines, presumably to revisit Fertig's wartime haunts and give him a better understanding of the environment in which the guerrilla movement on Mindanao took place. During this trip it is assumed that both had many conversations and notes were taken by Keats to better understand the history of the period and the dynamics that were at work in the guerrilla movement which Fertig commanded.

The first open and published criticism of Fertig and the book was not made until August 1989. Prior to this date the only criticism of Fertig was in the early 1960s, just before the publication of the book, when Fertig, at a reunion of the American Guerrillas of Mindanao (AGOM), the established veterans group of U.S. military who served in the Tenth Military District, circulated waivers on the use of material about them or information they may have provided to Fertig that he was using in the book. Many declined to sign the waiver. (Fertig died March 24, 1975, twelve years after the publication of Keats' book on the Mindanao guerrillas.)

The 1989 criticism erupted from a memorandum written by Clyde Childress that was included in a newsletter of AGOM. Following are portions of Childress's memorandum:

As I told you, I have been in correspondence with John Keats, the author of *They Fought Alone*. What motivated me to contact him is what I have considered an oversight these past years in the total lack of contact, as far as I know, of anyone in this organization with this author who wrote the definitive book about the AGOM experience. It is no secret among AGOMers that I hold Fertig in very low regard for cause. This I expressed in plain terms to Keats. In Keats's reply to me, among other things, he stated, "I should make clear that from the first to the last, the book is Fertig's story, not mine. I was just the writer." He also stated, "To my astonishment, Fertig had come out of the war with a diary and a footlocker full of daily situation reports for every day of the war."

Keats also said that his agent had put together a motion picture deal, that Hollywood wants to make a film (about the book) and are willing to put up a quarter of a million dollars for the rights to do so.

In research for the book, Keats said, "I checked at the Pentagon for the official history of that campaign, and found the military history was exactly what I had already found in the footlocker—for the very good reason that Fertig had supplied the Pentagon with all they knew about the Mindanao campaign." In my letter to Keats, I said, "Are you sure what he supplied to the Pentagon is the true unvarnished story of the campaign or was it doctored to fit Fertig's preferred version of his activities? The reason why I ask this—from my association with Fertig—I don't trust him for one minute to give a true history of the Tenth Military District."[1]

In the January 1990 issue of the AGOM newsletter John Keats had the following to say:

> I took particular notice of what Jordan Hamner, Bob Spielman and what you had to say with respect to Col. Fertig and your desire to set the record straight. Not until Col. Childress wrote to me last summer did I have any idea of your feelings. He and I had considerable correspondence about this.

Keats goes on:

> As I said in my letters to Col. Childress, I am sorry to learn so late about the bitter views of Fertig as a commanding officer. As far as I am concerned, and as my letters to Col. Childress show, I have nothing but admiration for all of you.[2]

The most intense criticism of Fertig and his book was to appear thirteen years later. It was contained in Clyde Childress's article "Wendell Fertig's Fictional 'Autobiography': A Critical Review of *They Fought Alone*." The article was published in the *Bulletin of the American Historical Collection* in 2003. Childress had served under Fertig as deputy of the 110th Division along with Lieutenant Colonel Ernest McClish, the commander. Both were subjects of critical comments by Fertig in his diary and draft book. Later, when Childress became the division commander of the 107th, the critical comments continued. One might ask why Childress waited so long to publish his criticism. Only in recent years had the MacArthur Memorial Library in Norfolk acquired Fertig's wartime papers, including his diary and draft manuscript, which had been retained by his family after his death in 1975. When Childress became aware of this acquisition he visited there to view firsthand the documents which had not been available to the public earlier. This review process must have been an especially galling experience for Childress. Moreover, when Childress and McClish were detached from Fertig's command and sent to the U.S. Army command in Leyte for re-assignment, they read for the first time their individual performance evaluations authored by Fertig. These evaluations contained statements about being disloyal, incompetent and their having done little for the effort on Mindanao. It is little wonder that Childress became caustic after reading these same comments in Fertig's diaries and papers.

Another development that may have expanded Childress's criticism of Fertig was Keats' comments about efforts to produce a movie on Fertig's wartime exploits as described in Keats' book. While this did not come about, it must have been disturbing to Childress, who must have felt that a film based on Fertig's recollections to Keats would have distorted even more the actual history of the Mindanao guerrillas.

Childress's article in the historical bulletin addresses some 42 "inaccuracies and false statements" that were contained in the Fertig book written by Keats. This chapter will not endeavor to discuss these, many of which were minor in content. Instead, it is believed more useful at the outset to review Childress's most forceful critique of Fertig's weakness to command that was contained in the article.

> Apparently Fertig's civilian and military background, life experiences and psychological makeup had not prepared him for such a large and important independent military command. He performed the technical aspects of his job well but failed miserably in his personal relationships and displayed serious character flaws that were inconsistent with the professionalism expected of a United States Army officer. He appeared to be unaware of, or at least ignored, the normal customs of the service involving the proper relationship between himself and the officers and personnel under him, to the extent of being disdainful of the abilities of people in the military, even including the theater commander, General Douglas MacArthur, and his staff, about whom he wasn't abashed at making his usual deprecatory remarks. He solicited all the perquisites he felt were his due to his position, while doing nothing for the welfare of his subordinates. His worst trait was an underhanded predilection for entering undeserved defamatory reports on his people without their knowledge in his dispatches to headquarters SWPA and their papers when they departed from Mindanao for repatriation. I was one of those people to whom he did this; I did not find out about it until much later.[3]

To better understand the dynamics at play here between Childress/McClish on one side and Fertig on the other, the following might provide an interesting historical perspective. The beginning point for this friction might be traced back to the time when Fertig issued his proclamation concerning his assumption of command of the guerrilla movement. In September 1942 McClish had begun organizing guerrilla units in the Bukidnon area of Mindanao. In November, upon learning of the proclamation that Fertig had issued on September 18, he traveled to Misamis City to meet with Fertig himself. At this meeting he also met Childress whom he had not seen since the Japanese invasion of Malabang. Both had served as battalion commanders in the 61st Infantry Regiment (PA). This must have been an awkward meeting—here are two experienced infantry officers meeting with a reserve Army Corps of Engineers lieutenant colonel who has promoted himself to general. This self-promotion could have exacerbated further the developing conflict between the two combat arms officers and Fertig.

At this meeting it was agreed that Fertig would command the guerrillas on Mindanao (later to be designated as the Tenth Military District). McClish was promoted to lieutenant colonel, commanding the 110th Division which would encompass Misamis Oriental, Agusan, Surigao and Davao provinces; Childress would be his chief of staff. Fertig accomplished two things by these appointments. First, he assigned two experienced officers to consolidate the guerrilla movement in northern Mindanao, thereby expanding his overall area of command. Second, he removed from the geographic area of his headquarters the officers who could have caused problems by questions emerging about his competency to command military units. This only postponed a growing feud between Fertig and the two officers. This problem became greater when Fertig was forced to move his headquarters from Misamis Occidental province to the Agusan River valley—the very backyard of McClish and Childress.

There are numerous comments in Fertig's diary and draft narrative regarding what he considered to be sub-standard performance by McClish and Childress. In a diary entry for November 28, 1942, Fertig states:

> McClish has done some organizing but has been taken in by some crooks from Bohol. He apparently has already moved against the wrong elements in Talisayan and Camuigin Island, but does act impulsively and does not know the Filipinos as he should.[4]

It should be noted that McClish and Childress had just met with Fertig and they were being designated as commander and deputy, respectively, of the 110th Division. Just a few days later (November 30) Fertig makes an interesting notation in his diary to the effect that he wrote a memo of instruction for Colonel McClish. He also remarks that Childress is the stronger of the two.[5]

A diary entry for December 7 states the following:

> Some rather nasty reports about McClish which I hope are not true for he has to do this job with Filipino troops. Filipino women appear to conquer American men more readily than Japanese.

Through the years there had been talk that McClish had an ongoing relationship with a Filipina in the Agusan area. I have seen nothing written in the research I have consulted to substantiate the rumor that is referred to in Fertig's diary entry.[6]

In a diary entry on December 20 Fertig states:

> Dictated all the letters, of criticism mainly to Col. McClish. Believe he means well but at times his methods are those of a bull in a china shop.[7]

A later diary entry on February 9 mentions the following:

> McClish has a mutiny and everything else on his hands in the 110th. Collado and several officers are under arrest. Charges will be preferred against them by him. He is apparently hopeless.[8]

Relative to this incident, the following entry is made by Fertig on February 11:

> Seems McClish has moved his headquarters over near Gingoog and that Collado and others were placed under arrest and generally a messy situation.[9]

Later in March a major issue arises when the 110th Division undertook an operation against the Japanese that resulted in a number of them being trapped in a schoolhouse. Out of this operational initiative emerges a request from the 110th Division for more ammunition. With stocks low, Fertig is furious with the request and rejects it outright. In Fertig's mind this is a wasteful and non-productive initiative, causing the attacking guerrilla units to run out of ammunition and forcing them to withdraw.[10]

During the reception of a SPYRON supply mission involving the USS *Narwhal* in November 1943, Fertig notes in his draft manuscript that he was somewhat irked at McClish's performance. He makes it quite clear that he does not like McClish's last-minute preparations where the margin of error increases substantially. Fertig is rightly concerned given that a large U.S. Navy submarine is landing at a pier under the noses of the Japanese. Besides the angst over the security of the submarine, Fertig has concerns for the safety of the 32 American civilians awaiting evacuation by the *Narwhal*. In Fertig's eyes, McClish is oblivious to the danger of errors that could cascade into failure for this sensitive operation. One could only imagine the furor that was raised in Fertig's mind over McClish's attitude, particularly when President Roosevelt had to intervene to make the USS *Narwhal* available for the SPYRON program. Incidents such as these may have been noted in the final evaluation

Fertig made on McClish prior to his detachment from the Tenth Military District.[11]

Further to Fertig's concerns/doubts about McClish's leadership, there are comments about a message received from Chick Parsons in both his draft manuscript and diary. In this message Parsons states that he stopped McClish from making an attack on Surigao. Regarding the future, Fertig responds that McClish will remain since he must clean up the problems in his own area. Fertig notes that McClish's division had to absorb a great number of soldiers and sailors that did not surrender to the Japanese. They were untrained and aggressive, tending to take chances. Most were advanced in rank from NCO to officer status with approval of GHQ SWPA.[12]

At the end of 1943 Fertig summarized his accomplishments and failures of the year. Operations in the Davao area were one of his concerns. He described them as follows:

> I had hoped to use the forces of Colonel McClish as a basis from which to develop the necessary auxiliary units that would support such an operation. However I had never found McClish's own organization sufficiently substantial to allow separation of the cells necessary to form a new unit. I continued to wonder just what the difficulty was in this area yet I was never able to locate it exactly. This was to plague me for the many months to come and still in retrospect I do not know exactly what the difficulty was. Perhaps I should have been more brutal and sent senior officers out by submarine in early 1944 [sic] and attempted to reorganize the area from the ground up. This I did not do and as a result continued to operate inefficiently with an organization in which I had little faith and doubted its ability to carry out the mission which fell naturally to it by virtue of its location.[13]
>
> (I believe Fertig made a typographical error in the date of 1944. This entry was made in his summary of the year's events at the end of 1943.)

The major concern that Fertig had was that Japanese troops from the Davao area would move northward into the headwaters of the Agusan River valley. At the same time Japanese units from the Butuan area would move southward up the river (which flows northward toward Butuan). The unpleasant result would be guerrilla units, including Fertig's headquarters, being trapped between the two Japanese forces. In May 1944 Fertig did form the 107th Division to meet the threat from Davao, appointing Clyde Childress as its first division commander. This resulted in Childress being promoted to Lieutenant Colonel.

During the April 1944 time frame the Japanese troops were putting increased pressure on guerrilla units along the Agusan River. In this regard, Fertig made the following comments on the shortcomings of McClish's command:

During a period of envelopment in April 1944 Japanese patrols penetrated to Tungao from Rizal. They burned the new command post at Tungao and my premonitions are proven. Had McClish's division devoted more time to careful choice of site and preparation of evacuation instead of constructing nice headquarters buildings along the river they would have been in a much better position to face the months now upon us.[14]

The basis of this criticism probably comes from Fertig's Army Corps of Engineers background and his experiences in planning defensive positions in Bataan in early 1942.

In August 1944 Fertig commented on Clyde Childress's command performance of the 107th Division:

The 107th was badly organized and Colonel Childress was so jumpy that it was doubtful whether he or any of his troops would interpose any serious resistance should the Japanese drive northward from Davao. With that we would have been surrounded and eventually capture would have been a certainty.[15]

As mentioned previously, Fertig had a nightmarish fear of the Japanese advancing northward from Davao and enveloping guerrilla positions along the upper reaches of the Agusan River. Again, critical communications facilities of FRS and Fertig's headquarters were often located in the same area.

After the American invasion of Leyte Fertig relates that some of his officers have had an epidemic of poor judgment. He then cites the case of McClish:

Colonel McClish suddenly decided to re-establish civil government in the province of Agusan. Disregarding those appointees who had served for months, he re-established the provincial government, although Butuan was still occupied. At the same time he recalled to active duty two or three Philippine Army officers who had contributed nothing during the long fight and now were placed in positions of command over officers who had served loyally throughout the troubled period. Again it was necessary to order all of these instructions be rescinded and be returned to the status quo. As may be expected, this was difficult and pointed up the fact that it would be absolutely necessary to return my senior officers to Army control as early as possible.[16]

Several things may have gone through Fertig's mind at this juncture. It should be noted that after the liberation of Leyte, the Philippine government-in-exile had also returned. Earlier he had been cautioned by Chick Parsons about becoming too involved in civil government. Fertig probably felt it unwise to stir up the civil government issue at this point. When he talks about returning senior officers to Army control, he is, in effect, thinking of detaching McClish and sending him to Leyte for reassignment in the U.S. Army.

As U.S. forces consolidated its control of Leyte, some of Fertig's American officers could see the writing on the wall as far as their future was concerned. Almost 200 U.S. military were in key positions in the Tenth Military

District and most were keen to return to their parent services. When Childress visited Fertig following the Leyte campaign he was most interested in how things had progressed on that island. Within this conversation he brought up the possibility of returning to the U.S. for reassignment. It was Fertig's response that American personnel would be released as early as possible as long as it did affect operational capabilities.[17] Childress responded that he would continue to serve until he could be released. Fertig noted that it was the current talk in the officers' mess as to when they would be released. Then he remarked that some had come to him and said that they would stay until he himself had been released. Fertig further notes that it gratified him that his subordinates would stay until he himself had been released.[18] The way Fertig portrays these different attitudes of leaving the command suggests some bias was generated, particularly regarding Childress and his loyalty to Fertig. Probably at this point Fertig had made the decision to release both Childress and McClish at the earliest possible time. In Fertig's mind it appeared that both officers were, as it were, "joined at the hip" and had not helped Fertig in dealing with the command problems with which the Tenth Military District was faced.

At one point Major Larry Evans approached Fertig about visiting the 110th Division. Fertig's response was that Evans' visit "would help McClish see the whole picture instead of continuing to view his position as an isolated portion of 'blood and thunder adventure.'"[19]

After Evans returned from his visit to the 110th he reported to Fertig that "things were pretty well fouled up." He further reported that McClish had retained several officers on duty although they did not report for duty when needed. Fertig expands on this. "When he ordered a particularly worthless major to duty I burned him with the sharpest cable that I have ever sent."[20]

Fertig finally resolves to make a decision on the reassignment of Childress and McClish. While his decision was long in coming, he felt he had no other choice. Following are Fertig's comments on the issue:

> Lt. Colonel Childress apparently is determined to go out and I felt that McClish should go with him. The only officer available for that command is Lt. Colonel Paul Marshall.[21]

Fertig comments further on the replacement of Childress and McClish:

> My decision to replace Lt. Colonel Childress with Colonel Claro Laureta as commanding officer of the 107th Division pointed the way to the final solution of the nagging problem of command of the 110th Division. I had requested Colonel McClish to report to my headquarters for a conference and while he was there I told him he should return to military control. He agreed that Colonel Marshall was the only officer in his command capable of taking over the division. It was arranged for Marshall to take command on January 10, 1945. In this manner I expect to solve

many of the problems that had plagued eastern Mindanao for the past eighteen months. Later I regretted that I did not make the changes earlier but had to recognize the fact that Colonel Marshall was not ready to take command until he had been seasoned by successively commanding a battalion, regiment and finally a division. I had confidence in his ability to carry on now and was pleased that both Childress and McClish wanted to leave as soon as possible.[22]

Commander Parsons, during his visit with Fertig in January 1945, related that Clyde Childress was still in Leyte and that he was being debriefed by Colonel Steve Mellnik on conditions in Mindanao. This revelation disturbed Fertig greatly, to the degree that in his draft manuscript he had to vent his anger on this:

I felt this was unnecessary for Childress had been out of touch with my headquarters and the actual status of operations (except in his limited area) for so long, that he could offer little of interest. I did not feel he was completely loyal to me and I had never been impressed by Colonel Mellnik—the fact that the two were together in G-2 did not make me view the future with complacency. In addition Commander Fred Worcester (Fertig's intelligence officer in the early years of the guerrilla movement) was in Tacloban and certainly he had never made any effort to conceal his low opinion of my command ability. To further complicate the situation Chick told me that Colonel Morgan was at Tacloban assigned with the civil government section while Colonel Andrews was spending a considerable portion of his time with that same group. [Andrews, a close Philippine Air Force colleague of Major Villamor, had replaced him on Negros as chief of the AIB intelligence collection effort on that island. During the war he had voiced anti–American sentiments.] There was no question but that both hated my guts and anything they could do to foul up me or my operations would be done. It seems that my enemies are gathering in Leyte and I must get up there soon or they will be in ascendancy.[23]

It is somewhat surprising that Fertig would put pen to paper on this perceived threat to his professional reputation. The issue of making himself a general during the early days of the movement had been noted by senior officers at GHQ SWPA, but his command reputation had moved on and he was held in high respect by his seniors at GHQ SWPA. When Fertig visited with the military seniors in Tacloban in March 1945 there appeared to be no indications noted by Fertig that his military reputation had been affected by the detractors he noted in the foregoing paragraph.

Certainly the bad relationship that existed between Fertig on one hand and McClish/Childress on the other was not a good outcome or manifestation of leadership on Fertig's part. In reading Fertig's diaries one gets the impression that Fertig's disposition toward dealing with personnel problems was one of ignoring them with the hope that they might go away. By doing so, Fertig tarnished his own reputation as a leader. Moreover, he later gave evaluations that had a negative effect on the careers of two subordinate officers.

Some who knew Fertig described him as cool and somewhat aloof. However, in both his diary and draft manuscript he is objective in describing his disagreements with subordinates. His first intelligence officer, Navy commander Frederick Worcester, had come to Fertig's staff from central Bukidnon. He was a trained intelligence officer and had grown up in the Philippines. Moreover, he was widely known and respected and was particularly useful in seeking cooperation of Filipinos of all classes. Early in 1943 Fertig and Worcester had two differing views on how a guerrilla war should be fought. Worcester thought the development of sizeable units, with good defensive positions, was the solution. Fertig's view was just the opposite—working in small bands that could merge back into the population. Worcester also thought that the defense of Fertig's headquarters had been neglected, which Fertig admitted after the Japanese attacks in June and July 1943. With these continuing disagreements Worcester finally tendered his resignation. Fertig noted in his draft manuscript that it was with much regret that he accepted Worcester's resignation.

One has to ask why the chemistry in this situation was different than in the McClish/Childress problem. The answer may be in the proximity of the individuals involved. McClish and Childress did not see Fertig on a daily basis. Some of what Fertig heard about McClish and Childress was gossip and rumor. The reverse was probably true regarding impressions of Fertig by members of his staff. In the case of Worcester, he and Fertig discussed command issues on a daily basis. Both knew where each other stood and Fertig had respect for Worcester.

One of Fertig's closest colleagues during the war was Charles Hedges. In the early days of the war they were constantly together. Later, when the decision had to be made regarding joining Morgan's group, there were discussions between the two on the issues involved. Hedges was always frank with Fertig and cool to the idea of teaming up with Morgan and Fertig becoming the commander of his guerrilla group. He was also strongly against Fertig giving himself the rank of general. Despite these differences they appeared to have a strong relationship that could weather their contrary views of a problem or issue. When Fertig made the decision on splitting up the command, he preferred that Hedges be the deputy and commander of "A" Corps vice Bowler. However, he decided that Hedges was more valuable to the movement in a command position in Lanao, particularly in dealing with the Moros.

In both his diary and draft manuscript, Fertig notes that he has few people in which he can confide. In a letter to his wife in 1943 (not mailed until 1945) he makes the following comment:

> I am so tired, for more than a year I have borne burdens which continue to increase in complexity and during this entire time I have had no one with whom I could discuss the seriousness of my problems or share my burdens.[24]

By this time Hedges was in Lanao dealing with the Moro problem and Worchester had left his command.

With the arrival of LCDR Montgomery Wheeler on a SPYRON submarine in March 1944, Fertig seemed to have found an officer whom he could confide in and trust. Wheeler was sent by the Navy to establish a naval component within FRS because of the growing intelligence on surface ship sightings that the Tenth Military District was sending the submarine command in Fremantle. However, by the end of the year Fertig was so impressed with Wheeler that he designated him chief of staff. Moreover, as Wheeler assumed the chief of staff duties, the two men spent more time together, both on official duties and off-duty pursuits such as playing cards. They also shared the same quarters. This ability to relax with someone who was sharing weighty responsibilities must have been helpful to Fertig's mental outlook.

Arriving with Wheeler on the SPYRON mission was Second Lieutenant Saturnino Silva, a representative from AIB who was tasked to look after their intelligence collection interests. He was accompanied by four Filipino radio specialists. They would be assigned to (the) FRS. However, the assignment of Wheeler and Silva came with some restrictions and created an issue between Fertig and GHQ SWPA. Fertig balked at this; his position was that as the commander he would decide how these personnel would be used. After message exchanges the issue was resolved. As noted in the foregoing paragraph, eventually Wheeler would become Fertig's chief of staff. Silva joined Fertig's staff as the Plans and Training Officer. After serving in a number of staff and training positions, as well as being promoted to Major, Silva in April 1945 was given command of the 130th Infantry Regiment under the 107th Division. The 130th would later be noted for its combat against the Japanese at Ising and the final liberation of the Davao area.[25]

In early June 1945 Major Harold Rosenquist arrived on the USS *Narwhal* from GHQ SWPA with secret orders and an unusual mission. Australia had intelligence that the Japanese were planning to move all American POWs from the Davao Penal Colony (DAPECOL) to Formosa. However, before this information had been received, actual planning had commenced on an operation to remove all POWs from Japanese control in Davao. This planning had been generated by the debriefing of Major Mellnik by Rosenquist at the Pentagon. Mellnik was one of the 10 American POWs that had escaped from DAPECOL in April 1943. Later, both Mellnik and Rosenquist were assigned to GHQ SWPA where planning had continued for an operation to rescue the POWs. Rosenquist's travel to Mindanao had been approved at the highest level at GHQ SWPA. His purpose was to collect additional information on the Davao

POW camp and work with Fertig on an operational plan to rescue the POWs using guerrilla units before they could be moved by the Japanese. (By the time Rosenquist had arrived in Fertig's command the POWs had already been removed from DAPECOL.) In his first meeting with Rosenquist Fertig expressed his doubts about such an operation. His first question to Rosenquist was whether GHQ SWPA was prepared to send in a hospital ship to care for the hundreds of weak and sick POWs that would be removed. More to the point, the guerrillas would not have the capability to deal with the numbers that might be rescued. These important these issues shocked Rosenquist. Unlike Fertig, he had not experienced first-hand the condition of the POWs that had escaped from DAPECOL in April 1943. Moreover, Fertig was still reeling from a March 1944 POW escape attempt from DAPECOL where only six POWs out of eleven were successful in reaching the safety of Fertig's guerrillas. Regarding the other five, one had been killed and four were recaptured and faced probable execution. For Rosenquist, Fertig's comments and questions meant non-support for the proposal. However, Fertig said he would allow Rosenquist to mount a mission for intelligence collection on the POW camp. Back at GHQ SWPA Mellnik anxiously awaits the results of Rosenquist's mission. He quotes the message that reports Rosenquist's findings.

> "Walked around the Penal Colony. Found no, repeat no, POWs. Happy convicts say POW's evacuated ten days ago, probably to Manila. Recommend we scrub rescue project and work on strengthening the guerrillas."[26]

Despite this disappointing outcome Fertig nonetheless offered Rosenquist the position of G-2 on his staff.

Maurice Shoss, a POW who survived the sinking of the Japanese ship *Shinyo Maru* off Sindangan Point, describes the Japanese rationale for removing all POWs from DAPECOL.

> The Japs seemed afraid of an American landing on Mindanao so they closed the colony in mid–May. They sent the very sick POWs to Manila and put the balance, about eight hundred, to work around Davao City; I was in the second group. When U.S. planes appeared over Davao in July the Japs got jittery. Without warning they put us aboard a tramp steamer and let us bake in the Davao Gulf while they formed a convoy.[27]

According to Duane Heisinger's account of the POWs in DAPECOL and its closing, initially 650 POWs left the colony for airfield construction in the Lasang area and another 100 were detailed to the Davao City port. The remaining 1,250 POWs were trucked to Lasang Lumber Dock and departed for Manila on the *Yashu Maru* on June 12.[28] Later, in August the remaining

750 POWs working at Lasang and the Davao Port area were loaded on the *Tateishi Maru* departing Davao on August 20.

In early September 1944 Fertig's staff received a message from the Davao coast watcher station that 750 POWs had been put aboard two small Japanese freighters that were headed southward toward Zamboanga. This information was passed to the Navy. A hands-off policy alert was issued to U.S. submarines operating between Davao and Zamboanga. Because so many Japanese ships had been torpedoed in this area, ships were only traveling at night. When the small freighters carrying the POWs arrived in Zamboanga it was reported by the coast watcher station there. During the night the POWs were transferred to the *Shinyo Maru,* but because of darkness, heavy rains and the distance from the coast watcher station to the docks, the transfer of POWs was not observed and reported. On September 4 or 5 the *Shinyo Maru* departed Zamboanga. This was reported by the coast watcher station but, with no information that the POWs were aboard, the hands-off policy was not in effect for this ship. This ship and others in the convoy were subject to a torpedo attack by the USS *Paddle* (SS 263) on September 7 at Sindangan Point, off the west coast of Zamboanga province. The *Shinyo Maru* sank from this attack and only 83 POWs survived. During the period of the sinking the Zamboanga coast watcher station reported that sources in the port had observed the movement of the POWs from the freighters to the *Shinyo Maru*; unfortunately, this information was not received and disseminated in time to avoid the torpedoing by a U.S. submarine. One of the POW survivors later died of pneumonia, another opted to join Fertig's guerrillas.

After seeing the incoming reports about the sinking of the *Shinyo Maru* with the POWs aboard, Fertig asked Wheeler to accompany him on a walk. Entering a dense portion of jungle near the headquarters building, they both sat down on a fallen tree. According to Keats' book, at this point Wheeler observed Fertig's ashen and horror-stricken face. Fertig then spoke, accusing himself of not having done more with the plan, initially proposed by Rosenquist, to rescue the POWs. He and Hedges had seen many of these same POWs in the Japanese forced march along the Iligan road on July 4, 1942. Fertig openly wept over this tragic incident.[29]

While Fertig describes the sinking in his draft manuscript, the conversation with Wheeler on his grief about the incident is not mentioned. Did Keats make up Fertig's grief with respect to the incident, or was this expressed to Keats by Fertig in their many conversations about the book? After reading Fertig's diary and draft manuscript, it is quite possible to conclude that it had happened; however, Fertig may have felt that his image might have been negatively affected if it had been included in the manuscript.

It is interesting to note the contrast between the contentious McClish/ Childress issue and the positive Wheeler and Rosenquist relationships with Fertig. Understandably, Fertig had a growing confidence in these two officers regarding their ability to bring credit to his command after the Leyte invasion.

10

Magnitude of Responsibilities

Some critics of Fertig indicated that while he performed the technical aspects of his responsibilities well, he was lacking in his human and personal relationships. But if one were to prioritize the tasks at hand as a commander, where would the human element fall in the array of actions to be taken in order to accomplish a mission, particularly when building a guerrilla organization? While important, it would probably be relegated to a middle position on the priority list. Some commanders have a capability to do both and still accomplish the mission at hand. Others will be complete technicians and also achieve success but leave wrecked relationships that could threaten the future of that commander and the involved subordinates. A good example of such leadership in the fist instance would be General Eisenhower. In the second instance, it would be General Patton.

Once contact was made with MacArthur's headquarters in Australia, Fertig was charged by MacArthur to command the Tenth Military District (islands of Mindanao and Sulu), as well as establish an intelligence net covering the Ninth Military District (islands of Samar and Leyte). When MacArthur gave this order Fertig was already well on his way to building a military organization on a guerrilla movement that had the Filipino people as its base. He had, with the assistance of Major Luis Morgan, moved forward to establish a firm foundation for the Tenth Military District. Even so, many disparate groups had to be brought into the organization throughout the island of Mindanao—from the Sulu region in the south to the Agusan/Surigao region in the north. Regarding the latter region, in November 1942 Fertig appointed two experienced American battalion commanders, McClish and Childress, to consolidate the area of the 110th Division—Agusan, Surigao, parts of Misamis Oriental and Davao. Other commanders were appointed as divisions were designated. Fertig had an excellent group from which to appoint his commanders. Most had World War I experience as military officers and had become successful businessmen in the Philippines. One such choice for commander of the 106th Division, which had a large Moro population, was Frank McGee. He had lived and worked in the Cotabato area and was respected by the Moros in the province. Fertig realized early on that keeping the Moros in the guerrilla movement required an American commander and one that could capture the allegiance of the Moros. When asked by Fertig, talented Americans like McGee willingly accepted the responsibility of helping him build an effective guerrilla organization. But some had difficulty in doing so. Sam Wilson, a successful Manila businessman and millionaire, was a reluctant warrior because his family was interned at Santo Tomas. However, he finally agreed to assist Fertig with fiscal matters—printing money, ensuring that funding available to the Tenth Military District was within the approved guidelines mandated by the Philippine government-in-exile, and providing an accounting for all funds expended. Bringing these talented personnel into the organization was not a technical matter as his critics assert. It required vision and human persuasion.

There were many command problems and responsibilities facing Fertig which his critics were not privy to nor could appreciate. Moreover, they did not have access to the message traffic between Fertig's command and MacArthur's headquarters on these matters. That aside, the magnitude of the problems faced by Fertig required more than the skills of a technician.

Other problems and weighty responsibilities which confronted Fertig were relations with other military districts, particularly with Colonel Peralta's Sixth Military District on Panay. Fertig was accused by some of maneuvering to extend his command to other islands. On the other hand, in some cases guerrilla commanders from other islands were coming to Fertig and asking to be placed under his command. Policy guidance from Australia and Fertig's political instincts did temper his involvement with movements on the other islands. However, he did provide Colonel Ruperto Kangleon's Ninth Military District on Leyte with advice and materiel assistance. This was done through Kangleon's intelligence officer, Ensign Iliff David Richardson, a former PT boat officer who did not surrender to the Japanese. Coming from Leyte, Richardson spent time at Fertig's headquarters in Misamis City. In discussions with Fertig, Richardson was given the benefit of Fertig's own experiences in developing a guerrilla movement. Richardson was very complimentary of Fertig in this regard. He was impressed with Fertig's command and operations— he classified him as a real businessman that ran the guerrilla movement as a corporation. Returning to Leyte, Richardson carried with him a transmitter for communications that had been provided by Fertig.[1]

The planning, coordination and execution of submarine evacuation operations of American civilians was a sensitive as well as heartbreaking experience for Fertig. Moreover, the safety of civilians and the security of the submarine involved was a major responsibility. To say the very least, this was more than just a technical matter—it was a major command responsibility. Within this context, ensuring the security of the submarines themselves, bringing in supplies and evacuating personnel, had to be conducted with most exacting care. Loss of a submarine to Japanese actions could have jeopardized the SPYRON program.

While briefly mentioned in the early portions of this chapter, it is worth describing the command attention that Fertig had to devote to the process of handling of American civilians (including women and children) being evacuated by the SPYRON missions. Getting them safely to the meeting site for debarkation required detailed planning and execution. Prior to the November 1943 evacuation, Fertig met with some of the civilian evacuees from the Mindanao Mother Lode mine and made the following comments to them:

> I wish I could stay longer with you all—it's really been wonderful to be with such a large group of friends of former days, but I have a lot to get done before I can get you out of here. If your means of escape really does rendezvous with us, I have to get a crew organized that can move what comes in to places where it's needed. I hope you'll interpret what I am saying, as I don't want to speak directly. I'm sure you'll understand that. It's been a privilege to be with you, and good luck until we meet again.[2]

Fertig left the following letter with them to answer some of the questions:

November 9, 1943

To All Civilian Repatriates:

> You are being repatriated as a result of some very hard work on the part of personnel of the armed services of the United Sates. It is requested that you show your appreciation for these efforts by refraining from discussing any military or guerrilla activities in the Philippine Islands, especially those which have taken place since the surrender of our forces on May 10, 1942.

> The safety of our troops in the Tenth Military District may depend upon our ability to keep our activities out of the newspapers and off of the radio until such time as the War Department desires to release this information.

> You will find that every effort has been made to make you as comfortable as possible under the circumstances, and that General MacArthur, who is responsible for the repatriation of civilians, has completed the necessary arrangements for your trip to your final destination.

> With your kindest good wishes and the hope that your stay in the Tenth District has left at least a few good memories, I am,

Sincerely yours,

Wendell Fertig
Colonel, AUS, Commanding[3]

After arriving in Darwin in northern Australia, the American civilian repatriates were met by Colonel Allison Ind, Allied Intelligence Bureau, GHQ SWPA and immediately put aboard a C-47 and flown to Brisbane. GHQ SWPA did not want the repatriates identified with submarine activity operating out of Darwin. In Brisbane they were placed in the hands of the American Red Cross for medical treatment and processing for eventual travel to the United States. Since travel processing would take some time, the repatriates were housed in a Red Cross hostel some 70 miles from Brisbane. Here they were in a secure environment, away from the press and others that might be curious as to where they came from and how they traveled to Australia. These efforts protected both the SPYRON operation and the fact that MacArthur's command in Australia was secretly supporting guerrilla operations in the southern Philippines.[4]

One aspect of the U.S. military's advance through other parts of the Pacific was that it did not have a local guerrilla force with which to partner. However, once the invasion of the Philippines was near at hand the situation was quite different. Both on Luzon and on the islands in the southern Philippines, large and organized guerrilla forces had emerged from the ashes of defeat in 1942. Even so, there is an underlying question as to whether MacArthur's headquarters, GHQ SWPA, and its subordinated commands understood or were aware of the capabilities of the Philippine guerrilla units. Perhaps the general view of U.S. military planners was that guerrilla units would not be assigned specific supporting roles; their participation in the invasion would be limited to providing tactical intelligence on the Japanese dispositions. Little thought was given to assigning the guerrillas specific missions alongside the regular forces.

On Mindanao there were a number of missteps that would give credence to this thesis. Despite the intelligence provided by Fertig's command to GHQ SWPA, military planners at the corps and division levels formulated invasion plans, including bombardment from the air and sea, without including guerrilla intelligence or their offensive capabilities. Once American operations had commenced on Mindanao, Fertig had a continuing responsibility to point out to the task force commander the realities of the objective areas they were about to invade. An example of this was the Eighth Army's invasion of Malabang, Lanao. Fertig's forces virtually held this terrain and U.S. aircraft were able to operate from an airfield in the area. Only after Fertig sent a message to the Eighth Army and X Corps advising that they could land unopposed at Malabang did they modify their invasion plans. A similar situation developed during the campaign in Zamboanga. Guerrilla forces had complete control of the Dipolog airfield in northern Zamboanga. After being advised by the guerrillas, elements of the 24th Division were flown into the airfield via C-47 aircraft. This was followed by Marine Corps attack aircraft being deployed to the airfield to support the invasion of Zamboanga.

Despite GHQ SWPA's large staff, there were probably only a few compartmented components such as the Allied Intelligence Bureau and its subordinate Philippine Regional Section (PRS) that were aware of the specific capabilities of Fertig's Tenth Military District. Because of the "close hold" status of the SPYRON program and the focus on intelligence from guerrilla units and the coast watcher system, specific information on the guerrilla force structure and its operational capabilities did not go beyond PRS. This information in effect did not go to the GHQ planners or others drawing up specific invasion plans. The result was a void of information about the guerrillas that should have been disseminated to corps and division staffs for inclusion in their detailed planning. It was only on the spur of the moment that the invasion force could take advantage of the on-the-ground capabilities of the guerrilla units. Even so, the transition from a guerrilla force to that of a conventional force in warfare is most difficult. T. H. Lawrence, "Lawrence of Arabia," experienced this in the British campaign to capture Damascus in World War I. Lawrence was ordered by General Edmund Allenby to use his Arab guerrillas in 1918 against Turkish troops. In this case the Arabs would have to fight the Turks, take ground and hold it. This was a fundamental change in the tactics that had been previously used by Lawrence's Arab guerrillas.[5]

A similar transition for guerrilla troops in the Philippines would occur, particularly on Mindanao. As American forces became firmly established ashore, Fertig's guerrilla units were deployed in a conventional mode to support and assist these forces. This transition is discussed in detail in Chapter 11.

During August 1943 Fertig's relationship with his deputy, Lt. Col. Morgan, reached a very low point. This became the most frustrating and divisive command problem with Fertig had to deal. While he had heard rumors of Morgan's unhappiness with the way the movement was being run, his displeasure came to a head after the Japanese major offensive in Misamis Occidental province during July of 1943. After this had abated, Fertig received background information to the effect that Morgan was going to submit his resignation as chief of staff.[6] During the June–July Japanese attacks on Misamis Occidental province Morgan assumed Fertig was leaving and going to Australia with Smith and Parsons. With Fertig's appointment of Bowler to division commander in Bukidnon he jumped to the conclusion that if Fertig left for Australia Bowler would be placed in charge and he, Morgan, would be ignored. This, plus his heavy drinking bouts, prompted him to consider submitting his resignation. Fertig summarized his relationship with Morgan as follows:

> Looking back on the situation, I assure myself as well as other people that I dealt fairly and honestly throughout and that had he stayed with me there is no question he would have become one of the great heroes of the Philippine guerrilla movement. Very probably ending up in the National Assembly as many of his contemporaries have done. However, he was a warped, egocentric who could not consider that anyone could deal frankly and honestly with one whom he might consider an antagonist.[7]

It was Fertig's view that Morgan could not resign from the chief of staff position. Later Fertig received a proclamation purportedly signed by Morgan that he had assumed command of Mindanao but left Fertig in charge of the Tenth Military District. In his new capacity Morgan requested that Fertig meet with him on August 10 at Kolambugan. Fertig replied that any conference would be held on his order. A delegation of commanders requested permission to go to the conference that Morgan had called. Their rationale was that perhaps they could point out to Morgan the error of his ways; they attended.

Because various commanders had put pressure on Morgan (some of them were Moro), Morgan sent a letter to Fertig. His major point was that he had not been given the same treatment as others—he had not been given the honors due him and other Americans had been given command over him. Following is the entirety of the letter sent by Morgan to Fertig:

IN THE FIELD

10 August '43

(PERSONAL)

Lieut-Col. W.W. FERTIG:

> I and my people are very much disappointed in what has transpired in our organization. When I organized the forces in September last year I have only the welfare of the United States and the Philippines at heart. I did not have the least intention of making myself a big shot. Being part American and loyal to America, I did not like to put the Americans down. So against the protest of my fellow officers I requested you, a U.S. Army officer, to head our organization and placed myself as your chief of staff. By this arrangement, I thought I could bring about the cooperation of the Americans and Filipinos in this fight against our common enemy.
>
> Everything went well at first. I went on my trip to organize and coordinate all guerrilla forces under our headquarters. I even sent my instructions to Col. Hugh A. Straughn in Luzon, thus carrying your name in practically all parts of the Philippines. I even made plans to make you the Major General of our guerrilla forces upon the request of the various guerrilla leaders and the people. I defended you against harsh criticism from people who did not like you. I explained to Major Meider, AC. (who is antagonistic to you) and to Major Villamor why you are heading our forces.
>
> But during my long absence you practiced nepotism and sectionalism openly. You and your fellow Americans have the best arms, best accommodation, best clothes,

best shoes and best positions. Some of your American officers behave arrogantly toward Filipino officers and men. Tires and other supplies were taken from my house to accommodate your American Friends. When you received your appointment as district commander for the Tenth Military District you sidetracked me by appointing Lt-Col. Robert V. Bowler as your second in command. (see SO#116). When some Tommy guns arrived from Australia I was entirely neglected, though an American civilian, a non-combatant, was given one.

I realized that my position as chief of staff is treated with contempt. I made recommendations for commissions which in many cases were not approved but recommendations made by your American friends are given more weight. You gave me a rotten car while American officers inferior in rank than I, have nicer and better cars. I did not have my share of clothing and shoes though American enlisted men have their shares.

There is one honorable way out. Resign as chief of staff.

I blame, not you, but your advisers for most of these faults. Your Filipino advisers are injecting politics in the Army while your American advisers are utterly ignorant of local conditions and have done you more harm than good.

I am expecting you here in Kolambugan for a conference as per letter dated 4 August '43.

(SGD.) L. P. MORGAN
Lt-Col. Inf. USFIP[8]

Making matters worse, Morgan had assembled some provincial officials to announce his grievances, which were largely anti–American and petty personal insults.

Fertig invited Morgan to meet with him on August 11. Tait and two other officers accompanied him to this meeting. Fertig pointed out that Bowler, who had been appointed deputy commander, was a Lieutenant Colonel and senior to Morgan; therefore, he was most eligible to succeed him. Morgan was informed by Fertig that the substance of their conference would be made available to field commanders. The door was left open to Morgan on whether he would continue as chief of staff. Later Morgan issued an order on his own notifying all officers in Misamis Occidental to follow his orders "until friction concerning me is settled."

Though it is not known what effect it had on Morgan, on August 18, 1943, Fertig was awarded the Distinguished Service Cross by MacArthur's headquarters. Shortly after this event Fertig learned that Morgan's colleagues, including Tait, were withdrawing their support from Morgan.

Not hearing from Morgan, Fertig appointed Hedges to the office of chief of staff. Eventually a shocked Morgan came to see Fertig after he learned of Hedges' appointment. Fertig informed Morgan that since he had not communicated his decision after their August 11 meeting, he had no recourse but to appoint Hedges to the chief of staff position. Fertig then advised Morgan that he was glad that he desired to remain with the organization. He then indicated that he had found a new position for Morgan. GHQ SWPA, he related, had asked for a senior and experienced officer from this command to join their headquarters in Australia. Fertig then stated he had nominated Morgan for the position and that he would be on the next submarine to Australia.

As the guerrilla movement grew there were separatist tendencies on the part of several other guerrilla leaders. Apart from the Morgan problem, the revolt of Major Angeles Limena, commander of the 109th Regiment, was the most serious. This revolt lasted some four months but was finally brought under control by Bowler. This was fortunate because Limena would be key to ending the Morgan revolt in August 1943. For this he was given back his command. As more and more logistical support flowed into Mindanao from Australia, separatist tendencies began to wane. Commanders began to realize insubordination would not be tolerated; otherwise, they would not be sharing in the ammunition and weapons that were coming in via the SPYRON missions.

The escape of ten American POWs from the Davao Penal Colony (DAPECOL) and their eventual arrival at Fertig's headquarters would prove to be a delicate handling problem for Fertig. The ten Americans included the following service personnel:

> LCDR Melvin McCoy, U.S. Navy (senior officer in the group)
> Major Stephen Mellnik, U.S. Army
> Major William Dyess, U.S. Army Air Corps
> Captain Austin Shofner, U.S. Marine Corps
> Captain Samuel Grashio, U.S. Army Air Corps
> First Lieutenant Jack Hawkins, U.S. Marine Corps
> First Lieutenant Michael Dobervich, U.S. Marine Corps
> First Lieutenant Leo Boelens, U.S. Army Air Corps
> Sergeant Paul Marshall, U.S. Army
> Sergeant Robert Spielman, U.S. Army

After their escape from DAPEPCOL they became somewhat lost but later came in contact with guerrilla elements. All were escorted to the headquarters of the 110th Division in Medina. Hank Hansen happened to be at the division headquarters when the escapees arrived—tired, thin and bedraggled, some suffering from malaria. Their arms and legs were covered with infected sores, and their bare feet were cut and bleeding from the long hike over very rough terrain. Hank contacted a local carpenter and arranged for large-size wooden *bakyas* (slip-on footwear with wooden soles) to be fashioned for the ex–POWs.[9]

After discussions with Colonel McClish, they decided to give up their

Escaped American POWs at 110th Division Headquarters. Left–right: Major William Dyess (ex–POW), Lieutenant Colonel Ernest McClish (division commander), Lieutenant Commander "Chick" Parsons, Captain Charles Smith, Lieutenant Commander Melvyn McCoy (ex–POW), Major Stephen Mellnik (ex–POW) and Lieutenant Leo Boelens (ex–POW) (courtesy MacArthur Memorial Archives, Norfolk, Virginia).

original plan of finding a boat and sailing to Australia. They also learned that there was a communications capability at Fertig's headquarters and that the guerrillas were being supplied by submarine. Now aware of these possibilities, McCoy and Mellnik opted to travel at once to Fertig's headquarters in order to investigate the possibility of getting a message to GHQ SWPA and arranging repatriation back to their parent services. For the time being the remaining escapees would remain with the 110th Division.

When McCoy and Mellnik arrived at Tenth Military District headquarters in Misamis City, their demands for immediate communications with Australia and transportation on the next submarine returning to Australia were met with a cool reception by Fertig, who made it clear to the two that they and the other escapees were, for the time being, under his command. Furthermore, his communications with GHQ SWPA were marginal and a message about their arrival would not take precedence over more pressing operational and intelligence traffic. Moreover, their movement to Australia would be decided by GHQ SWPA. In response to Fertig's cautionary tone they made it clear to him that they were graduates of their respective service academies and did not think they should be taking orders from civilians now on active duty, particularly Fertig who had promoted himself to the rank of general. In a follow-on meeting with Fertig, McCoy and Mellnik were joined by Ed Dyess, who had just arrived with Chick Parsons from the Agusan provincial area. According to Mellnik, McCoy had a .45 on his lap during this meeting which focused on whether a message had been sent to GHQ SWPA and a response received.[10] Fertig reminded them that his communications with Australia were somewhat fragile but he would nonetheless remind GHQ SWPA to respond to his original message. In both his diary and draft manuscript Fertig states that at this point it was necessary to write a letter of instruction to McCoy (senior officer among the POWs that escaped) on how the POWs would conduct themselves while assigned to the Tenth Military District.

On June 10 GHQ SWPA responded to Fertig's communications, advising that POW's will be taken out at first opportunity.[11] Both McCoy and Mellnik were informed of the response from GHQ SWPA.

To say the very least, these issues over communications and repatriation could have been handled better by both sides. Fertig, before meeting with McCoy and Mellnik, should have thought through the mental state of these former POWs. Since their surrender they had suffered severe hardships at the hands of the Japanese. Added to this was the anxiety and physical challenge of making the escape. In addition, there was the frustration of having been lost in the jungle following their escape. After having made contact with the guerrillas, it must have been something of a shock to see American and Filipino guerrillas fighting the Japanese under an American commander and his experienced officers—and this was taking place not too distant from where they had been held as POWs. Added to this dimension was the surprise that these guerrillas had a communications capability and logistical support from MacArthur's headquarters. This new world of the guerrillas was probably too much for them to grasp without really thinking through their relationship with the guerrillas and Fertig. Little did McCoy and Mellnik understand how tenuous was the capabilities of the guerrillas to immediately respond to their desire to be repatriated. Moreover, both jumped to hasty and erroneous conclusions about Fertig and his officers. Fertig had been promoted to Lieutenant Colonel in December 1941 and was very much involved in the defense of Bataan. Both McClish and Childress had been battalion commanders in the defense of Mindanao. The authority to organize and lead the Tenth Military District had been given to Fertig by MacArthur. Perhaps they did not understand this or the military background and experience of the guerrilla leaders, jumping to conclusions because Fertig did not immediately respond to their requests. During this period Fertig had more important issues on his plate, such as completing the organization of the guerrilla force and establishing coast watcher stations that had been ordered by GHQ SWPA. In addition, the SPYRON program was in its early stages and only two submarine resupply missions had been made to Mindanao. For them to insist that they be on the next submarine returning to Australia was somewhat unrealistic, particularly since GHQ SWPA set the priorities for the evacuees.

It is interesting to note that the majority of the escapees did serve some time in the guerrilla ranks before being sent out by submarine at a later date. Only McCoy, Mellnik and Dyess went out early in July 1943 and did not spend any appreciable time with the guerrillas. Those that remained made themselves useful, providing experience, expertise and vital services for the guerrilla organization. Until he was repatriated in November 1943, Captain Austin Shofner was acting chief of staff for the 110th Division. Lieutenant Jack Hawkins also served in the division as the G-2. Captain Grashio and Lieutenant Leo Boelens worked on the airfield construction projects. Paul Marshall and Robert Spielman, both sergeants when they arrived, elected to

Three escaped POWs meet with General MacArthur in Brisbane, Australia. on July 30, 1943. Left–right: Major William Dyess, Lieutenant Commander Melvyn McCoy, General MacArthur, and Major Stephen Mellnik. The three were part of group of 12 POWs that successfully escaped from Davao Penal Colony in April 1943 (courtesy MacArthur Memorial Archives, Norfolk, Virginia).

stay with the guerrillas and not be evacuated. Both received commissions and held successive command positions that included battalion and regiment assignments. Spielman commanded the 114th Infantry Regiment of the 110th Division. Eventually Marshall was promoted to Lieutenant Colonel and replaced McClish as commander of the 110th Division in 1945. In that position he worked closely with the American forces in deploying his guerrillas to support U.S. Army operations. Later he would team up with the U.S. Navy to use his guerrilla forces in an impressive amphibious operation. Sadly, one of the escapees, Lieutenant Leo Boelens, was killed in a guerrilla operation. Despite some of the early missteps in the handling of the escapees, the group did make a vital contribution to the overall capabilities of the Tenth Military District.

11

Leadership Assessment

Perhaps the following leadership guidelines might be helpful in assessing Fertig's leadership of the Mindanao guerrillas. On May 27, 2011, Secretary of Defense Robert M. Gates was the commencement speaker at the U.S. Naval Academy. In the text of his speech Gates laid out his thoughts on leadership. His first point was that great leaders must have vision. This means that such leaders have the ability to see beyond their day-to-day tasks and responsibilities. These effective leaders look beyond tomorrow and see what others cannot.

A second element in effective leadership is conviction. This element in the mind of the leader will stimulate and excite those men and women around him and make them eager to follow.

Gates went on to list self-confidence as a third quality of leadership. This is not a quality of the ego but one of quiet self-assurance. With self-assurance, the leader can give others responsibilities that bring them credit and reward. At the same time such a leader will stand in the background and let the subordinates receive the praise and attention they deserve. In addition, this self-assurance means the leader trusts his subordinates but at the same time holds them accountable.

A fourth quality of leadership, as outlined by Gates, was courage. Such a leader will have the courage to take a new direction and possibly stand alone and not do what is currently popular. Also, a leader with courage will "speak truth to power" if the occasion demands it. In today's world, government, business and the military stress the importance of team building and group dynamics. Even so, a time will come when a leader must stand alone and say, "This is wrong." Such an act displays real courage.

Another quality of leadership is integrity. Honor and character are part of this. There are some who feel that they have a sense of entitlement and that rules are not made for them. Such would-be leaders will not in the end succeed. An effective leader will have in his personality the building blocks of integrity—self-reliance, self-control, honor, truthfulness and morality.

The final quality of leadership is common decency—treating those around you, particularly subordinates, with fairness and respect. In ending, Gates remarked that the true measure of leadership is not how you react in times of tranquility but how you react with to adversity.[1]

I will attempt in the following paragraphs to measure Fertig against the qualities of leadership as outlined by Gates in his 2011 commencement speech at the Naval Academy. Essentially this assessment is about Fertig's performance as a leader and his ability to inspire, organize and give purpose to a guerrilla movement. In this regard, Fertig did have vision regarding the future and how the Japanese occupation should be opposed. Timing in his efforts was critically important in gauging how the Filipino people reacted to the Japanese occupation. After talking with Catholic priests and American "old-timers" in the Misamis Occidental and Lanao provinces, he sensed the Filipino opposition to the Japanese occupation was building but was not yet at a critical stage. Initially the Filipinos took a wait and see attitude after the arrival of the Japanese. Certainly the Japanese propaganda, coupled with the visual scenes of the defeated U.S. and Filipino military being marched to internment camps, prompted the individual Filipino to reflect on what his life would be like during the Japanese occupation. However, once the harshness of the Japanese military rule was felt on the streets, with physical abuse and degrading treatment, the transition from passivity to anger began to grow. At some critical point in the near future, Fertig reasoned, there would be a growing will to resist. This would lead to a Filipino desire to see forceful action and leadership emerge. Fertig judged that if this leadership to resist did not emerge among the Filipinos themselves, the chances were good that they would come to an American military officer, like himself, who had not surrendered. Here again, Fertig had the vision to see what was ahead. The Filipinos would be looking for an officer with poise that could instill inspiration to organize and take action against the Japanese. That being said, it was important to Fertig that the initiative to organize such a movement, with an American officer in command, had to originate from the Filipinos themselves. As Fertig anticipated in his thinking about the way forward after the surrender of USAFFE forces, an appeal finally did come from Luis Morgan, a former Philippine constabulary officer who had organized a band of guerrillas.

The scenario that Morgan and his colleague Tait had laid out to Fertig included Fertig arriving on Mindanao as a general officer from Australia who had come to command the guerrilla opposition against the Japanese. Their rationale for this was that there were Filipino military officers trying to organize guerrilla groups who were giving themselves the rank of colonel. Only an American general could command respect and unite the disparate groups into an armed movement against the Japanese occupation. Knowing the Filipinos as he did, Fertig could understand their reasoning. For them a general officer being sent by MacArthur from Australia to consolidate the various guerrilla groups would signify that "the Aid" was coming and that the eventual liberation of the Philippines would be launched. This would be an essential and appealing factor for the creation of a guerrilla movement against the Japanese occupation which had been Fertig's ultimate vision. Thus, posing as a general without authorization would take courage, conviction and self-confidence.

The more pressing issue for Fertig was the reality of the Filipino/Moro problem. He realized that if he were to accept Morgan's offer of command, a number of reforms would have to be undertaken to offset the bad relations between the Filipinos and the Moros. Moreover, a major priority would be securing the allegiance of the Moro people and bringing them into the movement.

Fertig focused on the ongoing and vexing problem of the Moros—he could not go forward in accepting Morgan's offer until he had resolved this issue in his own mind. Again, the more pressing issue for Fertig was the reality of the Filipino/Moro problem. Morgan's organization continued to launch raids against Moros on behalf of Filipino settlers who were concerned about the actions of the Moros following the breakdown of law and order after the surrender. Fertig realized that a number of reforms would have to be undertaken to offset the bad relations between the Filipinos and the Moros. Moreover, a major priority would be securing the allegiance of the Moro people and bringing them into the movement. As mentioned previously, the Moros had been ambivalent about the arrival of the Japanese and, in fact, had taken advantage of the confusion in the wake of the surrender to give vent to their historical grievances against the Filipinos. Many had been killed in this outburst and Filipino/Moro relations were at a low point. With this point of departure in his thinking, he commenced having discussions with Moro leaders about the state of relations between these two peoples. On the positive side he found, through discussions with certain Moro leaders, that there was still some goodwill among the Moros for Americans. Several Moro datus recalled the respect that their forebears had for General Pershing following the agreement that had been worked out in 1913. The Americans from that point forward had given the Moros fair treatment. Fertig was led to understand that if Americans were in leadership roles in the guerrilla movement, it was likely that the Moros would support the movement and not side with the Japanese. As noted in previous chapters, Fertig was fortunate that there were experienced Americans who had worked with Moros that could fill guerrilla leadership roles in guerrilla units located in Moro areas, e.g., Charles Hedges and Frank

McGee. The goal here was to bring the Moros into the movement and not have them side with the Japanese. To achieve this Fertig was resolved to make the changes to the existing guerrilla organization that would make it more acceptable to both the Filipino and Moro populations.

Assuming a command role as a general arriving from Australia was somewhat audacious on Fertig's part; there would be resultant reaction from MacArthur's headquarters in Australia once communications were established. Nonetheless, Fertig judged that it was a gamble he was willing to take if a strong guerrilla movement were to come into being, particularly if the role he would play as a general from Australia would unite guerrillas throughout Mindanao. In this situation Fertig was looking at the end result which demonstrates a leadership trait of being able to visualize the final objective—a strong and viable guerrilla movement. This was his vision and conviction. The act of impersonating a general would, of course, take courage, but it would also haunt him in the future and dim his chances of ever being promoted to general officer status. Given the magnitude of the movement he would eventually create (various manpower estimates range from 25,000 to as high as 35,000), such an organization of this size would have easily justified a general officer in command. He would later pay the price by being denied promotion beyond the rank of full colonel. However, his accomplishment of organizing a guerrilla movement on Mindanao would be recognized by the awarding of the Distinguished Service Cross on August 18, 1943.[2]

How did Fertig perform relative to the leadership quality of integrity? When President Quezon approved a budget of ₱20 million for civilian and guerrilla operations, Fertig appointed a well qualified American businessman, Sam Wilson, as a technical adviser to the Mindanao Emergency Currency Board (MECB). In this capacity he would oversee the printing of the peso currency as well as establish a system to account for all monies expended on both the civilian and military sides. While there were a few cases of irregularities in accounting for monies expended, these were met with disciplinary action by Fertig. All officer personnel were put on notice that irregularities would not be tolerated in his command.

The element of common decency in leadership, as described by Gates, is somewhat vague. Essentially it means treating those around you, both colleagues and subordinates, with fairness and respect. On the surface, Fertig was cordial but somewhat distant and cool. His diary records occasions when he and his subordinates were enjoying social activities, but he would withdraw after only a short period of involvement. Was he concerned that "familiarity breeds contempt" would be a potential element restricting the fulfillment of his vision for the guerrilla movement?

At this juncture, it might be useful to quote, in part, the Clyde Childress comment from Chapter 9 of this book:

> He performed the technical aspects of his job well but failed miserably in his personal relationships and displayed serious character flaws that were inconsistent with the professionalism expected of a United States Army Officer. He appeared to be unaware of, or at least ignored, the normal customs of the service involving the proper relationship between himself and the office and personnel under him, to the extent of being disdainful of the abilities of people in the military, even including the theater commander, General Douglas MacArthur, and his staff, about whom he wasn't abashed at making his usual deprecatory remarks.

A very strong statement by Childress! However, I believe he ignores the reality of the guerrilla movement. This organization was conducting an irregular type of warfare and was not a part of the regular U.S. Army, although it was conforming to the policies and requirements of GHQ SWPA. It would seem that there is an interesting parallel between Fertig and T. H. Lawrence (of Arabia fame). Both were not professional military personnel. During the World War I British campaign in the Middle East Lawrence was cool and direct with his military seniors and contemporaries. He was often speaking truth to power and not following the British army norms. Even so, Lawrence was able to build an effective guerrilla force of disparate Arab groups that had a great deal of success against the regular Turkish army. He was a talented and gifted guerrilla leader. I believe the same could be said of Fertig. Again the question is whether both guerrilla leaders treated their subordinates with fairness and respect. While difficult to judge, one could venture an assessment of "C+" for both leaders. An "A" assessment would be reserved for a leader such General Dwight Eisenhower.

In his closing statements to the graduates of the U.S. Naval Academy Secretary Gates offered his final thoughts on leadership:

> Above all, remember that the true measure of leadership is not how you react in times of peace or times without peril. The true measure of leadership is how you react when the wind leaves your sails, when the tide turns against you.[3]

In the case of Fertig, the most difficult period for his movement was during the months of June and July 1943, when the Japanese launched a strong assault against his newly-formed organization. While the guerrillas were forced to flee and disperse from their headquarters in Misamis City, they were able to later regroup and fight the Japanese another day. Fertig's tactic of not building fixed facilities, but having the capability to quickly fold back into the jungle or population proved to be the effective course for the movement. This was a difficult time for Fertig and the movement but both recovered and became stronger in their efforts against the Japanese.

Decision on the Invasion of the Philippines

In reviewing Fertig's leadership accomplishments as commander of the Tenth Military District and all guerrilla units on Mindanao, it should be noted that decisions were being made in Washington and GHQ SWPA that would affect the original premise upon which assistance to the various guerrilla movements was made. After the American surrender in 1942, the objective for the U.S., in the eyes of MacArthur and GHQ SWPA, was to methodically remove the Japanese presence from islands in the Pacific, finally returning to the Philippines for its liberation from the Japanese. This had been a valid assumption or premise. All support for Fertig and other guerrilla leaders in the islands was based on this. Work to be accomplished by the guerrilla forces (force development, intelligence collection, preparations for the amphibious landings and the construction of emergency airfields) was all geared to an invasion of the entire archipelago.

However, early 1944 planning at the Joint Chief of Staff (JCS) level in Washington was not holding the same assumption as MacArthur and GHQ SWPA. Many JCS planners believed that Formosa was so important that bypassing the Philippines should be considered.[4] Much of the work the guerrilla commanders were doing was on the verge of becoming redundant if the Philippines were bypassed in favor of Formosa. Initially, the JCS ordered MacArthur to prepare plans to invade the Philippines on November 15, with the first landing in southeastern Mindanao. By September 1944 the Mindanao landing was still in the planning stage but an alternative landing on Leyte had been added. As deliberations continued in Washington senior American Officers voiced their opinions on bypassing the Philippines. Admiral Ernest King, Chief of Naval Operations, was a leading advocate of bypassing the Philippines. In late 1944 General George C. Marshall, chief of staff of the U.S. Army, supported bypassing both the Philippines and Formosa and going directly to Japan. Of course, General MacArthur was strongly opposed to the bypassing of any part of the Philippines. He met with President Roosevelt at Pearl Harbor in late July 1944 to discuss the future direction of the war in the Pacific. He made a very forceful argument to the president on not bypassing the Philippines. However, no final decision was made at the conference on strategy and whether the Philippines would be invaded. The debate continued at the Washington level.

Admiral Nimitz was circulating a report that a U.S. Navy carrier pilot (downed temporarily on Leyte) had reported, after his repatriation, that local Filipinos on Leyte had told him that there were no Japanese on Leyte. Whether or not this information affected the final decision is unclear. In any event, it is an interesting footnote to history. GHQ SWPA responded that the Navy pilot's report was untrue. In fact, the order of battle for the Japanese on Leyte, as compiled by Sixth Army G-2, was 21,700 troops. By contrast, the Japanese forces on the ground on Mindanao were estimated by different U.S. commands to range from 34,000 to 43,000 troops. Regarding the guerrilla troop numbers on these two islands, Leyte had 3,190 and Mindanao well in excess of 25,000. In any case, there were other factors beyond guerrilla strengths that were considered in selecting Leyte over Mindanao. By September 1944 both Mindanao and Leyte were still on the planning agenda—these operations would be in sequence with Mindanao going first. However, MacArthur wanted a time interval between the two. By eliminating Mindanao, this removed the time requirement. Also being considered were the availability of transport for assault craft, carrier forces to cover the land assault and forces available to make the landings. Making one landing at Leyte made the final decision easier. Finally, MacArthur proposed that JCS cancel the Mindanao landings and make the point of entry into the Philippines at Leyte on October 20.

Within days after the JCS decision on Leyte, MacArthur then proposed that the landings on Luzon begin on December 20, with possible Formosa landings in February 1945. On October 3, 1944, the JCS directed MacArthur to launch the invasion of Leyte and Luzon as he had proposed. Nothing was said about the other islands, including Mindanao. The direct outcome now was that Formosa would be bypassed. After the invasion of the Philippines, Iwo Jima and Okinawa would be the next objectives for Admiral Nimitz's forces. The overall result was that U.S. forces would recapture all of the Philippines as had been the vision of MacArthur when he left in March 1942.[5]

With the decision made on choosing Leyte as the entry point for retaking the Philippines, it is interesting to imagine the many adjustments that had to be made by the respective guerrilla organizations throughout the archipelago, particularly for Leyte, Luzon and Mindanao. The guerrilla organization on Leyte was still very much in a formative state. It was not until October 21, 1943, that Colonel Kangleon was recognized by MacArthur as the guerrilla leader on Leyte. By September 1944 its total strength was 3,190 personnel. The Leyte guerrillas had only a limited intelligence collection capability and logistical support from Australia had been minimal. Moreover, its communications capability was most fragile and had been provided by Fertig's organization on Mindanao. Once the American invasion began on Leyte Kangleon's guerrilla support was limited to tactical intelligence and having the guerrillas act as guides for U.S. Army assault units.

On all islands in the Philippines where there was an active guerrilla movement, the American invasion on Leyte was a clarion call to arms for all these organizations. It encouraged them to be ready on short notice to support the invasion when it came to their island. In northern Luzon, in the early days of liberation there, General Walter Krueger, Sixth Army commander, was most concerned about the Japanese 19th Division. It was decided to use the guerrilla organization USAFIP (NL), led by Colonel Russell W. Volkmann, to assist the Sixth Army elements against the 19th Division. When the Americans arrived in Luzon in January 1945, Volkmann's guerrilla forces numbered 8,000. After the invasion, the Sixth Army commenced active logistical support to Volkmann's guerrillas using over-the-beach resupply on the coastline that they controlled as well as with C-47 support aircraft flying into remote landing strips. Two months after the U.S. Army's landings at Lingayen Gulf, Volkmann's total guerrilla force had grown to 18,000 men. The combat personnel were divided into five infantry regiments, each having 2,900, for a total armed force of 14,500. The mission of the expanded guerrilla force was to gather intelligence, ambush Japanese elements, disrupt lines of communication and block Japanese troop movements in and out of the Cagayan Valley. While it was not intended that Volkmann's guerrillas would sustain their operations against the Japanese, they in fact exceeded their mission by clearing much of the west coast of Luzon north of San Fernando. The guerrilla forces became the equivalent of a full division that General Krueger did not have.[6]

Before completing the retaking of Luzon, MacArthur turned his attention to the southern part of the Philippines. While this would divert resources away from the completion of the Luzon operation, he felt that the Filipinos in the south would be in growing danger of brutal retaliation by the frustrated Japanese troops who realized that they had no favorable outcome in their situation. Even though Fertig's Tenth Military District had sadly accepted the invasion of Leyte and Luzon ahead of Mindanao, six months would pass before Fertig's guerrillas would have the opportunity to support an invasion.

Mindanao Guerrilla Support for the Invasion

The following guerrilla support for American landings on Mindanao demonstrates the effectiveness of Fertig's leadership in building a force that could partner with the regular American military in removing the Japanese presence from all of Mindanao. Samuel Eliot Morison's book, *The Liberation of the Philippines*, suggests that it was not necessary for GHQ SWPA to commit American troops to Mindanao because the estimated 34,000–45,000 Japanese troops remaining on the island were restricted to the major towns and cities. According to Morison, Fertig's guerrillas numbered 25,000 but controlled 95 percent of the country. He further cites an Eighth Army report saying that Mindanao did not have strategic importance once Luzon and the Visayas were secured. Morison's thesis might be disputed if one were to give full weight to the capabilities of the Japanese troops with their superior firepower and training. While the SPYRON missions had provided the guerrillas with improved weapons like the M-1 Thompson machine gun and the carbine, only a small portion of guerrillas had these newer weapons—many were still using World War I vintage weapons. Without the liberation of Mindanao by American troops, the Japanese could have carried on a suicidal insurgency that would have overwhelmed the newly liberated government of the Philippines. Such a situation might have required the re-introduction of American troops in the postwar era to eradicate the last vestiges of the Japanese presence.[7]

In March 1945, the campaign to liberate Mindanao would commence in Zamboanga, in the western part of the island. The Tenth Military District's 121st Infantry Regiment of the 105th Division under the command of Captain Donald Le Couvre in Zamboanga would have the honor of being the first Fertig-led guerrilla unit to support the invasion. Unlike northern Luzon, a fully operational guerrilla force was ready to assist the U.S. Army forces. The Eighth Army did not have the air support needed for the operation because the airstrip on Palawan was not complete. Fortunately, Fertig's 105th Division had control of the Dipolog airstrip, 145 miles to the north of Zamboanga City; in fact, the strip had been used to support the guerrillas since late 1944. With this capability in place, one squadron of Marine tactical fighters was deployed to the airfield to support the invasion of Zamboanga. To assist the guerrillas in maintaining the security of Dipolog, reinforced companies from the 24th Division were airlifted into the strip. In the south, guerrilla units were assisting the underwater demolition teams and engineers in preparation for the landings that would take place on the beaches near Zamboanga City.[8]

On March 8 troops of the 162nd Infantry Regiment of the 41st Division landed northwest of Zamboanga City, followed shortly thereafter by the 163rd Infantry Regiment. Guerrillas of the 105th Division provided blocking support for the 163rd Infantry Regiment's sweep northward from Zamboanga City. By April 2, with the combined efforts of the 41st Division's two regiments and the guerrillas, the Japanese presence was forced northward toward Dipolog. There, elements of the guerrilla 105th Division contained the Japanese advance.[9]

The retaking of eastern Mindanao would fall to the U.S. Eighth Army. Originally it was planned that the 24th Division would land at Malabang with a traditional amphibious landing, including pre-bombardment and tactical air support. However, on April 15 changes were made. Eighth Army headquarters decided to limit the landing to just one battalion from the 24th Division

Directing American air support for the guerrillas. Left–right: Unidentified Army Air Corps controller, Major Rex Blow (Australian army), Lieutenant Colonel Charles Hedges, Colonel Wendell Fertig (Australian War Memorial).

based on a report by Fertig that the 108th Division, under Lieutenant Colonel Hedges, had secured and occupied the Malabang region and had control of the Malabang airfield.

Throughout much of eastern Mindanao Fertig's guerrillas greatly contributed to the inability of the Japanese to maneuver—they constructed roadblocks and destroyed bridges, supply dumps and communications facilities. These actions made it difficult for the Japanese to move trucks throughout the region; in fact, the movement of Japanese patrols on these roads had not been possible for months.[10]

The U.S. Eighth Army's 108th Infantry Regiment, 40th Division, landed unopposed on Macajalar Bay on May 10, and contact was immediately made with the Tenth Military District's 110th Division guerrillas commanded by Lieutenant Colonel Paul Marshall. At the end of June both the guerrilla 109th and 110th Divisions took over the area east of the Sayre Highway from Maramag north to Malaybalay. In the Agusan River valley guerrillas of the 113th Infantry Regiment of the 110th Division, commanded by Major Khalil Khodr, were harassing the Japanese throughout the valley.[11]

Taking over from the 24th Division in late July, guerrillas of the 107th Division, Colonel McGee now in command, continued to pursue Japanese remnants. In this process the guerrillas were able to exert control over the southwestern section of the Kibawe-Talomo trail.[12]

The guerrilla component in the operation was the 118th Infantry Regiment, 106th Division, now being led by Colonel Bowler. The unit came overland from Pikit. They moved southwest toward Sarangani Bay. On July 15 the guerrilla 116th Infantry Regiment and a combat team from the 24th Division engaged the Japanese. By July 25 the Japanese resistance collapsed. This concluded the campaign on Mindanao.[13]

Reviewing the U.S. campaign in the Philippine liberation—Leyte, northern Luzon and Mindanao—it is clear that the planned phases of the U.S. liberation of the Philippines did not match the relative strengths and capabilities of the respective guerrilla movements. Leyte, the first campaign, was the least prepared and provided only minimal guerrilla support to the American invasion. In northern Luzon, a modest guerrilla organization, once supplied, was able to surge and perform operations at a sustained level that was the equivalent of a U.S. Army division. Certainly, Colonel Volkmann's leadership was a vital element in the success of the guerrilla support activities.

The Mindanao guerrillas were the largest and best organized of the three guerrilla movements discussed. This was in no small measure due to the leadership of Fertig. His guerrilla organization was able to respond immediately to planning gaps that existed in X Corps operations. Certainly they exceeded the expectation that GHQ SWPA had for them when logistical support commenced in March 1943. Moreover, their intelligence coverage of the island, particularly the maritime passages, was superior to the other guerrilla movements. Their communications capability, backing up intelligence collection and operations, was robust and without parallel among guerrilla organizations found in the Philippines. Again, these superior capabilities were due to the leadership of Fertig—he had carried out the original GHQ SWPA guidance for the Tenth Military District, particularly in developing a substantive intelligence collection capability. The coast watcher element of this collection effort earned its keep with its timely reporting on the major Japanese naval movements in the archipelago. This made a major contribution to the U.S. success in the first battle of the Philippine Sea, well-known in U.S. Navy annals as the "Marianas Turkey Shoot." This action inflicted major damage to the Japanese carrier-based aircraft capability in the Pacific, with over 400 aircraft destroyed.[14]

The effectiveness of both Fertig's and Volkmann's guerrilla organizations in supporting the liberation of the Philippines is thoroughly discussed in the foregoing. However, only in a minimal way has the effectiveness of other guerrilla leaders such as Colonel Macario Peralta on Panay and Colonel Ruperto Kangleon on Leyte been covered. This is not to say that they did not make contributions to intelligence collection and other operational activities. However, their substantive use in a combat role with the American forces was not demonstrated. For example, when the U.S. Army's 40th infantry Division landed on the Panay beaches they were met by Peralta's guerrillas, lined up in parade formations. Later the guerrillas did harass retreating Japanese forces.[15] Though Peralta's guerrilla organization was one of the first recognized by GHQ SWPA and had radio contact with Australia, they did not distinguish themselves in the liberation. There could be several reasons for this. It should be recalled that Peralta was the G-3 for the USAFFE garrison when the Japanese invaded. Colonel Albert Christie was the commanding officer. Early on he had withdrawn his forces into the mountains and was prepared to conduct guerrilla operations against the Japanese until he was ordered to surrender in May 1942. Only 10 percent of the force surrendered; the remainder, led by Peralta, did not. With USAFFE radio equipment and ciphers destroyed prior to the surrender, they were able to assemble a radio utilizing pieces of equipment from local sources and successfully effected communication with Australia by November 1942. Peralta named himself commander of this guerrilla force which now consisted mainly of former USAFFE soldiers.

Herein is a major distinction between Peralta's organization and Fertig's guerrilla movement. Fertig started with only a few guerrillas that included both civilians and former soldiers. While the majority was Filipino, there was a solid use of Americans with former military experience in command positions. Fertig patterned his six area divisions after U.S. Army reserve divisions. By contrast, Per-

Colonel Wendell W. Fertig, 1945 (American Guerrillas of Mindanao Records, AGOM Descendants Group, Falls Church, Virginia).

alta made very limited use of Americans in his organization, keeping command positions for Filipinos. He ruled with a heavy hand and in a czar-like fashion.[16] What made him respond in this fashion may be rooted in his background. He was a graduate of the Philippine Military Academy which may have contributed to an elitist and almost anti–American attitude. Even so, being the G-3 for Christie would have been a substantive accomplishment. It is unclear is why Peralta did not surrender. Given Peralta's many advantages for his organization, including communications capability and resupply by submarine, one would have expected that the guerrillas on Panay would have played a larger role in the liberation.

As mentioned previously, Kangleon's guerrilla force on Leyte came to the guerrilla table at a very late period of the war. It was not until October 1943 that his group was recognized by GHQ SWPA. Much of his support from Australia came through Fertig's Tenth Military District. When available, he used effectively the few Americans that were available on the island A good example of this was Ensign Iliff David Richardson who had been a PT boat officer and served as Kangleon's intelligence officer. With the American landings on Leyte in October 1944 guerrilla support was limited to tactical intelligence and guide assistance for U.S. Army tactical units.

Guerrilla contribution to U.S. Army liberation efforts on Mindoro, Negros Occidental, Negros Oriental and Cebu mirrored very much the same level of support that was available on Leyte—tactical intelligence, guide assistance for U.S. Army tactical units and residual mopping efforts against Japanese units. As previously pointed out, major operational capabilities by guerrillas to the liberation of the Philippines by American forces were only demonstrated in northern Luzon and Mindanao. Again, the credit for these capabilities should go to Volkmann on Luzon and Fertig on Mindanao.

12

Legacy and Reflections on Guerrilla Warfare in the Philippines

This effort commences with some reflections and comments by Fertig on guerrilla warfare as he experienced it in the early phases of his movement. In Fertig's draft manuscript he sets forth some basic principles of guerrilla warfare. These principles were never articulated in his diary, probably because he had not sufficient time to think about them or subject them to the test of time.

- In order to prosecute a successful guerrilla war, a clandestine organization should be developed before the emergency. In our case this had not been done and it was necessary to develop the clandestine organization before we could move into the field of guerrilla warfare.
- A guerrilla force consisting of only native troops has seldom achieved success unless they have support from an outside power. This support can be either covert or overt but such support must be there to provide adequate supplies and funds if the guerrillas are to succeed.
- A means of communications must be available, not only internally but with the outside power which is providing the supplies and financial help. Serving as a force of many eyes the guerrillas can see and use the radio to report information to the central command which will result in extremely complete intelligence coverage of the enemy and its capabilities.
- Terrain plays an extremely important part in guerrilla warfare operations and the more favorable terrain utilized is readily reflected in the character of the operations. As a general rule the people who inhabit the mountains or swampy areas are more hardy and self-sufficient than urban citizens.
- A good and widespread food supply is essential to the successful prosecution of guerrilla warfare. In an area such as that over which we had fought,

food was produced on a year round basis, and except for unseasonable floods or infestations, was available in sufficient quantities to support the small units assigned to the various areas.

• Last, but not least, the guerrilla must have the support of a loyal and willing populace. The loyalty and support must be given freely while at the same time the local population must accept the risk of reprisal should they support the guerrillas in a too open manner.[1]

In the comments leading up to the foregoing principles, Fertig notes the following concerning Filipinos in the movement:

> Initially, the Filipino soldier and officers followed me as the only leader available, but as time passed they followed me because they felt my command was enhancing the prestige of the Philippines as a country and the Filipinos as a nation. It has ceased to be a Filipino-American effort and has become a Filipino effort still guided and directed by the few Americans merely because the Filipinos had not yet developed the leadership.[2]

It should be noted that Fertig's principles and his views on Filipino participation were drafted in 1958. They were sandwiched between his chronologies of events in September 1944, just prior to the American invasion of Leyte. It may be that Fertig's thoughts on guerrilla warfare at that point in 1958 were generated by his participation with Colonel Russell W. Volkmann, American guerrilla commander in northern Luzon (see Chapter 10), in the U.S. Army's study on "Special Operations."[3] Significantly, this study would become the basis for the establishment of the U.S. Army's Special Forces. It is ironic, but appropriate, that the two most effective American guerrilla commanders in the Philippines during World War II would collaborate to build the framework for today's Special Forces.

During and after the Korean War the U.S. Army sought to develop guidance on Special Operations, particularly as it might relate to counterinsurgency. The result was Field Manual (FM 31–20) *Operations Against Guerrilla Forces* (September 1950). Colonel Volkmann was the author of this field manual.[4] After returning from a tour of duty in Korea, Volkmann also authored FM 31–21, *Organization and Conduct of Guerrilla Warfare*. Following the publication of FM 31–21, Volkmann became Chief of Plans for the U.S. Army's Office of the Chief of Psychological Warfare (OCPW). Other members of OCPW included Fertig and Colonel Melvin Blair, a veteran of "Merrill's Marauders." It was probably this participation in the work of OCPW that prompted Fertig to articulate the principles of guerrilla warfare in his draft manuscript.[5]

The work of Volkmann and his OCPW staff on Special Operations came to the attention of the Army chief of staff, General J. Lawton Collins. He would later approve a 2,300 manning level for the first Special Forces unit being formed at Fort Bragg. The first Special Forces unit was activated on June 19, 1952. During the remainder of the 1950s Special Forces units would be assigned to both Europe and the Far East.[6]

At this juncture it is fitting to include a few comments concerning Fertig's career following World War II. He decided to accept a permanent commission in the regular Army. In an early assignment he was officer-in-charge of the ROTC unit of the Colorado School of Mines and would later serve as a professor of Military Science and Tactics at the school. Other assignments took him to Washington for work with Volkmann and the OCPW group; he was also an adviser in the establishment of the Army Special Warfare School at Fort Bragg, North Carolina. After retirement he worked as a consulting engineer and ran a Colorado mining company until his death on March 14, 1975.

At the start of President John F. Kennedy's administration the Special Forces had established themselves as the Army's elite unit to counter insurgent threats that were emerging in the Cold War period, particularly in developing countries. When Kennedy visited Fort Bragg he was most impressed with what he saw in this elite force. With Kennedy's interest in counterinsurgency, he felt that the Special Forces could be an effective tool in defeating Communist-inspired guerrilla movements. With presidential support, the U.S. Army increased the size and role of Special Forces, particularly as the U.S. role expanded in South Vietnam.

The legacy of guerrilla operations in the Philippines during World War II had a strong influence, especially through Volkmann, on the development of the Department of Defense (DOD) Special Operations. It would also shape the Central Intelligence Agency's (CIA) paramilitary capabilities in the emerging Cold War. As the reader will recall, CIA was established by the National Security Act of 1947 during President Truman's administration. The director of Central Intelligence became the primary adviser to the president and the National Security Council (NSC) on foreign intelligence matters. An Executive Order authorized only CIA to conduct special activities, including clandestine and covert paramilitary operations. As the Cold War progressed CIA was involved in covert paramilitary activities in China, Tibet, Cuba, Afghanistan and Indonesia.

The largest and longest paramilitary operation conducted by CIA was in Laos, 1961–1975. Initially, the NSC and White House approved only a modest amount of support to train and arm the Hmong, one of several hill tribes that live at the higher elevations of Laos. This was prompted by the expanding presence of North Vietnamese Army (NVA) forces in northern

Laos. The Hmong are fiercely anti–Vietnamese and, under the leadership of General Vang Pao, resisted the encroachment of North Vietnamese cadres into northern Laos. Under supervision of CIA trainers, the Hmong guerrillas were trained by U.S. Army Special Forces and Thai border police personnel. Here is a case in the Cold War when both CIA and DOD Special Operations components worked together.

In June 1961 President Kennedy met with Prime Minister Nikita Khrushchev in Vienna. During their discussions the two leaders agreed that they would work together in support of a neutral and independent Laos. In the meantime, CIA continued armed support to the now 9,000 man Hmong guerrilla force. After months of discussions in Geneva the two sides worked out a settlement and in July 23, 1962, an agreement was signed by both the Soviet Union and the U.S. Unfortunately, the North Vietnamese were in the driver's seat as far as Laos was concerned. Regardless of what the Americans and Soviets agreed to, the Vietnamese would violate the agreement if it suited their interests. In compliance with the agreement the U.S. pulled out 666 military advisers and support staff. Only a few NVA were counted by the International Control Commission as having been withdrawn. CIA at this point halted support to Vang Pao's forces. The State Department permitted two CIA officers to remain in Laos to monitor the NVA compliance. Later intelligence reporting indicated that over 7,000 troops remained in Laos. As Hanoi continued to send additional troops into Laos, the Kennedy administration in 1963 authorized CIA to resume support to the Hmong guerrilla force. Also, the size of the force was increased to 20,000. While considering reactivating the DOD support for Laos, Washington decided instead to expand the role of CIA. This clandestine paramilitary role became known as the "Secret War in Laos." The use of CIA provided a "fig leaf" for the U.S. government as it continued to support the Geneva Accords on Laos while at the same time providing covert military assistance to the Lao, Hmong and other hill tribes.

(The author was involved with CIA's paramilitary operations in Laos from 1969 to 1973. Initially, he was deputy at the Lao Task Force at CIA headquarters. Later, during the period 1971–1973, he was the senior paramilitary officer in Military Region I.)

Returning to Fertig's principles of guerrilla warfare mentioned on page 1, CIA followed very much his basic thoughts on secret guerrilla operations, especially maintaining the secrecy of the support so that plausible denial could be articulated. Realizing (as did Fertig) the importance of outside logistical support, CIA utilized airlifts to transport supplies and personnel to the Hmong guerrilla outposts. In Laos, because of few roads and rugged terrain, CIA's proprietary airline, Air America, became an important element in bringing the needed support to the guerrillas. Hundreds of short take-off and landing (STOL) airfields were carved out of the jungle by local villagers. STOL aircraft such as the Swiss Pilatus Porter became the mainstay for transporting arms/ammunition and troops into remote areas. Rice for the guerrillas and their families was dropped without parachutes using double bag packaging. World War II reliable transport like the C-46 and C-47 were ideal for this effort. As the program expanded, newer aircraft were added to the program such as the C-130, Twin Otter, Huey and H-34 helicopters. By 1971 almost 2,000 tons of rice per month were being transported or dropped by Air America's fleet of 80 aircraft. As the war in Vietnam expanded, Air America aircraft in Laos were rescuing downed American military pilots, conducting photo intelligence missions and inserting intelligence teams along the famous Ho Chi Minh Trail. Over 300 Air America personnel were involved in this unique capability with flight time per year reaching 4,000 hours. During this period Long Tieng, General Vang Pao's major base, was one of the busiest airfields in Southeast Asia—one landing or take-off every minute during daylight hours.

As spelled out in the cease-fire agreement signed in Paris in February 1973, all U.S. military support was gradually wound down and finally ended

Air America Pilatus Porter aircraft, mainstay for transporting arms and ammunition to guerrillas in Laos (author's collection).

in 1975. Nonetheless, from 1961 until 1975 the CIA's paramilitary program in Laos had maintained the country's independence and constrained NVA domination of the country. Moreover, the guerrilla program had tied down three NVA divisions that would have otherwise been deployed to South Vietnam.

With 9/11 and the war on terrorism, special operations for both DOD and CIA brought new frontiers in this mode of fighting non-traditional warfare. However, much of the legacy from the Philippine World War II guerrilla experience still remains and is valid. A few weeks after 9/11 CIA was able to insert paramilitary teams into remote areas of Afghanistan and link up with tribal leaders to carry the war to Al Qaeda and the Taliban. Unfortunately it would be several weeks before DOD could insert Special Forces and forward air controllers to assist the CIA teams in coordinating the air war against the terrorist remnants.

However, as the war on terror has continued there has been closer coordination between DOD's Special Operations Command and CIA. The high point of this cooperation was the killing on May 1, 2011, of Usama Bin Laden in Pakistan. Even so, a gulf remains between DOD and CIA on legal authorities to carry out special operations. This will surely intensify as the global war on terrorism moves to other Middle East countries such as Yemen and Somalia. Most recently the actions of the Syria-based Islamic State of Iraq and the Levant (ISIL) in taking over large portions of northern Iraq, including Mosul, have prompted the U.S. government to expand its military presence in Iraq by about 1,500 personnel, primarily at the U.S. Embassy in Baghdad and the consulate in Irbil. A September 11, 2014, CIA estimate states that ISIL can muster between 20,000 and 31,500 fighters across Iraq and Syria.[7] On September 10 President Barack Obama, in an address to the nation, said, "American will lead a broad coalition to roll back this terrorist threat. Our objective is clear. We will degrade, and ultimately destroy, ISIL."[8]

A part of the president's recent initiative will be increased support for the Free Syrian Army. The CIA has been supporting this group in a limited capacity for more than a year. Whether the CIA will continue this program in an expanded mode is in question as the White House has indicated that DOD will now be responsible for the expanded program.[9]

The policy of "No U.S. boots on the ground" will continue to be followed in President Obama's various programs against ISIL. This will necessitate more DOD special operations and CIA covert action programs and could highlight the debate on DOD-led "Title 10" operations versus CIA "Title 50" operations. These refer to the two U.S. Code titles that give DOD and CIA their respective authorities. CIA's authorities go back to its founding in 1947 when it was first given authority to conduct covert action, including paramilitary operations. To carry out such operations requires the Agency to seek a Presidential Finding and briefing of appropriate Congressional committees. For the military, conducting special operations where the U.S. role is unacknowledged is permitted as long as those missions are under the command and control of a military commander that is in support of possible future hostilities. Neither a Presidential Finding nor notification to Congress is required.[10]

Until Congress modifies or clarifies the Title 10 and Title 50 authorities, both agencies will continue to have different authorities and approvals relative to carrying out special operations. However, with the immediacy of the ISIL threat, there could be another option available that would not violate the White House pledge of "No U.S. boots on the ground." As was done with the Usama bin Laden raid in May 2011, Special Operations Command personnel could be placed under the command of CIA for a covert paramilitary operation under Title 50. This would give CIA the presidential authority under a finding to deploy the special operations personnel in a covert paramilitary operation against ISIL.

Appendix

History of the Mindanao Guerrillas

Compiled by the Historical Section, Tenth Military District
(MacArthur Memorial Museum and Archives, Norfolk, Virginia)

Section C. 187 American Guerrillas on Mindanao

Clyde M. Abbot

ASN 6553635, 1st Lieut, Inf. Reported to Tenth Military District on 15 Oct 1942. Born in Cuba, New Mexico, on 30 Oct 1917. Second Year High School; speaks English and Spanish; 6 years as Pvt, USAC: Commissioned 2nd Lieut, Inf, Tenth Military District, USFIP, on 28 Nov 1942; promoted 1st Lieut, Inf, on 27 Feb 1943; served as 1st Lieut until he proceeded to the Replacement Depot on 14 Jan 1945. Executive Officer, 110th Infantry, 1 Dec 1942; responsible for mutual understanding of the civilians and the Army—settling troubles between civilians and the Army. Responsible for locating suitable places for intermediary radio stations in the 2nd Battalion area, 110th Infantry. Ordered to proceed to USAFFE Headquarters on 10 Jan 1945.

Michael J. Amrich

ASN 6895873, Private, USAC. Evacuated 2 December 1943.

Robert Andrews

ASN 19115375, Corporal, Allied Air Force. Reported to the Tenth Military District on 26 Feb 1945. On DS with the Force Radio Section, Tenth Military District, for two months. Evacuated on 26 Apr 1945.

Robert B. Ball

ASN O-888819m Captain, Signal Corps. Reported to Tenth Military District on 3 Dec 1942. Pfc in the Hqs, 5th Air Base Group. Captured by the Japs; escaped

191

and joined the Mindanao Guerrillas. Commissioned 2nd Lieut, Inf, USFIP, on 3 Dec 1942. Commissioned temporary 2nd Lieut, AUS, Hq, USAFFE, on 4 Jan 1944. CO, Signal Detachment and Radio Officer on 24 Dec 1942. CO, FRS, Tenth Military District, on 8 May 1943. Promoted 1st Lieut on 26 April 1943; promoted Captain, Signal Corps, on 11 Sept 1943. Sent on mission to the areas garrisoned by the Tenth Military District on 30 Dec 1943. Relieved as CO, FRS, Tenth Military District, on 13 Dec 1943 to report to Maj CHARLES, CE, AUS, for assignment.

Howard Bates

Private, Air Corps; died 10 July 1942.

Thomas R. Baxter

ASN 19014929, Captain, Inf. Reported to the Tenth Military District, 1 Dec 1942. Born in Mt. Trumble, Arizona, 24 Dec 1916; High School Student; a Private in the 89th USAAC; promoted to Sgt, USAAC. Commissioned 2nd Lieut, Tenth MD, on 1 Dec 1942; promoted 1st Lieut, 1 Oct 1943; promoted Captain, CO, Anakan Sector, 110th Division; Liaison Officer for the Commanding Officer, Tenth Military District, with the 13th Air Force, USAFFE, and ordered to report to Commanding General, USAFFE, in March 1945.

Kenneth L. Bayley

ASN 6296797, 2nd Lieut, Inf. Reported to the Tenth Military District on 1 Jun 1943. Born in Plainview, Texas, on 11 Nov. 1921. High School graduate; 10 months in 131st Field Artillery, Texas. Enlisted in USAAC on 16 Nov 1939. 2nd Class Aircraft Mechanic; Graduate Air Corps Teach. School of Engineer; 14th Bomb Squad, 19th Group, AC. Commissioned 2nd Lieut, Tenth Military District, USFIP, on 7 Nov 1943. From Pfc, AC, assigned in FRS, Tenth Military District. Evacuated on 27 Feb 1944.

Julian Benac

ASN 19051297, 2nd Lieut, Inf. Reported to the Tenth Military District. Born in Allison, New Mexico, on 3 Jun 1919. Enlisted USAC on 10 Jan 1941 as Pvt; Mechanic, 32nd and 30th Bombard Squad, 19th Bombardment Group. Commissioned 2nd Lieut Inf on 1 Jun 1943, Tenth Military District. Executive Officer, 112th Regt, 109th Division.

Leo A. Bolens

ASN O-426888, Capt. Inf. Reported to the Tenth Military District on 15 May 1943. Reported and assigned to the 110th Division, Tenth Military District, after his escape from the enemy concentration camp. Commissioned 1st Lieut on 15 May 1943; Agent Officer, Farm Project (Landing Field) No. 1; transferred to Hq, Tenth Military District; promoted Captain 1 Sep 1943. His former organization was the 21st Pursuit Squadron. Killed in action in Balingbing, Kolambugan, Lanao on 22 Jan 1944.

Alexander Rankin Bonner

ASN 6583746, Capt Inf. Reported to the Tenth Military District on 1 June 1943. Born in Calgary, Alt., Canada on 31 Jan 1920. ACTS graduate on 2 Aug 1944. Enlisted in the Army on 20 Nov 1939. Reported to the Tenth Military District and commissioned 2nd Lieut on 1 Jun 1943; promoted 1st Lieut on 16 Aug 1944. Commanding Officer, MT Bn, Tenth Military District. Promoted Capt Inf on 6 May 1945. Ordered to report to the 4th Replacement Depot USAFFE ON 5 May 1945.

Robert V. Bowler

ASN O-294619, Colonel, reported to the Tenth Military District in Nov 1942. Born in Medical Lake, Washington; Major, assigned Commanding Officer of the 111th Inf Regt on 15 Nov 1942. Promoted Lt-Col on 14 Dec 1943; Commanding Officer, 109th Division, on 14 Mar 1943; Chief of Staff, HQ, Tenth Military District; promoted Colonel on 1 Mar 1945; Liaison Officer for Commanding Officer, 106th Division, on 8 May 1945. Placed on temporary duty with Hq, Tenth Corps on 23 June 1945.

Durward L. Brooks

ASN 6281619, 1st Lieut. Reported to the Tenth Military District on 1 Jun 1943. Born in Lohn, Texas, on 14 Feb 1916. Sgt, Air Corps, 28th Bombardment Squadron, 19th Group. Commissioned 2nd Lieut, Tenth Military District, USFIP; Signal Officer, 106th Division; attached to Radio Section as Code Officer on 8 Sept 1944. Promoted 1st Lieut 16 Aug 1944. Enlisted USA on 31 Nov 1937 to 26 Jan 1939. Graduated Clark Field Radio General School. Ordered to report to 4th Replacement Depot on 5 May 1945.

Oscar G. Brown

ASN 18046073, Private USAC. Born in Oakland Avenue on 22 May 1942. 440th Ordnance Co; High School graduate. Enlisted at Fort Logan, Colorado. Left for SWPA on 28 Dec 1944.

Edward W. Browning

ASN 13034981, 2nd Lieut, Inf. Reported to the Tenth Military District on 1 July 1942. Born in War Eagle, West Virginia on 20 Apr 1920. 4th year High School. Enlisted in the Army on 13 Jun 1941 in Roanoke, Virginia, as Pvt, 30th Squad, 19th Bomb, arrived Manila 27 Oct 1941 and stationed at Clark Field; Mindanao 1 Jan 1942, stationed at Bugo. Did not surrender. Commissioned 2nd Lieut from Sergeant on 1 Jul 1943. 5Assigned to 109th Division on 10 Aug 1943; Corps Radio Section "A" Corps on 5 Aug 1944. On duty with G-3, Tenth Military District on 27 Oct 1944. Ordered to proceed to Hq, USAFFE, on 19 February 1945.

Anthony Bujnowski

ASN 6828122, 2nd Lieut, Inf. Reported to the Tenth Military District on 1

Aug 1943; on duty with 109th Division for one year and five months. Evacuated on 4 January 1945.

Andrew Thomas Bukovinsky

ASN O-890200, 2nd Lieut, Inf. Reported to the Tenth Military District in May 1944. Born in Greensburg, Penn. 2nd Lieut Inf 101st Field Artillery, 101st Division on 10 May 1942, stationed at Aroman, Bukidnon. Requested repatriation. Assigned to 106th Division due to poor health; ordered to proceed to Leyte on 15 December 1944.

John F. Cain

ASN 6906281, 2nd Lieut, Inf, reported to the Tenth Military District on 5 May 1944. Assigned to the FRS, Tenth Military District.

Marvin Head Campbell

ASN O-890421, 2nd Lieut, Inf, reported to the Tenth Military District 6 May 1944. Assigned Ordnance Officer, 106th Division for 8 months. Evacuated 21 Feb 1945. Born in Meansville, Ga., 17 March 1912. Enlisted as Pvt in "A" Troop, 11th Cavalry on 25 November 1938. Discharged and reinstated 31st Inf, "A" Co, 26 Feb 1940. Transferred to 808 MP Company (Manila) in September 1941; 3 years High School. Commissioned 2nd Lieut, Inf, USAFFE, 51st Regt, 51st Division 5 Mar 1942, Bataan. Reported to 118th Regt, 106th Div, 6 May 1944; Agent Officer for 106th Division; transferred to "A" Corps Headquarters. Ordered to report to Commanding General, USAFFE 21 Feb 1945.

Lucien V. Campeau

ASN W2115938, 2nd Lieut, Sig C, reported to the Tenth Military District on 1 June 1944. Warrant Officer, AUS, 5217 Reconnaissance Battalion, appointed 2nd Lieut, Sig C, 1 May 1945. Instructed to report to the Hq, 8th Army, 19 March 1944.

Timothy C. Casey

ASN 6954402, 1st Lieut, Inf, reported to the Tenth Military District on 1 Jun 1943. Born in Akron, Colorado on 12 Feb 1920. Enlisted Pvt, 351st Ordnance Co, 19th Bombardment Group at Fort Logan, Colorado, 24 May 1940; promoted to Pfc in March 1941; to Corporal in December 1941. Commissioned 2nd Lieut 1 Jun 1943, Tenth Military District; promoted 1st Lieut 16 Aug 1944. Chief Water Transport, 106th Division; Code Officer, Radio Station. Ordered to report to 4th Replacement Depot on 27 Apr 1945.

Reid C. Chamberlain

ASN 265983, USMC, 1st Lieut, reported to the Tenth Military District on 15 Jan 1943. Born in Parkin, Arkansas, 1 Apr 1919. Trained 1 year in the Infantry and 9 months in anti-aircraft. Commissioned 2nd Lieut, Inf, 5 Jan 1943, Tenth Military District, USFIP; promoted 1st Lieut on 1 Oct 1943; 3 years and 6 months active duty with the Marine Corps; 2 years Reserve Marine Corps. 4½ years High School. On duty with the Tenth Military District. Repatriated 14 Nov 1943.

Bruce Chapman

Private 1st class, AUS. Died 14 April 1943.

Gerald S. Chapman

ASN O-1686506, 2nd Lieut OS, reported to the Tenth Military District on 28 Mar 1943. S/Sgt, 440th Ordnance Company Aviation Bombardment. Commissioned 2nd Lieut, AUS, Ordnance Dept, 24 Dec 1944. Advance Echelon, USAFFE. Radio Section, Tenth Military District Headquarters.

Clyde Clement Childress

ASN O-371217, Lieut-Col, Inf, reported to Tenth Military District on 20 Nov 1942. Born in Ft. Worth, Texas, on 22 Jul 1917. Junior Officer of "C" Co, 31st Inf, Manila on 8 May 1941 to 25 Aug 1941. On DS with the 2nd Bn, 61st Inf, PA. Machine Instructor at Dingle, Iloilo, Philippines, from 1 Sep to 30 Oct 1941; Bn Cmdr, 2nd Bn, 61st Inf, PA, Lanao on 10 May 1942. Capt, 61st Inf, PA. Chief of Staff, 110th Division, Tenth Military District, from Nov 1942 to May 1944; Commanding Officer, 107th Division. Promoted to Maj, Tenth Military District on 20 Nov 1942; Maj AUS on 20 Dec 1943; Hq USAFFE; Lt-Col, Tenth Military District on 20 Sep 1944. Relieved CO, 107th Division, 29 Dec. 1944.

Noel R. Chiota

Private. Died on 14 April 1943.

Edward O. Chmielewski

2nd Lieut, Sig C, reported to the 10th MD on 6 Dec 1942. Assigned Radio Operator, FRS, 10th MD for 1 year and 2 months.

Michael Chuckray

ASN 668–55, Radio Technician, Seventh Intelligence Fleet. Reported to Tenth Military District on 1 Jan 1945, assigned DS with FRS, Tenth MD. In charge of Radio Maintenance Section, FRS.

Jack Roland Clarke

ASN 6936730, 1st Lieut, Inf, reported to the 10th MD, 23 Apr 1943. Born in Topeka, Kansas, 24 Feb 1919. High School graduate; Civilian pilot; Pvt, USAC, 13th Bombardment Squad, from 20 Dec 1939 to 3 May 1941. Commissioned 2nd Lieut, Inf, 10th MD, on 23 Apr 1943; promoted 1st Lieut, 31 Jan 1944. Commanding Officer "I" Co, 112th Inf, 109th Division in Dec 1943. In charge of Radio Station TAB, 109th Division, March 1944. Executive Officer, 112th Inf June 1944 until ordered to proceed to GHQ, USAFFE, on 18 Feb 1945.

Joseph Philip Coe

ASN 7000444. 1st Lieut, Sig C, reported to the 10th MD on 29 Oct 1944. Born in Coleanor, Alabama 27 Jan 1920. High School graduate; Staff Sgt, USAC, 91st Bombardment Squad. Survivor of POW Transport sunk of Sindangan, Zamboanga, in September 1944. Joined Mindanao Guerrillas with FRS, 10th MD. Commissioned 2nd Lieut, Sig C 24 Nov 1944; promoted 1st Lieut 20 Apr 1945. Requested repatriation and left 20 April 1945.

Earl A. Cook

ASN 6130149, Pfc, AC, reported to the 10th MD, 19 Oct 1945, assigned in 108th Division; evacuated on 22 Jan 1944.

Richard L. Cook

ASN O-377258, 1st Lieut, reported to 10 MD on 20 Sept 1944. 1st Lieut, 59th Inf (PS) USA. Survivor of POW Transport sunk off Sindangan, Zamboanga in Sept 1944; on duty with G-3 Tenth MD; promoted 1st Lieut 21 Jan 1942; left for GHQ 6 Dec 1944.

Robert Myres Crump

ASN O-1688141, Capt Inf. Reported to the 10th MD on 8 Nov 1943. Born in Brazil, Indiana, on 5 Jun 1915. Degrees: B.A., M.A. Volunteered for service 9 Dec 1941 as civilian. Commissioned 2nd Lieut 10 Jan 1943; assigned Transportation Officer, Hq Bamar Prox Brigade. Reverted. Served the 110th Division, 10th MD, and called back to active duty as 2nd Lieut, Inf, 10th MD on 1 Jul 1943. Assigned as Asst FOM, 10th MD, 17 Nov 1943. Commission of 8 Nov 1943 confirmed by Hq, USAFFE, 4 Sep 1944. Promoted 1st Lieut 9 Mar 1944 and Capt on 1 Apr 1945. Ordered to report to 4th Replacement Depot 15 April 1945.

Bill Emery Dallenback

ASN 17027499, 2nd Lieut Inf. Reported to the 10 MD 1 Jun 1943, assigned Radio Operator, 109th Division for 6 months. Evacuated 22 Jan 1944.

Lincoln Hall Da Pron

ASN 6980094, Capt, Sig C, reported to the 10th MD on 23 Jun 1943. Born in St. Paul, Minn., on 10 Aug 1916; High School graduate. Studied journalism; 3 years service in the Air Corp as Sgt. Joined Air Corps in 1939. Commissioned 2nd Lieut on 23 Jun 1943. Promoted to 1st Lieut on 19 Jan 1944; Capt on 18 Jan 1945. On duty 109th Division and FRS, Tenth MD. Ordered to report to 3th Replacement Depot, Ha USAFFE on 30 Jun 1945.

George B. Davis

ASN 295828, 2nd Lieut Inf. Reported to the 10th MD on 3 Oct 1943. On duty with 125th Inf.

Marvin H. De Vries

ASN 2233318, 1st Lieut, USN Sig C, reported to the 10th MD 16 Dec 1942. Commissioned 2nd Lieut 16 Dec 1942. Assigned with MT Co, Hq 10th MD; assigned with 108th Division, 10th MD on 25 Sep 1943; to FRS, 10th MD 3 Nov 1943. Promoted 1st Lieut 11 Sep 1943. Evacuated 27 Feb 1944.

Frank Divino

ASN 19038803, 2nd Lieut Inf. Reported to the 10th MD 1 Oct 1943. Assigned in the FRS 10th MD for 1 year and 3 months. Born in Garfield, Utah, 6 Feb 1921. Enlisted at "MARCH" Field, California on 3 Mar 1941 in the QMS, 89th LM Battalion. Pvt in USAC. Commissioned as 2nd Lieut 1 Oct 1943. Assigned to duty with 110th Division 10th MD 2 Oct 1943. Transferred to duty with FRS 1 Nov 1943. Evacuated 6 Feb 1944.

Michael Dobervich

Capt, Infantry. Reported to the 10th MD 11 May 1943. Born in Iventon, Minnesota on 10 Oct 1915. A years college R.O.T.C. B.S. in Agricultural Engineering. Commissioned 1st Lt, Marine Corps 1 Jul 1939; promoted Capt, USFIP, 10th MD, 11 May 1943; Liaison Officer and FFO. Evacuated on 14 November 1943.

Vincent K. Douglass

ASN 6579268 Capt, Sig reported to the 10th MD on 1 Dec 1942. Born in Dalles, Oregon on 8 Apr 1914; High School graduate; Air Corps Mechanic; Sgt, 30th Bombardment Squad. Commissioned 2nd Lieut, USFIP, 10th MD, 1 Dec 1942. Assigned Provost Marshal 2nd Bn, 111th Inf Regt. Assigned in the Communication Section, 109th Div on 2 April. Promoted 1st Lt on 17 Dec 1943; changed his branch of service to Sig C on 10 Jan 1945; assigned Signal Supply Section in charge 109th Division on 3 Jan 1945; promoted Captain. Ordered to proceed to 4th Replacement Depot, Hq, USAFFE.

Frank W. Duff

ASN 6296419, 1st Lieut QMS, reported to the 10th MD 1 April 1943. Born in Childress, Texas on 9 Jun 1918. S/Sgt USAC on 4 Oct 1939. Commissioned 2nd Lt, Inf, 5 Jan 1943; Branch of service changed to QMS, 1 Apr 1943. Promoted 1st Lieut 1 April 1943. Acting S-4, Imbatug Sector 9 Nov 1942 to 5 Jan 1943; Procurement Officer, HQ 10th MD, 18 Mar 1943 to 2 Aug 1943; G-4, 108th Division from 2 Aug 1943 to 13 Sep 1943; Finance Officer, Farm Project (Landing Field) #1 from 13 Sep 1945 to Oct 1945. Ordered to proceed to SWPA on 14 Nov 1945.

William E. Dyess

ASN O-22526, Major, Inf, reported to the 10th MD on 15 May 1943; on duty with 110th Division; evacuated in July 1943.

Bruce G. Elliott

ASN 3762211, USN. Reported to the 10th MD, 8 Jul 1943. Born in Garden City, Kansas in 1923. Coxswain, USN, USS "TANKER." Arrived 8 Aug 1943 from Palawan. Surrendered on the fall of Corregidor on 6 May 1942 and concentrated in Princesa Concentration Camp, Palawan. Escaped and reported to the 10th MD. Assigned on duty with 125th Inf Regt. Evacuated on 17 February 1944.

James L. Evans Jr.

ASN O-556781, Maj MC. Reported to the 10th MD on 13 Dec 1944. Born in Philadelphia, Pa., on 6 Dec 1912. MD, Bachelor of Science in Biology and English, licensed Radio Operator; commissioned 1st Lieut ORC June 1937, promoted Captain (permanent) July 1941, 2nd Corps Area; Post Surgeon, Ft. Tilden, N.Y., on 31 Jan 1941 to 20 Jun 1948. Detachment Commander and Chief Neuropsychiatric Section, 5th Station Hospital, Australia from 13 Feb 1942 to July 1942; Surgeon and Adjutant, Hq Base Section 6, Australia from July 1942 to 25 Jan 1943; Chief of Record Section, 3rd Medical Supply Depot, Base Section 5, 25 Jan 1943. Assigned by the GHQ to the 10th MD and was designated Acting CO, FRS, 10th MD; promoted to Major, AUS by GHQ, USAFFE, 28 Jan 1944; ordered to proceed to GHQ, USAFFE for sick leave on 17 Jan 1945.

Beverly Perry Farrens

ASN 6953549, reported to the 10th MD on 16 Feb 1943. Born in Marysville, Missouri on 30 May 1917. Pfc in the Air Corps, 14th Bombardment Squad, 19th Group. Commissioned 2nd Lieut in the 10th MD on 16 Feb 1943; promoted 1st Lieut, Sig C on 8 Mar 1944; Capt on 1 May 1945. Assigned G-4, Hq 10 MD on 16 Feb 1943; to Force Radio Net on 1 Oct 1943. Ordered to proceed to 4th Replacement Depot on 30 Jun 1943.

Fred Sims Faust

ASN 6929112, 1st Lieut, Inf. Reported to the 10th MD on 19 Feb 1943. Born in South Carolina 27 Aug 1921. High School graduate. Commissioned 2nd Lieut 19 Feb 1943; promoted to 1st Lieut 1 Oct 1943. CO, 110th Division Special Troops. Commended for his attack on Buenavista, Agusan, inflicting 40 to 50 wounded or killed. Repatriated 10 Jan 1945.

Frederick A. Feigel

Capt, QMS, reported to the 10th MD on 1 Oct 1943. Born in Louisville, KY., on 5 Jan 1901; served as civilian in the 81st Inf, USAFFE. Commissioned 1st Lieut on 1 Oct 1943, QMS, in the 10th MD; promoted Capt on 15 Feb 1944. Assigned in the QMS and then 107th Division; Chief of Staff and G-4 on 4 May 1944. Killed in action on 26 Jul 1944 while on inspection trip.

Alfred Fernandez

ASN 6517769, 1st Lieut. Reported to 10th MD 1 Dec 1942. Born in Hilo, Hawaii on 8 Jan 1905. M/Sgt, USAC. CO, 1st Bn, 110th Inf Div. Ordered to report to SWPA, 17 Dec 1944.

Wendell W. Fertig

ASN O-254976, Colonel, Corps of Engineers, led the Mindanao Guerrillas on 18 Sep 1942 and organized the 10th Military District (MD). Relieved by Colonel Charles W. Hedges on 23 Jun 1945.

George Finnegan

ASN 121394211, 2nd Lieut, Sig C. Reported to the 10th MD on 1 Jun 1944. Born in Geneva, New York 13 Mar 1921. S/Sgt, USAAF; commissioned 2nd Lieut, Sig C, 4 Dec 1944. On DS with FRS, 10th MD. Ordered to proceed to Hq, Far Eastern Air Force Weather Group, 26 Apr 1945.

Paul F. Flowers

ASN 19049569, Pvt USAC. Died 27 July 1942.

Glen E. Gamber

ASN 13024686, 2ne Lieut, Inf. Reported to the 10th MD on 15 Jan 1943. Assigned Code Officer, 110th Division for 10 months. Evacuated 17 Jan 1945.

James Leonard Garland

ASN 7003822, Capt, Sig C. Reported to the 10th MD on 1 Jun 1943. Born in Erwin, Tennessee on 1 Mar 1921. High School graduate; graduated USAC Technical School, Hickam Field, Hawaii. Pfc in the Air Corps. Commissioned 2nd Lieut, Inf, 1Jun 1943; promoted 1st Lieut, Inf, 1 Jun 1944; Capt on 18 Jan 1945. Change of branch of service to Signal Corps on 18 Jan 1945; on duty with 109th Division 1 Jun 1943; FRS on 25 Oct 1943; Officer in Charge Message Center FRS on 6 Jan 1945; Commanding Officer, FRS and Communication Officer, 10th MD on 30 Jun 1945.

Robert E. Gentry

ASN O-288840, 1st Lieut, Inf. Reported to the 10th MD, 1 Nov 1942. CO, "D" Co, 115th Inf, for 5 months; on duty with G-4, 10th MD, for 5 months. Repatriated 15 Feb 1944.

Paul A. Gill

ASN 6570724, 2nd Lieut, Sig C. Assigned on duty with FRS, 10th MD for one year. Evacuated 7 Feb 1944.

Dewitt Glover

ASN 3758436, 1st Lieut, Inf. Reported to the 10th MD, 6 Dec 1942. On duty with Hq 10th MD. Repatriated 29 Sept 1943.

John W. Grant

ASN 6999542, 2nd Lieut, Inf. Reported to the 10th MD on 1 June 1943. Assigned to 109th Division. Died on 1 Nov 1943.

Samuel Grashio

ASN O-412503, Capt, Inf. Reported to the 110th Division, 10th MD in May 1943; assigned in Farm Project (Landing Field) #1, 10th MD on 1 Jul 1943. Born in Spokane, Washington on 1 Apr 1918. Two years in college. Commissioned 2nd Lieut 26 Apr 1941, AC. Promoted 1st Lieut 11 May 1943; Captain 1 Sep 1943. Proceeded to Hq USAFFE, 29 Sep 1943.

James R. Grinstead

ASN O-888857, LT-Col, AUS. Reported to the 10th MD on 19 Feb 1943. Born in Ridgeway, Mo., 5 Nov 1897. Served in "M" Co, 1st Inf, Oklahoma, 1st Raillery as 1st Lieut from Dec 1919 to 1921. Assigned in "D" Co, 15th Inf, Headquarters Company, 31st Inf, from April 1923 to 1926 as Private, Corporal, Sergeant and Staff Sergeant; with Philippine Constabulary from April 1926 to November 1931 as 3rd Lieut, 2nd Lieut, 1st Lieut and Captain. Student of the Philippine Constabulary Academy; on duty with the Provincial Commander, Lanao; with the Intelligence Division, Manila; participated in Mindanao and Sulu Campaign. Resigned in Nov 1931 to engage in business; established a coconut plantation in Malabang, Davao, Salaman, Cotabato. Reserve Officer in the United States Army; 2nd Lieut March 1924 to 1926, 1st Lieut from March 1926 to 1941. Battle campaigns; Mexican Border in 1913, AEF in France—April 1918 to January 1919 in St. Mihiel and Mousse-Argonne.

High School graduate, 1914; University of Kansas, September 1914 to April 1917; called to duty as Capt, Inf 19 Feb 1943. Captaincy in AUS confirmed by Hq, USAFFE 16 Feb 1944; promoted Major, Inf June 1943; confirmed by USAFFE 5 May 1944; promoted to Lt-Col 2 Nov 1943.

Assignments: Temporary assignment with the Headquarters, 10 MD on 19 Feb 1943; to the 109th Division on 25 Mar 1943; Commanding Officer, 109th Inf Regt, 109 Division on 7 Apr 1943; Chief of Staff, 109th Division on 25 Jun 1943; Commanding Officer, 109th Division 1 Nov 1943; Commanding Officer, 106th Inf Div, PA, 10th MD, 25 Jun 1945. Commended as good organizer and had the finest intelligence coverage in Mindanao.

Cyrill A. Grosh

ASN 19028955, 2nd Lieut, Inf. Reported to the 10th MD on 1 Nov 1942. Assigned to 110th Division as contact man for one year. Evacuated 16 Nov 1943.

James D. Haburne

ASN O-890327, 1st Lieut, Inf. Reported to the 10th MD 9 Feb 1944. Assigned Code Officer, FRS, 10th MD. Repatriated 2 Dec. 1944.

Arthur R. Hage, Jr.

ASN 7022833, 1st Lieut, Inf. Reported to the 10th MD on 9 Feb 1944. Assigned Code Officer, FRS, 10th MD. Evacuated 19 Dec 1944.

James E. Halkyard

2nd Lieut, Inf. Reported to the 10th MD in Dec 1942. Evacuated in Jan 1943.

George O. Hall

ASN 6938070, 1st Lieut, Sig C. Reported to the 10th MD on 5 Jan 1943. On duty with FRS, 10th MD for 2 years and 8 months. Evacuated 20 Jan 1945.

Charles Hansen

ASN O-600183, Capt, OS. Reported to the 10th MD 11 Apr 1943. Born in Syracuse, N.Y. on 4 March 1890; High School graduate. Studied M.E. University of Syracuse; Commissioned USA, Reserve Capt, OS in August 1919; called to active duty on 8 Dec 1941 but unable to report. Reported to 110th Division 10th MD 11 Apr 1943, assigned Procurement Officer; assigned Liaison Officer 110th Division on 11 Dec 1944. Evacuated 10 Jan 1945.

Anton J. Haratik

ASN O-1686153, Capt, Inf. Reported to the 10 MD on 1 Dec 1942. Born in Philipps, Wisconsin on 4 May 1916; High School graduate. Airplane Mechanic, 19th Bombardment Group, Hq & Hq Co, as Pvt. Joined the USFIP, 10th MD, and commissioned 2nd Lieutenant on 1 Dec 1942. USFIP; commissioned 2nd Lieut, AUS on 11 Jul 1944; promoted 1st Lieut on 1 Oct 1943, USFIP; promoted Capt. USFIP on 1 Jan 1944; assigned Agent Officer, 110th Div, 24 Dec 1943; CO, 112th Prov Bn, 107th Inf. Rated an excellent Commanding Officer by his Chief.

Frank Harayda

ASN 6978648, 2nd Lieut, Inf. Reported to the 10th MD on 16 Nov 1943.

Jack Hawkins

Capt, Ing. Reported to the 10th MD 11 May 1943. Born in Teston, Texas on 25 Oct 1916, Graduated from U.S. Naval School; commissioned 2nd Lieut (Reg) USMC 1 Jun 1939; promoted 1st Lieut (Reg) 2 Dec 1941; served in 4th Marines Shanghai from 17 Jul 1940 to 27 Nov 1941; served in Bataan and Corregidor during this war and captured by the Japs on 6 May 1942. Reported to 10th MD and promoted Capt 11 May 1943; assigned with G-2 Section, 110th Div, 10 MD. Proceeded to GHQ, USAFFE, 14 Nov 1943.

Elmer R. Hayes

ASN 19024031, Corp, USAC. Reported to the 10th MD on 1 Jan 1944. Assigned in 110th Div. Evacuated on 15 Dec. 1944.

Charles William Hedges

ASN O-540796, Colonel, Inf. Reported to the 10th MD on 2 Oct 1942; born in Springdale, Washington 14 Sep 1896; Mechanic Engineer Certificate and License, 3½ years in the United States Army from 1917 to 1920; Capt, Inf,, AUS, USAFFE on 18 Nov 1943; promoted Major, USFIP 18 Nov 1942 and Lt-Col, USFIP, 13 Dec 1942; promoted to Colonel, Inf, 16 May 1945. Helped Col FERTIG in organizing the guerrillas, 10 MD; Commanding Officer, 108th Division, 13 Dec 1942 and at same time Deputy Chief of Staff, 10th MD on 14 Oct 1943. Chief of Staff, "A" Corps, West Mindanao (WM), 10th MD on 9 Oct 1944; Commanding Officer, 10th MD, relieving Col Fertig.

Truman Heminway

ASN 6081224, 1st Lieut, Inf. Reported to the 10th MD 1 Dec 1942. Assigned with the Coast Watcher Station FRS 10 MD for 10 months. Evacuated on 20 Oct 1944.

Earl G. Hilliard

ASN 19000241, 1st Lieut, Inf, reported to the 10 MD on 1 Jun 1943. On duty, Corps Radio Station, "A" Corps, Western Mindanao, for 6 months. Evacuated on 15 Jan 1945.

Jack W. Hoffman

ASN 636779, 2nd Lieut, Inf, 1 Jun 1943. Assigned in 109th Div for one year and six months. Evacuated 25 Dec 1944.

Mc (Max) E. Hoke

ASN 16041689, 2nd Lieut, Sig C. Reported to 10th MD 1 Jun 1944. Officer in Charge, Weather Control, Corps Radio Station, "A" Corps, Western Mindanao. Evacuated 16 Apr 1945.

Lowell G. Holder

ASN 6983959, Capt, Inf. Reported to 10th MD 24 Feb 1943. Born in Evansville, Indiana on 12 Apr 1921. High School graduate of AC Technical School; enlisted in the ?C, 13 Nov 1939 as Sergeant. Reported to 10th MD 24 Feb 1943 and commissioned 2nd Lieut on 25 Feb 1943. Promoted to 1st Lieut on 19 Jan 1944; promoted Capt 1 Apr 1945. Also assigned JO in the MT Co, 10th MD Hq on 24 Feb 1943. Also a Code Officer on 27 Nov 1943 and assigned to Davao area in March 1944. Ordered to proceed to the 4th Replacement Depot, Hq, USAFFE on 26 Jun 1945.

Earl C. Homan, Jr.

ASN 6946985, 2nd Lieut, Inf. Reported to the 10th MD 1 Nov 1943. Assigned in the FRS for one year and five months. Evacuated 28 Feb 1944.

John L. Houlihan

ASN 212469, 2nd Lieut, Inf. Reported to the 10 MD in Dec 1942. On duty with 110th Div, G-3 Section for six months. Evacuated 14 Nov 1943.

Forrest A. Howard

ASN 19002853, 1st Lieut, Inf. Reported to 10 MD on 6 Jan 1943. On duty for nine months with 109th Div; with Corps Radio Section, "A" Corps, Western Mindanao for nine months. Evacuated on 12 May 1945.

William H. Johnson

USN SN 2832703, 1st Lieut, Sig C. Reported to 10th MD 3 Dec 1942. Assigned with the Coast Watch Station, FRS, 10th MD in Zamboanga area for 2 years and 2 months. Evacuated 9 May 1945.

Erling H. Jonassen

ASN 6937757, 1st Lieut, Inf. Reported to 10th MD on 1 Jun 1943. CO, Sig Co, 109th Division.

Thomas Walker Jurika

ASN O-890348, Capt, QMC. Reported to 10th MD, 3 May 1943. Born in Zamboanga, Philippines on 9 Jan 1914. High School graduate; two years College, USA. Commissioned 1st Lieut, QMC, 19 Feb 1942 by Philippine Dept, USA. Assigned U.S. Army Transport Service, Philippines. Promoted Capt, 5 May 1943 in the USFIP, 10th MD. Assigned in the 108th Div, 10th MD on 3 May 1943; on SD with GHQ, 10th MD 5 May 1943. Assigned in the Hq, 10th MD, 5 Nov 1943.

Albert Roy Kirby, Jr.

ASN 6291177, Sgt, USAC. Reported to 10th MD 12 Apr 1943. Born in Colorado Springs, Colorado on 29 Sep 1919; High School graduate; 3 years in USAC Bomb Squad, as Flying Chief Crew, in Charge of Motor Maintenance, 110th Div on 6 May 1943. Killed in action 3 Sep 1943.

William A. Knortz

ASN 6909312, Capt Inf. Reported to the 10th MD and commissioned 2nd Lieut on 1 Dec 1942; promoted to 1st Lieut on 12 Jan 1943; promoted to Capt, 10 Feb 1943. Assigned Agent Officer, 114th Inf Regt. Died 11 Sep 1943.

John Kolodie

ASN 6877573, Pvt, QMSC. Evacuated 2 Dec 1943.

William F. Konko

ASN 2831701., 1st Lieut, Sig C. Reported to the 10th MD 26 Dec 1942. Assigned Radio Operator, FRS, 10th MD for 1 year and 8 months. Evacuated on 29 Dec 1944.

John Korysinski

ASN 16021372, 2nd Lieut, Inf.

Richard B. Lang

ASN 6571980, 1st Lieut, Inf. Reported to 10th MD, 1 May 1943. On duty with the 107th Div for 8 months; 110th Div for 1 year. Evacuated on 5 Jan 1945.

Donald J. Le Couvre

ASN 13011259, Major, Inf. Reported to 10th MD, 1 Dec 1942. Born in Bulgar, Penn., on 19 Feb 1916; attended Ordnance School, FA, Hawaii; AC Aviation Mechanic; Clark Field, Philippines, Pvt, AC; Commissioned 2nd Lieut, Inf, 10 MD on 1 Feb 1943; promoted 1st Lieut, Inf, 1 Oct 1943; promoted Captain 19 Aug 1944; promoted Major, Inf, 15 Apr 1945. Assignments: 9 Mar 1943, Observer in areas of 3rd Bn, 115th Inf, 105th Div; Ex O, FRS, 10th MD on 14 Oct 1943; CO, 1st Sep Bn; CO, 121st Inf Regt, on 20 Aug 1944; ordered to proceed to CINCAF-PAC on 17 Jun 1945.

Leonard Le Couvre

ASN 13009106, 1st Lieut, Sig C. Reported to 10th MD, 29 Jan 1943. Assigned as Code Officer, FRS, 10th MD. Evacuated on 5 Jan 1945.

John L. Lewis

ASN 3455913, 1st Lieut, Inf. Reported to 10th MD 12 Dec 1942. CO MTC, 10th MD for 1 year. CO, CTC, "A" Corps, Western Mindanao for 2 months. Evacuated 3 Apr 1945.

William Watt Lowry

ASN O-268916, Capt, ON. Reported to the 10th MD, 13 Apr 1943. Born in Brooklyn, N.Y. 1st Lieut, CE; changed his branch of service when he reported to the 10 MD from CE to Inf, 13 Apr 1943; promoted to Capt, 1 May 1943; assigned on SD with Hq 10th MD. In charge of Farm Project (Landing Field) #2, Balingbing, Lanao. Died 19 June 1943.

Ray J. Lozano

ASN 18155440, 2nd Lieut, Sig C. Reported to 10th MD on 1 Jun 1944. Weather Control Officer, 121st Inf, for 9 months. Evacuated 4 Apr 1945.

Aldo F. Maccagli

ASN 6980070, Pfc. Assigned to 110th Div. Evacuated 15 Nov 1943.

William Madison

ASN 36048730, S/Sgt. Reported to 10th MD on 26 Feb 1945. Assigned in the FRS, 10th MD. Evacuated 26 Apr 1945.

Andrew Mancuso

ASN 32028092, 2nd Lieut, Inf. Reported to the 10th MD on 1 Dec 1942. Assigned to 110th Div for 2 years and 2 months. Evacuated 10 Jan 1945.

Clayton A. Manners, Jr.

ASN 6914375, 1st Lieut, Inf, reported to 10th MD 1 Jun 1943. On duty with 109th Div for 3 months. In charge, Manticao Farm Project (Landing Field). Evacuated on 29 Apr 1945.

Paul H. Marshall

ASN O-1686161, Lt-Col, Inf. Reported to 10th MD on 11 May 1943. Born in McCows, Kansas on 27 Jun 1911. High School. Commanding Officer, 114th Inf for 1 year and 4 months; Commanding Officer, 110th Div for 5 months.

Harold D. Martin

ASN O-888847, Capt Sig C. Reported to 10th MD 16 Dec 1942. Born in Mayfield, Kentucky 7 Jul 1919. High School graduate. Enlisted USAAC on 28 Nov 1939; attended Army Air Corps Technical School for 7 months as Air Mechanic; Sgt, 1st Class, Air Mechanic in the USAAC. Commissioned 2nd Lieut in the 10th MD on 16 Dec 1942. Promoted 1st Lieut, USFIP 1 Sep 1943 and Capt, USFIP 1 Oct 1944. Commissioned 2nd Lieut AUS by GHQ, USAFFE, 9 Feb 1944; promoted 1st Lieut AUS by GHQ, USAFFE 24 May 1944.

Ernest E. McClish

ASN O296967, Lt-Col, Inf. Reported to 10th MD on 19 Nov 1942. Born in Wilburton, Oklahoma on 22 Feb 1910; College graduate; senior ROTC graduate; commissioned 2nd Lieut in April 1932 Reserve. Promoted to 1st Lieut in 1934; Capt in Aug 1939, permanent grade. Major on 23 Dec 1941; Lt-Col AUS 20 Nov 1942, USFIP, 10th MD; Lt-Col (temporary) AUS on 2 Dec 1943; promoted Major by Gen WAINWRIGHT, to Lt-Col, AUS by GHQ, USAFFE; assumed command of 110th Div, 10th MD on 20 Nov 1942. Relieved CO, 110th Div 23 January 1945.

James McClure

ASN O-990193, 1st Lieut, Inf. Reported to 10th MD on 1 Oct 1944. On duty G-2 Section, 10th MD for 2 months. Evacuated 2 Dec 1944.

Melvin H. McCoy

Lt-Comdr, USN. Proceeded to Hq, USAFFE in July 1943.

Warren L. McFadden

ASN 19028883, Pfc, USAC. Died on 10 May 1942.

Frank D. McGee

ASN O-3865, Lt-Col, Cavalry. Reported to 10th MD 10 Jan 1943. Born in Claremont, S.D., USA on 6 Sep 1889; U.S.-M.A. (West Point) 1915; 1st Lieut in 1916; Captain in 1917; Major in 1918—National Army; Major, USAFFE on 23 Dec 1941. Did not surrender. Commanding Officer, 2nd Inf Regt, Bukidnon-Cotabao Force on 10 Jan 1943. On SC with the 109th Div, 10 MD, 30 Jul 1943; Commanding Officer, 106th Div on 7 Oct 1943. Promoted Lt-Col on 1 Jul 1943; confirmed by USAFFE on 20 Dec 1943; on temporary duty with Tenth Corps Hq on 8 May 1945. Commanding Officer, 107th Inf, PA, 10th MD on 1 Jul 1945. Killed in action 7 Aug 1945.

Charles E. McGrath

ASN 13081616, 2nd Lieut, Sig C. Reported to 10th MD on 1 Jun 1944. Assigned Weather Control Officer, FRS, 10th MD for 10 months. Evacuated 26 Apr 1945.

Weyman L.McGuire

ASN 6266335, 2nd Lieut, MAC. Reported to 10th MD on 13 Dec 1942. Assigned Medical Supply Officer, 105th Div for 11 months; Medical Supply Officer, 10 MD. Evacuated 26 Mar 1945.

James E. McIntyre

ASN 6582459, 1st Lieut, Inf. Reported to 10th MD on 1 Dec 1942. Assigned Bn Comdr, 110th Inf, for 2 years. Evacuated 17 Dec 1944.

William F. McLaughlin

ASN O-890331, Major, Inf. Reported to 10th MD on 1 Oct 1942. Born in McKeesport, Pa., on 1 Aug 1918; attended High School in Chemical Warfare from 1937 to 1939; QM, 1939–1940—Inf, 1943; Instructor Chemical Warfare, PA; Ex O, 3rd Bn, 103rd Bn, 103rd Inf 1 Jan to 28 Feb 1942 as 2nd Lt; promoted to 1st Lt on 14 Mar 1943, 10th MD; promoted Capt on 1 Nov 1943; Major on 24 Sep 1944; promoted temporary 1st Lt AUS, by GHQ, USAFFE, 11 Jul 1944. CO, 112th Inf Regt, 109th Div; ordered to proceed to Hq, USAFFE on 28 May 1945.

James McNeil

ASN 658285, 1st Lieut, Inf. Reported to 10th MD on 1 Dec 1942. Assigned as Code Officer, Radio Section, 110th Div. Evacuated on 20 Apr 1945.

Stephen Mellnik

Major, CAC, passed the 110th Div before leaving for Australia in July 1943 without any personal record.

Leonard L. Merchant

ASN 62255032, 2nd Lieut, Inf. Reported to 10th MD 1 Jun 1943. Assigned MT CO, 110th Div. Evacuated 26 Jan 1944.

Walter R. Mester

1st Lieut. Reported to 10th MD on 19 Feb 1943. Assigned S-4 113th Inf for 1 year and 6 months. Evacuated on 27 Apr 1945.

Alma Bud Mills

ASN 6581151, Capt, Sig C. Reported to 10th MD 1 Aug 1943. Born in Evanston, Wyoming in 1920; High School student. With the Army Air Corps since 16 Oct 1939 as Corp; commissioned 2nd Lieut Sig C, 10th MD on 1 Aug 1943; promoted 1st Lieut on 19 Jan 1944; promoted Capt on 23 Jan 1945. Assigned in FRS, 10 MD, on 19 August 1943; on duty with FQM, 10th MD.

Leonard Minter

ASN 6223333, Sgt, USAC. Evacuated 29 Sep 1943.

Glynn W. Mitchell

ASN 6275077, Capt, Sig C. Reported to 10th MD on 24 May 1943; on duty with the FRS, 10th MD for 2 years; served in the Davao area. Proceeded to 4th Replacement Depot on 25 Jun 1945.

Thomas Mitsos

ASN 6914252, 1st Lieut, Inf. Reported to 10th MD 16 Dec 1942. Assigned Code Officer, FRS for 2 years. Evacuated 29 Dec 1944.

Willard Landis Money

ASN 6998768, Capt, Sig C. Reported to 10th MD in Dec 1942. Born in Point of Rocks, Maryland in 1923. Sgt in the USAC, 14th Bombardment Squad. Commissioned 2nd Lieut in the 10 MD on 1 Dec 1942; promoted 1st Lieut on 12 Jan 1943; promoted Capt on 1 Apr 1945. Assigned in FRS, 10th MD 1 Nov 1943. On duty with "A" Corps, Western Mindanao on 22 Jun 1944; Radio Officer of the 106th Div on 1 Jan 1945 to 22 Jun 1945.

Francis Napolillo, Jr.

ASN 2580667, 1st Lieut, Sig C. Reported to the 10th MD 16 Dec 1942. On duty with FRS, 10th MD for 10 months. Evacuated on 29 Sept 1943.

Bernard B. Nemzura

ASN 36006198, Pvt. Died 26 Feb 1943.

William L. Newman (or Neumann)

Pvt, USAC. Died in Nov 1942.

Frank O. Noel

ASN 2419049, 1st Lieut, Inf. Reported to 10th MD 26 Nov 1942. On duty with Div Provost Marshal, 110th Div for 10 months. Evacuated on 29 Sep 1943.

Leo O'Connor

ASN 14025849, 2nd Lieut, Inf. Reported to 10th MD on 15 Mar 1943. Assigned to the FRS, 10th MD for 8 months. Evacuated on 14 Nov 1943.

Elwood H. Offrett

ASN 3681644, 1st Lieut, QMS. Reported to 10th MD on 26 Oct 1942. On duty with G-4, 10th MD for 10 months. Evacuated on 29 Sep 1943.

Reece Agustus Oliver

Capt, Inf. Reported to 10th MD on 19 Apr 1943. Born in Akron (Fulton Co) Indiana on 1 Aug 1891. High School Graduate and Post Graduate work in Education. Attended Cadet Officer School, Philippine National Guard 5 Jul 1918. Commissioned 1st Lieut and assigned Adjutant, 1st Field Signal Bn, Philippine National Guard. Aide-de-Camp to Brig-Gen DENNIS P. QUINLAN, Camp Claudie. Promoted Capt, Supply Co. Assigned in the 1st Brigade Hqs, Philippine National Guard. Principal Teacher of various High Schools and Div Supt of Schools, Bureau of Education. Offered his services in any capacity to Col BEN CHASTAINE, CO, Prov Samar Brigade on 15 Jan 1942 and recommended to Gen SHARP for commission when the order of general surrender before any reply could be made. Commissioned 2nd Lieut in the 10th MD on 19 Apr 1943; promoted 1st Lt on 25 May 1943; promoted Capt on 1 Jan 1944. Assigned in 110th Div 19 Apr 1943.

Paul A. Owen

ASN 2718816, 2nd Lieut, Inf. Reported to 10th MD on 26 Mar 1943. Evacuated 29 Sep 1943.

Herbert Page

ASN O-1053, Major Inf, reported to 10th MD on 26 Apr 1943. Born in Petersburg, Va. on 17 Sep 1877; speaks English, Spanish, little Tao-Sug Moro. Graduated Constabulary, 1906, Manila. Pvt, Corp, Acting Sgt Major, Field Co "A," 8th United States Inf, 4 Aug 1904 to 24 Sep 1907; 3rd Lieut, 3 Oct 1907, promoted 2nd Lieut 1 Jul 1908; resigned 20 Oct 1911; active duty as 3rd Lieut on Sep 23, 1913; 2nd Lieut on 1 Apr 1915; 1st Lieut on 5 Jun 1917; Capt on 29 Jul 1919; retired as Major, 13

Feb 1941. Recalled on 26 Apr 1943 to 10th MD; CO, 116th Inf Regt, 25 Apr 1945. Appointed Acting Justice of the Peace ex-officio, Glan and Kiamba, Cotabato 9 Nov 1943. Terminated on 30 May 1945. Ordered to report to the 4th Replacement Depot for processing 11 Jul 1945.

Charles "Chick" Parsons

Lt-Comdr, USN, reported to 10th MD on 17 Mar 1943. On duty with 10th MD, G-2 Section.

Frank Y. Patten

Seaman, 2nd Class, reported to 10th MD on 4 Sep 1944. On DS with Special Intelligence Detachment. Evacuated on 30 Mar 1945.

Robert L. Pease

ASN 19052905, 2nd Lieut, QMS. Reported to 10th MD 17 Jan 1944. Assigned to QMS, 107th Div for 11 months up to 28 Dec 1944.

Dalcua A. Phillips

ASN 6414343, Radio Mechanic, 2nd Class. Reported to 10 MD 7 Jan 1945. On DS with the FRS, 10th MD for 4 months. Evacuated on 11 May 1945.

Nicholas D. Pociluyko

ASN 7021439, 1st Lieut, Inf. Reported to 10th MD on 18 March 1943. Radio Station Incharge, Dipolog, Zamboanga.

Michael Pritz, Jr.

ASN O-890333, 1st Lieut, Inf. On duty 110th Div. Killed 3 Sep 1943.

Lee C. Ragsdale

ASN 19013450, 2nd Lieut, Inf. Reported to 10 MD 3 Dec 1942. Assigned to the G-4, 10th MD. Committed suicide on 15 Aug 1943.

Iliff Richardson

Major, Inf, reported to 10th MD on 1 Nov 1943. Born in Denver, Colorado in 1918; on DS with 9th MD for 8 months; on duty with 10 MD, 10 Sep 1944.

Louis Robertson

ASN 19017768, 1st Lieut, Inf. Reported to 10th MD 1 Apr 1943. Assigned as Provost Marshal, 113th Inf.

Charles E. Robinson

ASN 35706008, Radio Mechanic 2nd Class. Reported to 10 MD on 7 Jan 1945. On DS with the FRS, 10th MD for 4 months. Evacuated on 11 May 1945.

Henry C. Rooke

ASN 2622774, 1st Lieut, Inf. Reported to 10th MD on 16 Dec 1942. On duty Farm Project (Landing Field) No. 2 and stayed for 6 months. Assigned in FRS and served for 2 months.

Harold A. Rosenquist

ASN O-278037, Major, FA. Reported to 10th MD on 1 Jun 1944. Born in Providence, R.I. on 28 Nov 1903; speaks French. Recalled to active duty 8 Jun 1942 as 2nd Lieut, AUS; promoted Capt 29 Jan 1944; assigned USAFFE in Oct 1943; ordered by Hq USAFFE to report to 10th MD, assigned Acting AC of S, G-2, 1 Jun 1944. Promoted Major, JA, 1 Nov 1944; AC of S, G-2, 10th MD, 1 Apr 1945; relieved of assignment 10th MD and ordered to proceed GHQ, SWPA, to C-in-C, 5 Jan 1945. Reassigned on temporary duty with 10th MD through request of Col FERTIG per letter order, 22 Mar 1945, USAFFE Hq; Deputy Chief of Staff, 10th MD.

Lewis C. Roybal

ASN 6961559, 1st Lieut, Inf. Reported to 10th MD on 1 Jun 1943. Assigned in 106th Div. Evacuated 22 Jan 1945.

Elwood A. Royer

ASN 6893017, 2nd Lieut, Inf. Reported to 10th MD on 12 May 1943. Assigned to the 110th Div. Evacuated 11 mar 1944.

Lee R. Rutherford

ASN 18029967, 2nd Lieut, Inf. Reported to 10th MD on 1 Jun 1943. Assigned to Corps Radio Section, "A" Corps, Western Mindanao for 7 months. Evacuated 25 Dec 1944.

John E. Ruziecki

ASN 19002877, 2nd Lieut, Inf. Reported to the 10th MD on 1 Jun 1943. Assigned to Corps Radio Section, "A" Corps, Western Mindanao for 4 months. Evacuated 1 Jun 1944.

Joseph St. John

ASN 6909351, 2nd Lieut, Inf. Reported to 10 MD on 26 Jul 1943; detached service 9th MD, Radio Section.

Jack Lawrence Samples

ASN 18046030, Capt, Inf. Reported to 10th MD on 1 Jun 1943. Born in Loveland, Colorado on 3 Aug 1919. High School graduate; one year ROTC, one year college. Pvt 3rd Special, 400 Ordnance. Commissioned 2nd Lieut in the USFIP, 10 MD on 1 Jun 1943; promoted 1st Lieut on 15 Feb 1944; promoted Capt Inf on 1

Apr 1945. Assigned in the FRS, 10th MD on 24 Oct 1943. CO of the Force Ordnance Co on 3 Nov 1943. Ordered to proceed to Hq, USAFFE on 8 Apr 1945.

Walter W. Sanders

ASN 6937917, 1st Lieut, Inf. Reported to 10th MD on 1 Jun 1943. Assigned CO, Sig C, 109th Div and Radio Section.

James E. Schoen

ASN 6657691, 1st Lieut, Inf. Reported to 10th MD on 1 Dec 1942. Assigned in the FRS, 10th MD for 2 years and 4 months. Evacuated 5 Feb 1945.

Austin Conner Shofner

Major, USMC. Reported to 10th MD on 11 May 1943. Born in Chattanooga, Tenn. on 3 Mar 1916. Graduated University of Tennessee. Professional Marine. Attended Marine Officer Basic School from August 1937 to May 1938; with the USS "Oklahoma" from August 1938 to June 1939; with the Fleet Marine Force in Jun 1939 to May 1941; with the 4th Reg. Luzon, Shanghai, etc., in May 1941. Commissioned regular in Aug 1937; reported as Capt, USMC, Apr 1943 with 110th Div. Major in the 10th MD, USFIP.

Peter Schur

ASN 6718063, 2nd Lieut, Inf. Reported to 10th MD on 7 Nov 1942. Assigned as S-2, 107th Inf, 105th Div for 1½ years. Assigned Regtl S-3 for 6 months. Evacuated 22 Dec 1944.

John David Simmons

USN SN 120868, Capt, Sig C. Reported to 10 MD 24 Jul 1944. Born in Columbus, Ohio on 16 Dec 1919. Degree: B.A. graduate, one and one-half years graduate school. Speaks English and Papuan. Graduate of Naval Reserve Midshipman School. Commissioned Ensign D-V (G) USNR. Two years in Southwest Pacific, attached to Staff, Com, 7th Fleet, duty on board ship and with radio station in New Guinea. Given the equivalent grade in the Army as Capt, Sig C, Reserve Force, USFIP, 10th MD, 18 Dec 1944. Ex O., FRS and Communication Officer of the "A" Corps, Western Mindanao on 7 Jul 1944. Ordered to proceed to HQ, Seventh Fleet at the instance of letter dated 14 May 1945, issued by HQ, Seventh Fleet.

Thomas Lowry Sinclair

ASN 117873, Capt, Inf. Reported to 10th MD 15 Oct 1944. Born in Yangehow, China on 14 Feb 1914. B.A. Graduate. Speaks Chinese (Mandarin), French. Two months in South China guerrilla from Jul to Aug 1939. Commissioned Ensign, Y-V (3), United States Navy Reserve on 1 Nov 1941. On active duty 19 Jan 1942. Ordered to proceed to GHQ, USAFFE 20 Feb. 1945.

Charles Smith

ASN O-888471, Maj, CE. Called to the Hq USAFFE 23 Dec 1943. (No further record).

James S. Smith

ASN 19038509, 2nd Lieut, Inf. Reported to 10th MD on 20 Nov 1942. Assigned in the District Motor Pool for 3 months and transferred to 110th Div, serving thereat for 8 months. Evacuated 2 Dec 1944.

Oscar F. Smith

ASN 1604078, Pvt, USAC. Reported to 10th MD on 1 May 1943. On duty with 110th Inf Regt for 1 month. Evacuated on 14 Nov 1943.

Russell Howard Smith

ASN 6291002, Capt, Sig C. Reported to the 110th Div, 10th MD on 1 Sep 1943. Born in Farmingdale, South Dakota on 16 Nov 1919. 1st year college. Sgt in the AC. Commissioned 2nd Lieut on 1 Oct 1943, USFIP, 10th MD; promoted 1st Lieut 1 Oct 1944; promoted Capt 6 May 1945. Assigned in the 110th Div on 2 Oct 1943. Asst Div Prov Marshal, 110th Div, 18 Sep 1943; assigned in the FRS, 10th MD on 1 Nov 1943. Ordered to proceed to Hq, USAFFE on 11 May 1945.

Robert O. Snyder

ASN 13016435, 1st Lieut, Sig C. Reported to 10th MD on 1 Jun 1943. Assigned in the FRS, 10th MD; served for one year and 11 months. Evacuated on 1 Jun 1945.

Robert B. Spielman

ASN O-1686152, Major, Inf. Reported to 10th MD 11 May 1943. Born in Leigh, Iowa in Jun 1921; 1st year C.E., Texas. Enlisted 17 Sep 1940; served Luzon campaign up to 24 Dec 1941; in Corregidor from 25 Dec 1941 to 6 May 1942. Commissioned 2nd Lieut in the 10 MD, 11 May 1943. Promoted 1st Lieut 1 Oct 1943; promoted Capt 1 Nov 1944; promoted Major 15 Apr 1945. Assigned as Asst G-3, 110th Div, 12 May 1943; AC of S, G-3, 110th Div, 1 May 1945; CO, 114th Inf 8 Jan 1945; ordered to proceed to 4th Replacement Depot 15 Jul 1945.

John E. Spruill

ASN 629476, Sgt, OS. Reported to 10th MD, 7 Dec 1942. Designated Mess Officer, American Mess for 6 months; Ordnance Supply Officer, 10th MD for 9 months; evacuated on 22 Jan 1944.

Robert E. Stahl

ASN 32236898, 2nd Lieut, Sig C. Reported to 10th MD on 15 Dec 1943 with Col SMITH.

John W. Starkey

ASN 18036776, 1st Lieut. Reported to 10th MD on 1 Jun 1943. Assigned on duty with 109th Div for 1 year and 7 months. Evacuated 5 May 1945.

Adolph Ernest Sternberg, Jr.

ASN 6587239, Capt, Inf. Reported to 10th MD on 1 Feb 1944. Born in Sidney, Nebraska on 9 Sep 1917. Speaks English and German; High School graduate; carpenter; 4 years, USAC Mechanic, Crew Chief and Engineer; Sgt in the 20th Bombardment Squad, 19th Bombardment Group, USAC. Joined the 10th MD on 28 May 1942. Commissioned on 1 Feb 1944 as 2nd Lieut;, promoted 1st Lieut, 1 Nov 1944; promoted Capt on 15 Apr 1945. CO of the Special Intelligence Detachment, 107th Div, 10th MD on 1 Feb 1944. Assigned to Radio Section and Utility, Hq, 107th Div on 1 May 1944. Ordered to 4th Replacement Depot on 27 Apr 1945.

Tommy Stewart

ASN 19050535, Pvt, USAC. Reported to 10th MD on 19 Jul 1943. Assigned in Signal Company for one month. Evacuated on 14 Nov 1944.

Oscar E. Swanson

ASN 6507759, Capt, Inf. Reported 1 May 1944. Born in Sweden on 18 Jul 1900. High School student; 10½ years in the USAC; Sgt in the USAC, 66th Service Sq. Discharged 1 Feb 1935; called to Davao by Col R. S. HILLSMAN on 14 Dec 1941. Served as Technical Adviser Aeronautical and Ordnance on 10 Jan 1942 to May 1942 with Gen SHARP; commissioned 1st Lieut on 1 May 1944; promoted Capt on 15 Apr 1945. On duty with 107th Div, 10th MD on 1 May 1944. Assigned Transportation Officer, QMS, 10th MD on 10 Jan 1945. In charge of the QMS Service Depot at Bahi and Bahi Landing Field from 1 Jan 1945 to 15 May 1945. Ordered to 4th Replacement Depot on 25 May 1945.

Frederick Marston Taylor

ASN 6581597, Capt, Inf. Reported to the 10th MD 1 Jun 1943. Born in Fort Scott, Kansas 16 Aug 1921. Graduate in ACTS; 3 years and 8 months in the Air Corps. Reported to CO, 10th MD on 3 Nov 1943. Temporarily assigned to the Div Signal Unit, 110th Div. Commissioned 2nd Lt. 11 Jun 1943. Promoted 1st Lt. 20 Feb 1945; promoted Captain 1 May 1945. CO, La Paz Military Area 5 Mar 1945; relieved as CO, La Paz Military Area on 17 May 1945.

Chandler B. Thomas

ASN O-418183, Major, AC. Reported to 10th MD on 4 Nov 1942. Born in Seattle, Washington on 11 Nov 1916. Degrees: B.A., Washington University 1937; graduated Army Air Corps 29 May 1941 with the 14th Bombardment Sq., 19th Group, promoted to 1st Lieut, 10th MD on 21 Dec 1942; promoted Capt, Hq

USAFFE, 24 May 1944. Promoted Maj 18 Nov 1944; assigned Asst AC of S, G-2, 10th MD on 6 Dec 1942; in charge of Farm Project (Landing Field) No.1, 10th MD on 19 May 1943. DC of S, "A" Corps, on 12 Dec 1944. On duty with G-2, 10th MD on 30 Oct 1944. Liaison Officer for the CO, 10th MD, with the 13th Air Force, 31 Mar 1945.

Richard Leonard Thommes

ASN 19032233, Capt, Inf. Reported to 10th MD on 28 Nov 1942. Born in Lastrup, Minnesota on 6 Apr 1919. High School graduate and 5 years in Pre-Divinity. Speaks German, English and Latin. Pfc in the 38th Reconnaissance Sq., 19th Bombardment Group. Commissioned 2nd Lieut, Inf, USFIP, 10th MD, 28 Feb 1943. Promoted 1st Lieut 11 Feb 1944; promoted Capt on 15 Apr 1945 and assigned as CO, Hq Bn, 110th Inf. Assigned to FRS, 10th MD on 1 Nov 1943. Ordered to proceed to Hq, USAFFE on 8 Jun 1945.

Carlyle G. Townswick

ASN 6938081, 1st Lieut. Reported to 10th MD on 1 Jun 1943. Communication Officer, "A" Corps, Western Mindanao and 109th Div. Evacuated 12 May 1945.

Franklin J. Trammel

ASN 6465880, 1st Lieut, Inf. Reported to 10th MD on 1 Jun 1943. On duty with 109th Division, Corps Radio Section "A" Corps. Evacuated 1 Jun 1944.

Tracy S. Tucker

ASN 19016176, 2nd Lieut, Inf. Reported to 10th MD on 1 Feb 1943. Assigned on duty with 109th Div. Evacuated 29 Sep 1943.

John Lincoln Tuggle

USN SN 265–74–29, Capt, Inf. Reported to 10th MD, 6 Dec 1942. Born in Chesterfield County, Va. on 3 Mar 1916. 6 years United States Army Mechanic 1st Class B., Sq 3. Commissioned 2nd Lieut in the 10th MD on 6 Dec 1942; promoted 1st Lieut on 1 Oct 1943; promoted Capt on 16 May 1945. Assigned in GHQ, 10th MD on 6 Dec 1942. Assigned to the 108th Div; designated Agent Officer, Farm Project (Landing Field) No. 2, 10th MD on 3 Sep 1943; Acting Administrator, Farm Project No. 2, "A" Corps, 8 Oct 1944. On 13 Jan 1945, assigned to Labo Landing Field. Ordered to proceed to Hq, USAFFE on 12 May 1945.

Glen S. Turner

ASN 19030146, Pvt, USAC. Corps, Casual EWP.

Fred W. Varney

ASN O-953161, Capt, QMC. Reported to 10 MD on 1 Jan 1942. Commissioned 1st Lieut, QMS, AUS, on 1 Jan 1942. Discharged by Col BEN H. CHAS-

TAINE on 9 May 1942 with instruction to report for duty at Anakan where he served continuously until called to 110th Div, 10 MD on 1 Oct 1943. Promoted Capt on 1 Jan 1944 and confirmed by GHQ, USAFFE; on 13 Sep 1944 assigned to the FRS, 10th MD.

Cecil E. Walter

ASN O-1686140, Major, CE. Reported to 10th MD on 1 Jan 1944. Born in Portland, Oregon 21 Feb 1891; degrees: Economics, Engineering and Forestry. Called to active duty on 1 Jan 1944 as Capt, Hq, 10th MD; rank confirmed by GHQ, USAFFE. Promoted Maj CE, 10th MD on 6 Dec 1944; promoted Lt-Col on 1 Jul 1945; Liaison Officer for CC, 10th MD, with the 108th RCT on 15 May 1945. CO, 109th Div, 10th MD on 25 Jan 1945.

Loyd Waters

ASN 6298002, 1st Lieut, Inf. Reported to 10th MD 1 Dec 1952. Assigned in the FRS, 10th MD for one year and nine months. Evacuated 29 Dec 1944.

Hadley C. Watson

ASN O-890290, 1st Lieut, Inf. Reported to 10th MD on 28 Apr 1944. Assigned in the Hq, 10th MD. Evacuated 28 Dec 1944.

Howard R. Watson

ASN 6581144, 1st Lieut, Inf. Reported to 10th MD 1 Jun 1943. Assigned in the 109th Div for one year, in charge of the Code Section, Corps Radio Section "A" Corps, Western Mindanao Net Control Station for 6 months. Evacuated 8 Apr 1945.

Roy E. Welbon

1st Lieut, Inf. Reported to 10th MD on 1 Oct 1943. Communications Officer, FRS, 10th MD. Died on 25 Jan 1944.

Royce F. Wendover

Capt, CE. Reported to 10th MD on 26 May 1943. Degree: B.S., Oregon State College. Born in Logging, Kansas on 6 Nov 1897. Joined Philippine Scouts USA at Zamboanga on 7 Mar.

Major M. (Montgomery) Wheeler

USN SN 149981, Lt-Comdr, USNR. Reported to 10th MD on 4 Mar 1944; Lieut—DVS USNR; promoted Lt-Comdr, USNR 26 Sep 1944. Promoted Maj, USFIP, 10th MD, Sig C, 15 Sep 1944; promoted Lt-Col, GSO on 1 Jun 1945. Assigned in FRS, 10th MD on 4 Mar 1944 and CO FRS on 1 Jul 1944. Designated DC of S, 10th MD on 1 Jan 1945; C of S, 10th MD on 1 Mar 1945.

Perry T. Whitley

ASN 627596, T/Sgt USAC. Reported to 10th MD on 1 Dec 1942. Assigned in the 110th Div; Asst in charge of the Machine Shop, 10th MD. Evacuated 17 Dec 1944.

William W. Williams

ASN 6576079, 2nd Lieut, Inf. Reported to 10th MD on 1 Jun 1943. Assigned in FRS, 10th MD for five months. Assigned on duty with 109th Div for one year and three months. Evacuated 8 Feb 1944.

Donald H. Wills

ASN O-389373, Major, Cavalry. Reported to 10th MD on 1 Jan 1944. Born in Lynchburg, Va. on 23 May 1918; degree: BSC. Graduated 4 years Virginia Military Institute; 1 year 14th Cavalry Graduate; Cavalry Motor School 1 year—26 Cavalry, Philippine Scouts. Called to active duty in Jun 1940. Promoted Capt, Cav on 22 Oct 1944; promoted Major Cav on 20 Mar 1945; Prisoner of War who jumped overboard prison ship off Coronado Point, Zamboanga. AC of S, G-3, "A" Corps, 16 Dec 1944. AC of S, G-3, 10th MD on 1 April 1945. Ordered to report to 4th Replacement Depot, USAFFE, on 17 April 1945.

Owen Paul Wilson

ASN O-888985, Capt, Sig C. Reported to 10th MD on 21 Dec 1943. S/Sgt, AC, born in McCrory, Arkansas on 23 Dec 1911. Enlisted in the AC in 1937. Finished the Air Base Radio School. Radio Com Teletype operator course graduate. Instructor in the 10th Group Radio School. Chief of Section (Radio) until the surrender. Commissioned 2nd Lieut, 10th MD on 21 Dec 1943. Promoted 1st Lieut on 1 Oct 1944; promoted Capt, Sig C, on 15 Apr 1945. Assigned 107th Div on 22 Jun 1944. CO, 111th Prov Bn, 110th Div, on 15 Jan 1944. Assigned to FRS, 10th MD on 10 Apr 1945.

Sam J. Wilson

USN SN 71404, Lt-Col, GSC. Reported to 10th MD on 21 Feb 1943. Born in Philadelphia, Pa., on 18 Feb 1897. High School and Economics business Courses: U.P. and Columbia University; attended Naval Training Station 5 months and Special Naval Course in Howard University in May 1918 to 1919. With USN in May 1917 to Apr 1919 (sub-chaser). In Oct 1932, a Lieut in USNR; on active duty 8 Dec 1941 in Manila, Philippines, assigned to the Censorship and Naval Intelligence.

George W. Winget

S/N 2232549, MM1c. PT-35 crew member.

Mark M. Wohlfield

S/N O-314054, escaped from Davao Penal Colony 27 Mar 1943.

John F. Wood Jr.

S/N 6961568, AFP O-63372, 2nd Lieut.

Halbert E. Woodruff

Maj

Frederick L. Worcester

Maj, reported to 10th MD Jan 1943.

Sidney T. Wright

Escaped from Puerto Princesa Concentration Camp, Palawan.

Chapter Notes

Chapter 1

1. David Tan, *Mining Engineer Job Descriptions*, http://www.org/mining_engineer_job_descriptions (accessed March 2, 2011).

2. Wendell W. Fertig, Personal Diary, 1941–1945 (MacArthur Memorial Archives and Library, Norfolk, VA), 2.

3. Wendell W. Fertig, Draft Manuscript (MacArthur Memorial Archives and Library, Norfolk, VA), 165.

4. Fertig, Personal Diary, 5.

5. Louis Morton, *The Fall of the Philippines: U.S. Army in World War II: The War in the Pacific* (Washington, D.C.: Center of Military History, U.S. Army, 1989), 259.

6. Fertig, Draft Manuscript, 1–2.

7. Ibid., 2.

8. Ibid., 7.

9. Ibid, 7–8.

10. Ibid., 9–10.

11. Scott Walker, *The Edge of Terror* (New York: Thomas Dunne Books, St. Martin's Press, 2009), 73–75.

12. Geoffrey Perret, *Old Soldiers Never Die, The Life of Douglas MacArthur* (New York: Random House), 270.

13. Ibid., 273.

14. Richard Connaughton, *MacArthur and the Defeat in the Philippines*, 2001. (New York: Overlook Press), 287.

15. Malcolm M. Champlin. Unpublished account of Champlin's experience in the Philippines, including biography of Rear Admiral John D. Bulkeley, USN. (Office of Information, Internal Relations Division, Naval History Division, 1965), 70–71.

16. Connaughton, *MacArthur and the Defeat in the Philippines*, 284.

17. Thomas Mitsos, "Guerrilla Radio—AGOM, American Guerrillas of Mindanao, Philippine Islands 1941–1945," unpublished collection of articles and letters between members regarding World War II, chapter 10, 7.

18. Perret, *Old Soldiers Never Die*, 279.

19. Mitsos, Guerrilla Radio—AGOM, chapter 10, 7.

20. Perret, *Old Soldiers Never Die*, 279.

21. Ibid., 281–282.

22. Ibid.

23. Mitsos, Guerrilla Radio—AGOM, chapter 10, 7.

Chapter 2

1. Fertig, Draft Manuscript, 17.

2. Ibid., 16–25.

3. John Keats, *They Fought Alone* (New York: J. B. Lippincott, 1963), 77.

4. Ibid., 81.

5. Ibid.

6. Mitsos, "Guerrilla Radio—AGOM, chapter 10, 5.

7. Wendell Fertig, Letter to General Hugh J. Casey, dated 1 July 1943, Fertig papers (MacArthur Memorial Archives and Library, Norfolk, VA).

8. Keats, *They Fought Alone*, 86.

9. Ibid., 87.

10. Ibid., 89.

11. Fertig, Draft Manuscript, 87.

12. Ibid.

13. Ibid., 88.

14. Ibid.

15. Ibid., 83.

16. Ibid., 90.

17. Ibid., 91.

18. Ibid.

19. Ibid., 92.

20. Ibid., 95.
21. Keats, *They Fought Alone*, 100.

Chapter 3

1. Larry Schmidt, "American Involvement in the Filipino Resistance Movement on Mindanao During the Japanese Occupation, 1942–1945" (MA thesis, U.S. Army Command and General Staff College, Fort Leavenworth, KS, 1982), 92–93.
2. Fertig, Personal Diary, 16.
3. Ibid.
4. Ibid., 18.
5. Ibid., 21.
6. Ibid., 24.
7. Ibid., 27.
8. Ibid., 28.
9. Fertig, Letter to General Hugh J. Casey.
10. Keats, *They Fought Alone*, 103.
11. Edward Haggerty, *Guerrilla Padre in Mindanao* (New York: Longmans, Green & Co., Inc., 1946), 78.
12. Keats, *They Fought Alone*, 139.
13. Fertig, Draft Manuscript, 116.
14. Ibid., 138–140.
15. "History of the Mindanao Guerrillas" (MacArthur Memorial Archives and Library, Norfolk, VA), 125.
16. Keats, *They Fought Alone*, 199.
17. Charles Hansen Personal Papers, 1943–1945 (Virginia Hansen Holmes Collection, Falls Church, VA).

Chapter 4

1. History of the Mindanao Guerrillas, 62.
2. Mitsos, Guerrilla Radio–AGOM, chapter 4, 3.
3. History of the Mindanao Guerrillas, 62.
4. Bob Stahl, *Fugitives: Evading and Escaping the Japanese* (Lexington, KY: The University Press of Kentucky, 2001), 99.
5. History of the Mindanao Guerrillas, 63–64.
6. Rafael Steinberg, *Return to the Philippines* (Alexandria, VA: Time Life Books, 1979), 24.
7. Mitsos, Guerrilla Radio—AGOM, chapter 5, 1.
8. American Guerrillas of Mindanao (AGOM) Historical Records (AGOM Descendants Group, Falls Church, VA).
9. Mitsos, Guerrilla Radio—AGOM, chapter 5, 3–6.
10. Ibid.
11. Ibid.
12. Ibid.
13. Ibid.
14. Ibid.
15. Ibid.
16. History of the Mindanao Guerrillas, 66.
17. Ibid.
18. Ibid.
19. Ibid., 67.
20. Ibid., 66.
21. Fertig, Draft Manuscript, 391.
22. History of the Mindanao Guerrillas, 68.
23. Allison Ind, *Allied Intelligence Bureau, Our Secret Weapon in the War against Japan* (New York: David McKay, 1958), 163.
24. Ibid., 164.
25. Ibid., 165
26. Ibid., 166.
27. Keats, *They Fought Alone*, 193.
28. Fertig, Draft Manuscript, 179.
29. Keats, *They Fought Alone*, 194.
30. Ibid., 198.
31. Ind, 169.
32. Fertig, Draft Manuscript, 249.
33. Ibid., 366.
34. Bob Stahl, *You're No Good To Me Dead: Behind Japanese Lines in the Philippines* (Annapolis, MD: Naval Institute Press, 1995), 71.
35. Mitsos, Guerrilla Radio—AGOM, chapter 10, 11–12.
36. Fertig, Draft Manuscript, 315.

Chapter 5

1. Morton, *The Fall of the Philippines,* 112.
2. Schmidt, "American Involvement in the Philippines Resistance Movement on Mindanao," 67.
3. Fertig, Draft Manuscript, 212–213.
4. Robert Spielman, "The History of the 114th Regiment, United States Forces in the Philippines," MA Thesis, The University of Texas, Austin, Texas, 1953, 44.
5. Virginia Hansen Holmes, *Guerrilla Daughter* (Kent, OH: Kent State University Press, 2009), 115–117.

6. Charles Hansen Personal Papers, 1943–1945.

7. History of the Mindanao Guerrillas, 80–81.

8. Ibid., 90.

9. Samuel E. Morison, *The Liberation of the Philippines: Luzon, Mindanao, the Visayas, 1944–45* (Boston: Little Brown, 1959), 240.

10. Ibid., 240.

11. Robert Ross Smith, *Triumph in the Philippines The U.S. Army in World War II: The War in the Pacific* (Washington, D.C.: Center of Military History, U.S. Army, 1993), 622–623.

12. Ibid., 684–691.

13. Schmidt, "American Involvement in the Filipino Resistance Movement on Mindanao," 31–32.

14. Ibid., 33.

15. Ibid., 215.

16. History of the Mindanao Guerrillas, 93–94.

17. Schmidt, "American Involvement in the Filipino Resistance Movement on Mindanao," 216.

Chapter 6

1. Haggerty, *Guerrilla Padre in Mindanao*, 23.

2. Mitsos, Guerrilla Radio—AGOM, chapter 1, 1–6.

3. Hansen Holmes, *Guerrilla Daughter*, 2.

4. Fertig, Letter to General Hugh J. Casey, 3.

5. Schmidt, "American Involvement in the Filipino Resistance Movement on Mindanao," 211.

6. Mary McKay Maynard, *My Faraway Home* (Guilford, CT: Lyons, 2001), 267.

7. Mitsos, Guerrilla Radio—AGOM, chapter 10, 3–4.

8. Hansen Holmes, *Guerrilla Daughter*, 101–102.

9. Charles Hansen, "Memorandum for the Record" dated 18 October 1943, Charles Hansen Personal Papers, 1943–1945.

10. Fertig, Draft Manuscript, 277.

11. Ibid., 220.

12. Ibid., 259.

13. Ibid., 260.

14. Ibid.

15. Ibid., 266–268.

16. Ibid., 270.

17. Ibid., 323–330.

18. Ibid.

19. Fertig, Draft Manuscript, 403.

20. Ibid., 410.

21. Ibid., 415.

22. Ibid.

23. Hamlin M. Cannon, *Leyte: The Return to the Philippines: The U.S. Army in World War II: The War in the Pacific* (Washington, D.C., Center of Military History, U.S. Army, 1954), 42.

24. Ibid., 42–43.

25. Ibid.

26. Fertig, Draft Manuscript, 421.

27. Ibid.

28. Ibid.

29. Steinberg, *Return to the Philippines*, 52.

30. Ibid., 55.

31. Ibid., 57.

32. Ibid., 59.

33. Ibid., 61.

34. Cannon, *Leyte: The Return to the Philippines*, 92.

35. Fertig, Draft Manuscript, 453.

36. Ibid., 455.

37. Ibid., 468.

38. Ibid., 480.

39. Ibid., 501–508.

40. Ibid., 520–526.

41. Morison, *The Liberation of the Philippines*, 240.

42. History of the Mindanao Guerrillas, 32–46.

43. Keats, *They Fought Alone*, 307.

44. Ibid., 225–226.

45. Schmidt, "American Involvement in the Filipino Resistance Movement on Mindanao," 211.

46. Mitsos, Guerrilla Radio—AGOM, chapter 10, 6.

47. Schmidt, "American Involvement in the Filipino Resistance Movement on Mindanao," 211.

48. Ibid.

49. Ibid., 212.

50. History of the Mindanao Guerrillas, 93.

51. Ibid., 96–121.

52. Hansen Holmes, *Guerrilla Daughter*, 159.

53. Henry (Hank) Hansen, Personal Interview, Sunnyvale, CA, 2006

54. Hansen Holmes, *Guerrilla Daughter*, 162–163.

Chapter 7

1. Hansen Holmes, *Guerrilla Daughter*, 77.
2. Ibid, 74.
3. Edward Dissette and Hans Christian Adamson, *Guerrilla Submarines*. (New York: Bantam Books, 1980), 12–13.
4. Fertig, Draft Manuscript,188.
5. Haggerty, Guerrilla Padre, 194.
6. Mitsos, chapter 10, 7–8.
7. Haggerty, Guerrilla Padre, 195–197.
8. Schmidt, "American Involvement in the Filipino Resistance Movement on Mindanao," 173.
9. Keats, *They Fought Alone*, 202–203.
10. Dissette and Adamson, *Guerrilla Submarines*, 12–13.
11. Ibid, 72.
12. Ibid, 72–73.
13. Hansen Holmes, *Guerrilla Daughter*, 124–125.
14. Ibid., 122.

Chapter 8

1. American Practical Navigator (Defense Mapping Agency, Hydrographic/Topographic Center, Washington, D.C., 1981), 393.
2. Ind, *Allied Intelligence Bureau*, 169.
3. History of the Mindanao Guerrillas, 64.
4. Ibid., 65.
5. Ibid., 77.
6. Ibid., 78–89.
7. Fertig, Draft Manuscript, 417.
8. Stahl, *You're No Good To Me Dead*, 100.
9. Gerald Chapman, Interview by Kent Holmes, Oceanside, CA, April 12, 2012.

Chapter 9

1. Clyde Childress, "Memorandum Concerning Communications with John Keats," American Guerrillas on Mindanao (AGOM) Newsletter, August 4, 1989.
2. Clyde Childress, "Further Comments on Communications with John Keats," American Guerrillas on Mindanao (AGOM) Newsletter, January 1990.
3. Clyde Childress, "Wendell Fertig's Fictional Autobiography: A Critical Review of *They Fought Alone*," *Bulletin of the American Historical Collection*, Vol. 31, no. 1(123), January, 2003. Published by the American Association of the Philippines, Makati City, Philippines.
4. Fertig, Personal Diary, 81.
5. Ibid., 82.
6. Ibid., 88.
7. Ibid., 96.
8. Ibid., 24.
9. Ibid., 26.
10. Fertig, Draft Manuscript, 134.
11. Fertig, Personal Diary, 148.
12. Fertig, Draft Manuscript, 185.
13. Ibid., 332.
14. Ibid., 373.
15. Ibid., 390.
16. Ibid., 442.
17. Ibid., 443.
18. Ibid.
19. Ibid., 444.
20. Ibid., 472.
21. Ibid., 473.
22. Ibid., 474.
23. Ibid., 493–494.
24. Ibid., 186.
25. Marie Silva Vallejo, *Battle of Ising* (Eres Printing, 2009), 14.
26. Stephen M. Mellnik, *Philippine War Diary*, 1939–1945 (New York: Van Nostrand Reinhold, 1969), 315.
27. Ibid., 316.
28. Duane Heisinger, *Father Found* (XulonPress.com, 2003), 385.
29. Keats, *They Fought Alone*, 398.

Chapter 10

1. Ira Wolfert, *American Guerrilla in the Philippines* (New York: Simon and Shuster, 1945), 209.
2. Mary McKay Maynard, *My Faraway Home*, 210.
3. Ibid., 211.
4. Ibid., 210–211.
5. Michael Korda, *Hero—Life and Legend of T. H. Lawrence* (New York: Harper Collins, 2010), 359–360.
6. Fertig, Draft Manuscript, 234.
7. Ibid.
8. Luis Morgan, Letter to Wendell Fertig dated 10 August 1943 (MacArthur Memorial Archives and Library, Norfolk, VA).
9. Hansen Holmes, *Guerrilla Daughter*, 80.
10. Mellnik, Philippine War Diary, 287.
11. Fertig, Personal Diary, 86.

Chapter 11

1. The Washington Post, May 28, 2011.
2. Fertig, Draft Manuscript, 246.
3. The Washington Post, May 28, 2011.
4. Smith, *Triumph in the Philippines,* 4.
5. Cannon, *Leyte: The Return to the Philippines:* 1–9.
6. Smith, *Triumph in the Philippines,* 465–467.
7. Morison, *The Liberation of the Philippines,* 240.
8. Smith, *Triumph in the Philippines,* 591–596.
9. Ibid., 596–597.
10. Ibid., 623.
11. Ibid., 641–643.
12. Ibid., 644.
13. Ibid., 647.
14. History of the Mindanao Guerrillas, 71.
15. Morison, *The Liberation of the Philippines,* 230–31.
16. Ind, *Allied Intelligence Bureau,* 134–135.

Chapter 12

1. Fertig, Draft Manuscript, 406–407.
2. Ibid., 405.

3. Mike Guardia, *American Guerrilla: The Forgotten Heroics of Russell W. Volkmann,* (Havertown, PA: Casement, 2010), 171.
4. Ibid., 160.
5. Ibid., 170.
6. Special Operations Command, U.S. Army Special Forces, Special Operations. http://www.special/operations.com/Army/Special_Forces/SF_info/Detailed_History (accessed July 15, 2012).
7. The Washington Post, September 12, 2014, A-8.
8. The Washington Post, September 11, 2014, A-1.
9. The Washington Post, September 12, 2014, A-6.
10. Richard C. Goss, "Different Worlds: Unacknowledged Special Operations and Covert Action," (U.S. Army War College Strategy Research Project for Master of Strategic Studies degree, U.S. Army War College, Carlisle, PA, February 24, 2009), 2–3. http://www.Scibd.com/doc/94917822//US-Army-Special-Operations-covert-actions (accessed July 15, 2012).

Bibliography

Books and Theses

Connaughton, Richard. *MacArthur and the Defeat in the Philippines*. New York: Overlook Press, 2001.

Dissette, Edward, and Hans Christian Adamson. *Guerrilla Submarines*. New York: Bantam, 1980.

Goss, Richard C. "Different Worlds: Unacknowledged Special Operations and Covert Action." U.S. Army War College Strategy Research Project for Master of Strategic Studies degree, U.S. Army War College, Carlisle, Pennsylvania, February 24, 2009. http://.Scibd.com/doc/94917822//U.S.-Army-Special-Operations-covert-actions (accessed July 15, 2012).

Guardia, Mike. *American Guerrilla: The Forgotten Heroics of Russell W. Volkmann*. Havertown, PA: Casement, 2010.

Haggerty, Edward. *Guerrilla Padre in Mindanao*. New York: Longmans, Green, 1946.

Hansen Holmes, Virginia. *Guerrilla Daughter*. Kent, OH: Kent State University Press, 2009.

Heisinger, Duane. *Father Found*. Xulon Press.com, 2003.

Keats, John. *They Fought Alone*. Philadelphia: J. B. Lippincott, 1963.

Ind, Allison. *Allied Intelligence Bureau: Our Secret Weapon in the War Against Japan*. New York: David McKay, 1958.

Korda, Michael. *Hero—Life and Legend of T. H. Lawrence*. New York: HarperCollins, 2010.

Maynard, Mary McKay. *My Faraway Home*. Guilford, CT: Lyons, 2001.

Mellnik, Stephen M. *Philippine War Diary 1939–1945*. New York: Van Nostrand Reinhold, 1969.

Morison, Samuel E. *The Liberation of the Philippines: Luzon, Mindanao, the Visayas, 1944–45*. Boston: Little, Brown, 1959.

Perret, Geoffrey. *Old Soldiers Never Die, Life of Douglas MacArthur*. New York: Random House, 1996.

Schmidt, Larry S. "American Involvement in the Filipino Resistance Movement on Mindanao During the Japanese Occupation, 1942–1945." MA thesis, U.S. Army Command and General Staff College, Fort Leavenworth, Kansas, 1982.

Spielman, Robert. "The History of the 114th Regiment, United States Forces in the Philippines." MA thesis, The University of Texas, Austin, 1953.

Stahl, Bob. *Fugitives: Evading and Escaping the Japanese*. Lexington: University Press of Kentucky, 2001.

_____. *You're No Good to Me Dead: Behind the Lines in the Philippines*. Annapolis: Naval Institute Press, 1995.

Steinberg, Rafael. *Return to the Philippines*. Alexandria, VA: Time-Life Books, 1979.

Vallejo, Marie Silva. *Battle of Ising*. Eres Printing, 2009.

Walker, Scott. *The Edge of Terror*. New York: Thomas Dunne Books, St. Martin's Press, 2009.

Whitney, Courtney. *MacArthur—His Rendezvous with History*. New York: Alfred A. Knopf, 1956.

Wolfert, Ira. *American Guerrilla in the Philippines*. New York: Simon & Schuster, 1945.

U.S. Government Papers and Records

American Practical Navigator, Defense Mapping Agency, Hydrographic/Topographic Center, Washington, D.C, 1981.

Cannon, Hamlin M. *Leyte: The Return to the Philippines: The U.S. Army in World War II: The War in the Pacific.* Washington, D.C.: Center of Military History, U.S. Army, 1954.

Champlin, Malcolm M. Unpublished account of Champlin's experiences in the Philippines, including biography of Rear Admiral John D. Bulkeley, USN. Office of Information, Internal Relations Division, Naval History Division, 1965.

Morton, Louis. *The Fall of the Philippines: U.S. Army in World War II: The War in the Pacific*: Washington, D.C.: Center of Military History, U.S. Army, 1989.

Smith, Robert R. *Triumph in the Philippines. The U.S. Army in World War II: The War in the Pacific:* Washington, D.C.: Center of Military History, U.S. Army, 1993.

Archival Sources

American Guerrillas of Mindanao (AGOM) Historical Records. AGOM Descendants Group, Falls Church, Virginia.

Childress, Clyde C. "Further Comments on Communications with John Keats." American Guerrillas of Mindanao (AGOM), Newsletter, January 1990.

_____. "Memorandum Concerning Communications with John Keats," American Guerrillas of Mindanao (AGOM) Newsletter, August 4, 1989.

_____. "Wendell Fertig's Fictional Autobiography: A Critical Review of *They Fought Alone.*" Bulletin of the American *Historical Collection* 31, no. 1 (January 2003). Published by the American Association of the Philippines, Makati City, Philippines, 2003.

Fertig, Wendell W. Draft Manuscript (based on Personal Diary, 1941–1945). MacArthur Memorial Archives and Library, Norfolk, VA.

_____. Personal Diary, 1941–1945. MacArthur Memorial Archives and Library, Norfolk, VA.

_____. Letter to General Hugh J. Casey, dated 1 July 1943. MacArthur Memorial Archives and Library, Norfolk, VA.

Hansen, Charles. Personal Papers, 1943–1945. Virginia Hansen Holmes Collection, Falls Church, Virginia.

"History of the Mindanao Guerrillas." Compiled by the Historical Section, Tenth Military District. Includes a complete list of the Americans that reported to that district and when they were detached. MacArthur Memorial Museum and Library, Norfolk, Virginia.

Mitsos, Thomas. "Guerrilla Radio—AGOM, American Guerrillas of Mindanao, Philippines Islands, 1941–1945." A history of AGOM members during World War II.

Morgan, Luis. Memorandum to Wendell Fertig, dated 10 August 1943. MacArthur Memorial Archives and Library, Norfolk, Virginia.

Special Operations Command. U.S. Army Special Forces, Special Operations.com. http://Special_Forces/SF_Info/Detailed_History (accessed July 15, 2012)

Tan, David. "Mining Engineer Job Descriptions," http://www.or/miningengineer jobdescriptions (accessed March 2, 2011).

Xavier University—Ateneo de Cagayan web site, http://www.Xu.edu.phil/index.php/about-xu-history (accessed August 23, 2012).

Index

Numbers in *bold italics* indicate pages with photographs.

"A" Corps 45, 57, 58, 93, 94, 154
Abbott, Clyde M. 191
Afghanistan 186, 189
Agusan 70, 106
Agusan River 56, 92, 104, 105; valley 56, 101
the Aid 173
Air America 187
Albert McCarthy 8
Allenby, Edmund 163
Allied Intelligence Bureau 153, 163
Alma, Colorado 9
Almendras, Eleno 48–49
Almendras, Gerardo 48–49
Alubijid 93, 126
Amberley Field, Ipswich, Queensland, Australia 61, 132
American Association of the Philippines, Metro Manila 146
American Declaration of Independence 39
American Guerrillas of Mindanao 1, 145, 146
American Red Cross 162
American Silver Star Medal 85
Ammo, Cal. 30 M1 130
Amrich, Michael J. 191
Anakan Lumber Company 10, 50, 82
Andrews 153
Andrews, Robert 191
Aparri, Luzon 12
Army Reserve Officer Corps 9
Athena *93*, 110
Australia 5, 6

B-17 11, 12, 21, 109
B-24 97
B-25 81
Baguio Gold Mine 9
bakwitan 71
Balingasag 40
Ball, Robert B. 48, 49, 191
Bastard 110
Batan Island 12
Bates, Howard 192
Battle of Baga 115
Battle of Leyte Gulf 99–101; Cape Engaño

100; Samar 101; Sibuyan Sea 99; Surigao Strait 100
Baxter, Thomas R. 113, 192
Bayley, Kenneth L. 5, 192
Bell, Roy 49, 50
Benac, Julian 192
Berhala Island, Sandakan, North Borneo 85
Blackstone diesel engine, 71
Blair, Melvin 185
Blow, Rex 85, 180
Boelens, Leo A. 166, *167*, 169–170, 192
Bolt, Charles 30, 35
Bonifacio 49, 51, 52
Bonner, Alexander Rankin 193
Bontuyan, Alfredo 48
boots on the ground 189–190
Borbing Mountain, Davao 134
Bowfin 54, 126
Bowler, Robert V. 1, 45, 82, 92–*94*, 104, 154, 163, 181
Brisbane 5, 162
Brooks, Durward L. 193
Brown, Oscar G. 193
Browning, Edward W. 193
Browning Automatic Rifle 86
Bugo 81; Operation 120
Bujnowski, Anthony 193
Bukidnon 1, 40, 48, 105, 105
Bukovinsky, Andrew Thomas 194
Bulkeley, John 19, 20, 135
Bulletin of the American Historical Collection 7, 146, 203
Bureau of Constabulary 70
Bush, George H.W. 144
Butler, Rex 85
Butuan 81; Butuan Bay 126
Butuan, Siege of 112
Byers, Clovis 103

C-46 103
C-47 125, 162–163
C-130 188
Cabadbaran 126, 135
Cabadbaran Line 119
Cagayan 67, 97

Index

Cain, John F. 194
Camiguin Island 88
Camp Keithley 116
Campbell, Marvin 84, 194
Campeau, Lucien V. (Luke) 126, 132, 194
Caraga, Davao 126
cargadores 73, 129
Carmen Operation 120
Casey, Hugh J. 10, 38, 84
Casey, Timothy C. 194
Catholic Church 5, 130; priests 172; religion
123
cease-fire agreement 188
Cebu 70, 183
Central Force 99–101
Central Intelligence Agency 186, 187, 189, 190
Cervini, Andrew 23
Chamberlain, Reid C. 194
Chamberlain, Stephen 103
Chapman, Bruce 195
Chapman, Gerald S. 143, 195
Childress, Clyde Clement 7, 39, *62*, 105, 145–
148, 150, 152–154, 159, 168, 175, 195
China 186
Chiota, Noel R. 195
Chmielewski, Edmund O. 53, 195
Christian Filipinos 4
Chuckray, Michael 195
Clark Field 12, 51
Clarke, Jack Roland 195
Claver, Surigao 103
coast watcher station 95, 134
Coe, Joseph Philip 196
Collins, J. Lawton 186
Colorado 1, 18, 96
Colorado School of Mines 9
Commander, Submarines, Southwest Pacific
123
Conte Verde 60
Cook, Earl A. 196
Cook, Richard L. 196
copper stills 131
Corregidor 14–15, 18–20
counterfeit Japanese currency
crossing the enemy's "T" 100
Crump, Robert Myres 196
Cuba 186
currency, paper and plates 130

Dallenback, Wilbur Emery 53, 196
Dansalan 16, 86, 98
Da Pron, Lincoln Hall 53, 56, 196
Darwin 132, 162
Davao 59, 69, 97, 106
Davao City 105
Davao Gulf 56, 134
Davao Penal Colony 143, 155–156, 166
Davis, George B. 196
Deisher's Camp 24
Del Monte Airfield 11, 12, 48, 51
dental care, lack of 66

DeVries, Marvin H. 53, 197
Dimoroc Canyon 132
Dinagat 135
Dipolog 49, 179
Distinguished Service Cross 165
Divino, Frank 197
Dobervich, Michael 166, 197
DOD Special Oprations 186, 189
Doe, Jens 103
Donovan, William 67
Douglass, Vincent K. 197
Duff, Frank W. 197
Dyess, William 124, 126, 166, *167*, 168, *169*, 197

Eichelberger, Robert 103
Eisenhower, Dwight D. 159
Elizalde Corporation 10
Elliott, Bruce G. 198
Enfield rifle 4, 81, 122
Esperanza 51, 56, 95
Evans, James L. 56, 66, 126, 152, 198

farm projects 124; Project #2 124–125
Farrens, Beverly (Ben) Perry 51, *52*, 53, 55, 198
Faust, Fred Sims 198
Feigel, Frederick A. 198
Fernandez, Alfred 199
Fertig, Claude 9, 11, 18, 43, 44
Fertig, Laverne 9, 11, 18, 43, 44
Fertig, Mary Ann Esmond 9, 18, 49
Fertig, Olive Baxter 9
Fertig, Welby 9
Fertig, Wendell W. 1–7, 9–11, 13–15, 23–26,
30–31, *32*, 33–46, 48–50, 53, 56–59, 62, *63*,
64- 65, 69–70, 79, 81, 84–85, 88–93, 95, 98,
101–104, 106–107, 122–123, 128, 134, 145–
168, 171–179, *180*, 181, *182*, 183–187, 199
field manuals 185
Fifth Fleet 144
fig leaf 187
Filipino foot soldiers 5; guerrillas, Agusan
River Valley *92*
Finnegan, George 199
Flowers, Paul F. 199
Force Radio Section 48, 51, 93, 95, 123, 155
Formosa 60, 155, 176
Fort, Guy O. 17, 23
Fort Bragg, North Carolina 186
Fort Sam Houston 9
Free Syrian Army 189
Fremantle 123, 127, 134

Gamber, Glen E. 199
Garland, James L. 53, 199
Garma, Hipolito 105
Gates, Robert M. 171, 174–175
General Headquarters Southwest Pacific Area
(GHQ SWPA) 55, 64, 74, 84, 95, 103, 104,
107, 122, 123, 134, 144, 153, 155–156, 162–
163, 168–169, 175–178, 181
Gentry, Robert E. 199

Gill, Paul A. 199
Gillon, Leslie 85, 126
Glan, Invasion of 112
Glover, Dewitt 200
Grant, John W. 200
Grashio, Samuel 126, 166, 169, 200
Grinstead, James R. 82, 100, 115, 200
Gripsholm 60
Grosh, Cyrill A. 200
Guerrilla Daughter 1
Guerrilla divisions: 105th 104, 179; 106th 105;
    107th 105, 151–152, 155, 181; 108th 105;
    109th 105; 110th 7, 40–41, 57, 63, 70, 72, 86,
    102, 143, 149, 180
Guerrilla Navy 109
guerrilla postal stamp *44*
guerrilla tactics 107–108
Gustafson, Carl *83*

H-34 188
Haburne, James D. 83, 201
Hage, Arthur R. 201
Haggerty, Edward 124, 130
Halkyard, James E. 201
Hall, George O. 49, 201
Halsey, William F 96, 99–100
Hamner, Jordan A. (Ham) 49, 126, 146
Hansen, Charles 1, 37, 41, 46, 71–72, 82–*83*,
    86, 88, 122, 130
Hansen, Henry (Hank) 1, 41, 85–*87*, 88, 130
Hansen, Rudy 1, 41, 85–*87*, 88, 130
Hansen Holmes, Virginia 1, 130
Haratik, Anton J. 201
Harayda, Frank 201
Hawkins, Jack 82, 166, 169, 201
Hayes, Elmer R. 202
Hedges, Charles Wilhelm 17, 23–24, 81, 91–93,
    105–*106*, *180*, 202
Heisinger, Duane 156
Heminway, Truman 64, 135, 202
Hilliard, Earl G. 202
Hmong guerrilla force 187
Ho Chi Minh Trail 188
Hoffman, Jack W. 202
Hoke, Mc (Max) E. 202
Holder, Lowell G. 53, *55*, 202
Homan, Earl C. 203
Houlihan, John L. 203
Howard, Forrest A. 203
Huey 188

"I Shall Return" 131
Ind, Allison 127, 162
Indonesia 186
International Control Commission 187
Islamic State of Iraq and Levant (ISIL) 189–
    190

Japanese: aircraft activity 141; airfield activity
    146; Army's Air Regiment 69; bomb damage
    assessment 142; casualties 77; counter-
guerrilla tactics 76; 54th Independent Mixed
    Brigade 74; First Air Fleet 69; intelligence 70;
    Korean troops 75; military installations 138;
    occupation policies 75; 100th Infantry Divi-
    sion 74; presence in Mindanao 69; road and
    trail activity 141–142; 2nd Air Division 74;
    74th Infantry Regiment 74; shipping informa-
    tion 123; 16th Army detachment 69; 30th Di-
    vision 74; 32nd Naval Base 74; troop disposi-
    tions 139; troop strength in Mindanao 74
Johnson, William H. 22, 48–49, 135, 203
Joint Chiefs of Staff 70, 76
Jonassen, Erling H. 203
Jurika, Thomas Walker 203

Kabacan Siege 112
Kamikaze attacks 101
Kangleon, Ruperto 1, 160, 177, 182–183
Kapai valley 51
Kapatagan Valley 31, 32
KAZ 50
Keats, John 6, 38, 145–147
Kennecott Copper Company 1
Kennedy, James 85, 126
Kennedy, John F. 186–187
KFS (McKay Radio Station) 49–50, 144
Khodr, Khalil 85, 180
Khrushchev, Nikita 187
Kiamba 126
Kihawe-Talamo Trail 181
Kincaid, Thomas 101
King, Ernest 176
King Ibn Saud 131
Kirby, Albert Ray 203
Knortz, William A. 48, 86–88, 203
Kolambugan 69, 104, 164
Kolodie, John 203
Konko, William F. 22, 49, 53, 204
Korysinski, John 204
Krueger, Walter 102
Kuder, Edward 30

Labo Attack 113
La Junta, Colorado 9
Lake Lanao 16, 51, 69
Lanao 70, 104, 105, 172
Lang, Richard B. 204
Laos 186; DOD support for 187
La Paz 51, 59, 101
Lasang 156–157
Latta, Frank 128
Laureta, Claro 152
Lawrence, T.H. 163, 175
leadership elements 171
LeCouvre, Donald 103, 179, 204
LeCouvre, Leonard R. 53, *55*, 204
Lewis, John L. 204
Leyte campaign 102; invasion 96, 177
Liangan, attack on 114
Liberation of the Philippines 178
Life (magazine) 131

Lim, Glicerio 45
Limena, Angeles 166
Lingayen 51, 53, 56
Lingayen Gulf 178
liver fluke 66
Long Tieng 188
Lowry, William Watt 204
Lozano, Ray J. 204
Luzon 3, 101, 103, 177, 181
Luzon Stevedoring Company 60

Macajalar Bay 126
Macalibre Ambush 113
MacArthur, Douglas 3, 11, 18–19, 67, 104, 122–123, 127, 147, 160–161, *169*, 174, 176–178
MacArthur Memorial Archives and Library 7, 147
Maccagli, Aldo F. 205
Madison, William 205
Malabang 162, 179; airfield 162
malaria, epidemic 66
malnutrition and beriberi 66
Mambajao, Camiguin Island 135
Mancuso, Andrew 205
Manners, Clayton A. 205
Marianas Turkey Shoot 144
Marine Corps tactical fighters 179
Mariveles 14
Marshall, George C. 176
Marshall, Paul H. 82, 88, 102, 143, 152, 166, 170, 180, 205
Martin, Harold D. 53, *55*–56, 205
Mayon 80
McClish, Ernest 3, 39–40, 63, 86, 89, 106, 122, 146, 148–154, 158, 166, *167*–168, 205
McClure, James 82, 205
McCollum, Arthur H. 127
McCoy, Melvin H. *119*, 126, 166, *167*, 168–169, 206
McFadden, Warren L. 206
McGee, Frank D. 6, 81, 105, 160, 174, 206
McGrath, Charles E. 206
McGuire, Weyman L. 206
McIntyre, James E. 206
McLaren, Robert K. (Jock) 110
McLaughlin, William F. 206
McNeil, James 206
Mellnik, Steven 126, 153, 155, 166, *167*, 168–169, 207
Merchant, Leonard L. 207
Merrill's Marauders 185
Mester, Walter R. 207
Mills, Alma Bud 53, 207
Mina-Ano Encounter 116
Mindanao 1–5, 96, 136
Mindanao Emergency Currency Board 44–45, 174
Mindanao guerrillas, operational employment of 105
Mindanao Mining Company *83*
Mindanao Mother Lode mine 102, 110, 161

Mindanao Smith Fertig 49
Mindoro 80
Minter, Leonard 207
Misamis Occidental 5, 41, 69, 71
Misamis Oriental 490–41, 59, 70, 90–91, 95, 98, 106, 172
Mitchell, Glynn W. 50, 207
Mitscher, Marc 97
Mitsos, Thomas 53, *55*–56, 207
Money, Willard Landis 135, 207
Morgan, Luis 5–6, 26, 30–37, 41–42, 126, 153–154, 159, 163–166, 172–173
Morison, Samuel Eliot 178
Moros 26, 29–32, 35
Morotai 97
Morozumi, G. 74
Motor Torpedo Squadron 3 19–22, 48
Mountain Gun Battle 117

Napolillo, Francis, Jr. 22, 53, 207
Nara Maru 109
Narwhal 91, 95, 97, 105, 126, 128–*129*, 132, 149
Nasipit 126, 135
National Guardsman 68
National Security Act of 1947 186
National Security Council 166
Nautilus 97, 126, 128
Navy amphibious ships 119
Negros 21, 96, 101, 183
Nemzura, Bernard B. 208
Neveling, Waldo 85, 110
New Guinea 66
Newman (or Neumann), William L. 208
Nichols Field 12
Nimitz, Chester 128
Ninth Military District 159–160
Nipa and bamboo structure *92*
Noel, Frank O. 208
North Vietnam Army 186
Northern Force 100
Notification to Congress 190

Obama, Barack 189
O'Connor, Leo 208
Office of Strategic Services 67
Offrett, Elwood H. 22, 24, 208
old timers 81
Olendorf, Jesse 100
Oliver, Reece Augustus 208
Opendo, Florentino 48
Or Else 49
OSS radios 67
Owen, Paul A. 208
Ozamis, Carmen 41–42

P-46 pursuit aircraft
P-51 102
Pacana, F.D. 43
Paddle 157
padre kits 130
Pagadian Bay 61, 126; city 132; operation 116

Page, Herbert 82, 208
Palau 97
palay 72, 73
Panamanian Consul 60
Panaon Island 64
Panay 4, 182
Panguil Bay 37, 104
paramilitary teams in Afghanistan 189
Parang 17
Paris 188
Parsons, Charles (Chick) 46, 50, 59–61, 62–*63*, 64, *94*–95, 98, 103, 123, 125–126, 130–131, 134–135, 150–151, 153, *167*, 209
Patten, Frank Y. 209
Pease, Robert L. 82, 209
Pendatun, Salipada 30, *94*
Peralta, Macario 3, 44, 50, 160, 182–183
Pershing, John J. 4, 30, 173
Perth 65
Peso note, emergency *42*
Philadelphia 39
Philippine Census Bureau 69; constabulary 29, 99; constabulary template 45; emergency peso note *42*; radio specialists 155; Regional Section 163; 61st Infantry Regiment 44; telephone company 60
Phillips, Dalcua A. 209
Pikit 181
Pilatus Porter *188*
pillow defense 107
Pociluyko, Nicholas D. 209
Presidential Finding 190
Pritz, Michael, Jr. 209

Quezon, Manuel 43, 51, 128, 174

radios 65
Ragsdale, Lee C. 209
Ray, Arizona 9
Richardson, Iliff David 160, 183, 209
Robertson, Louis 209
Robinson, Charles E. 209
Rooke, Henry C. 22, 210
Roosevelt, Franklin D. 11, 128
Rosenquist, Harold A. 102, 126, 132, 143, 155, 158, 210
Roybal, Lewis C. 210
Royer, Elwood A. 210
Rutherford, Lee R. 210
Ruziecki, John E. 210

St. John, Joseph 210
Samar 101, 136, 143
Samar Iron Mines 10
Samples, Jack Lawrence 210
San Bernardino Strait 99–101, 143–144
San Fernando 12
Sanders, Walter W. 211
Santa Magdalena, Luzon 144
Sarangani Bay Operation 181
Sayre Highway 180

Schoen, James 143, 211
Schur, Peter 211
Secret War in Laos 187
Secretary of Defense 171
sewing machine needles 130
Shanghai 60
Sharp, William F. 17, 21, 23, 69
Shinyo Maru 126, 156–157
Shofner, Austin C. 82, 166, 169, 211
Shoss, Maurice 156
Silva, Saturnino 126, 155
Simmons, John David 58, 211
Sinclair, Thomas Lowry 211
Sixth Military District 44, 166
Smith, Athol Y. 49
Smith, Charles M. 23, 49, 59–63, 122–123, 125–126, 134, *167*, 212
Smith, James S. 212
Smith, Oscar F. 212
Smith, Robert Ross 75
Smith, Russell Howard 212
Snyder, Robert O. 213
So What 85, 110
Southern Force 99–100
Soviet Union 187
Special Forces 186
Spielman, Robert B. 71, 73, 82, 88, 146, 166, 170, 212
Springfield rifle 4, 81, 122
Spruance, Raymond A. 144
Spruill, John E. 212
SPYRON 64, 91–92, 95, 97, 125, 128, 130, 149, 155, 161, 179
Stahl, Robert E. (Bob) 65, 126, 144, 212
Starkey, John W. 213
State Department 187
Steele, Raymond 85, 126
Sternberg, Adolph Ernest, Jr. 213
Stewart, Tommy 213
Stivers, Charles 102
Straughn, Hugh 164
Surigao 70, 97–98
Surigao Road 113
Surigao Strait 63, 64, 100, 103
Sutherland, Richard 127
Swanson, Oscar E. 213

Tacloban 56, 98, 153
Tago 73
Tait, William 27–29, 33–38, 165, 172
Talacogon 51, 56–57, 95
Talakag Operation 114
Talisayan Operation 119
Tambor 60, 122, 125
Tandag 72
Tateishi Maru 157
Taylor, Frederick Marston 53, *55*, 213
Tenth Military District 3, 44–46, 48, 50, 72, 81, 84, 90, 102, 104–105, 130, 136, 145–146, 155, 159, 161, 163, 167, 176, 178–179, 181; organization chart *108*

Terrorism 9/11 189
Thai Border Police 187
Thanksgiving dinner 1944 102
They Fought Alone 1, 6–7, 24, 145–146
Third Fleet 99
Thomas, Chandler B. 124, 213
Thommes, Richard Leonard 214
Title 50 CIA Covert Operations 189–190
Title 10 DOD Special Operations 189–190
Torpedo Alley 135
Townswick, Carlyle G. 214
Trading Post Administration 45–46
Trammel, Franklin J. 214
Trout 126
Truman, Harry 186
Tucker, Tracy S. 214
Tuggle, John L. 22, 124, 214
Tungao 151
Turkish troops 186
Turner, Glen S. 214
Twin Otter 188

ulcers, tropical 66
Umayon 51, 58, 96
Umpa, Datu 32–33, 41
United States Army: command in Leyte 147;
    Expeditionary Force 82; Forces in the Far
    East (USAFFE) 4, 11, 13, 30, 79, 84, 89, 122,
    127, 172, 182; Forces in the Philippines
    (USFIP) 87; Office of the Chief of Psycho-
    logical Warfare 185; reserve division 34, 90,
    183; Special Forces 186–187; Special Warfare
    School; study on "Special Operations" 185
U.S. Eighth Army 103, 133, 180; 24th Infantry
    Division 179; 40th Infantry Division 179,
    180; X Corps 181
United States Naval Academy 171–172, 175
Ural Maru 60
Usama Bin Laden 189

Vang Pao 187
Varney, Fred W. 82–*83*, 214

Vienna 187
Vigan 12
Visayas 97
Vit-us Line Attack 118
Vladivostok 82
Volkmann, Russell W. 3, 178, 181, 183

Wagner, Charles 85
Wallace, Walter 85, 126
Waloe, 51, 57–58
Walter, Cecil E. 50, 82, 92, 215
War Department 123, 161
Waters, Loyd 50, 215
Watson, Hadley C. 215
Watson, Howard R. 215
weather forecasting station 131
Welbon, Roy E. 215
Wendover, Royce F. 215
Wheeler, Montgomery 57–58, 126, 155, 158,
    215
Whitley, Perry T. 216
Whitney, Courtney 103, 127
Williams, William W. 216
Willoughby, Charles 103, 127
Wills, Donald H. 216
Wilson, Owen Paul 216
Wilson, Sam J. 45, 53, 58, *62,* 82, 160, 174, 216
Wilson, Woodrow 82
Winget, George W. 216
Wohlfield, Mark M. 216
Wood, John F. 217
Wood, Leonard 60
Woodruff, Halbert E. 217
Worcester, Frederick L. 153–155, 217
wounds from enemy actions 66
Wright, Sidney T. 217

Yashu Maru 84, 156

Zamboanga 56, 103–105, 157, 162, 179
Zapanta, Vicente *93*, 110